HOW TO MAKE A
FORTUNE
ON THE
INTERNET

Martha Siegel

HarperPerennial
A Division of HarperCollinsPublishers

How to Make a Fortune on the Internet is a revised edition of a book published in 1994 under the title *How to Make a Fortune on the Information Superhighway.*

FIRST EDITION

Library of Congress Cataloging-in-Publication Data
Siegel, Martha S.
How to make a fortune on the Internet/Martha Siegel.—1st. ed.
p.   cm.
Rev. ed. of: How to make a fortune on the information superhighway/Laurence A. Canter and Martha S. Siegel, 1994.
Includes index.
ISBN 0-06-273466
1. Internet advertising. 2. Internet marketing. 3. Internet (Computer network) 4. Information technology—Economic aspects. 5. Information superhighway. I. Canter, Laurence A.   How to make a fortune on the information superhighway. II. Title.
HF6146.I5C36   1997   96-48979
658.8—dc21

97 98 99 00 01 ❖/RRD 10 9 8 7 6 5 4 3 2

FOR JEFF NEFF
MY BEST FRIEND

CONTENTS

ACKNOWLEDGMENTS

I would like to thank the following people who contributed to this book and its author with their minds, hearts, knowledge, and talent:

Mike Marzano, for the superb researching job, his conscientious sense of responsibility, his dedication to excellence, his commitment to the final quality of this book, and the many nights he didn't sleep because of it.

Robyn Bluth, for her perfectionism, patience, and dedication in typing and proofing the manuscript, as well as waking the rest of us up when it got late.

Tom Jackiewicz, Systems Security Administrator and Head Programmer of Goodnet, for his vast store of information on the technical intricacies of the Internet and his constant willingness to make himself available for this project.

Jeff Harris, for the contribution of his broad computer knowledge and good sense to many parts of this book, being a wonderful, loyal friend, and displaying an unfailing patience in bailing me out of a remarkably diverse variety of tight spots.

Steve Weinberg, Net and entertainment attorney extraordinaire for his help with difficult and barely formed legal concepts, as well as the supply of egg rolls.

Jim Dilettoso, president of Village Labs in Tempe, Arizona, for his contribution to the security and finance portions of this book, the sharing of his massive intellect on computers and any other subject you can mention, his always loving ways, and the music.

Rob Kaplan, my editor at HarperCollins, for his long-term support, encouragement, and patience in bad times and good.

Mark Edgerton, President of FiestaNet in Phoenix, for the important details on Microsoft products and cutting-edge Web information, as well as the overall assistance of his excellently run company.

Steve Cannon, for keeping both my computer and me operational, as well as his brilliant job of being the big brother I never had.

Gavan Weiser, for guruism above and beyond the call of duty.

Adam Holoway, for his helpfulness in simplifying the complex assortment of Web options available.

Fred von Graf, for his general technical computer expertise.

1
Getting Your Bearings on the Information Superhighway

IF YOU HAVEN'T HEARD OF THE INTERNET YOU CAN probably look up right now and see bats hanging upside down from the ceiling of the cave in which you live. Never in recent memory has the media taken any single new entity, blown it up so big, draped it with so much fancy rhetoric, and played it back to the public with such repetitiveness. The interesting part of all the hype arises because, although almost everyone has heard of the Internet, few seem to have a true understanding of what it really is. It was this lack of understanding that first brought about the creation and subsequent almost mind-numbing repetition of the pop phrase "Information Superhighway." The term, to the relief of more than a few, is progressively falling into disuse, but it was only two years ago that it, too, was a media darling.

The concept was meant to help explain to a largely bewildered public a revolutionary concept in communications. Rather than describing the actual Internet itself, instead you were asked to picture a big, familiar freeway, the kind you probably drive to work on everyday. Then, as you tried to digest the "Internet as superhighway" idea, you would somehow come to understand what it all meant. Then again, you might also begin to wonder about some other things as well. For instance, where was this so-called highway? Where did it lead? How did you get on it? What would you find as you traveled along the Information Superhighway? If you had no answers to these questions, you were not alone by any means, and if you continue to be puzzled, you still have plenty of company.

Then again, maybe you are not thinking at all "What is the Information Superhighway?" Instead, perhaps the question that first comes to mind is "Who cares?" Of course, you probably wouldn't be reading this if you didn't care, and you should, for lots of reasons. The Information Superhighway has already affected your life and will continue to do so to an ever-increasing degree, whether you like it or not. If you have until now managed to avoid the Internet fast track, in the very near future you will invariably find yourself talking to your friends and family, sending letters, going shopping, getting news, finding answers to questions, drawing pictures, solving problems, even gambling, and more, all on the Internet. Not least, you can make a lot of money.

"But," you say, "I can do the things you've mentioned perfectly well already. Why should I bother learning a new way when things are working fine just as they are?" The answer to this very good question is, again, simple. The Internet is, now and for the foreseeable future, where the action is. More and more it is becoming a vital and integral part of everyone's work and home life. If you join in the fun and excitement—not to mention the profit potential—of this great new resource, you will benefit in more ways than you can imagine. Here you will find out that taking advantage of all the Internet has to offer is well worth the trouble. On the other hand, if you choose not to embrace this undeniable wave of the future, while nearly everyone else is busily climbing on the computer bandwagon, you will surely be left behind. There you will be, huddled in your cave, alone with your new best friends, the bats. Maybe you think that's an overstatement. It's not. The ubiquitous infiltration of the Internet into nearly every aspect of communication that has taken place in only the past two years would indicate that overestimating its importance is extremely difficult to do.

There are endless numbers of missions you can accomplish while traveling the Information Superhighway, and you should know about all of them. But the one you will learn most about here will help you to achieve a goal close to all our hearts—making money! Money. Is there ever enough of it? You know the answer. If you're anything like most people, you've been looking for a good way to increase your moneymaking ability for a long time. Many tried it as I did by going to college and learning a profession. Everyone thinks all lawyers are rich. If only it were true. Rich lawyers are rich. The rest struggle just like anyone else. And so I and those around me struggled. I wrote a law book for lay people on immigration and sold it for extra income. The book was a critical success and became very popular throughout the world, but it was expensive to promote and had a limited market. Contrary to what you read in the newspapers, not every living soul in the world wants to move to the United States. For that matter, not everyone who wants to move to the United States is willing or even able to read a book about it, especially one written in English. Moreover, as time goes by, legal restrictions on immigration become tighter, and enforcement against illegals increases. Like many other professions these days, this one seemed headed for oblivion. And so in the face of new developments like these we all go right on struggling. In the course of a lifetime, you might, as I did, come across lots of ideas on how to get rich. On close inspection, however, none of them really seem to make much sense. You may want to make a change but find that it's hard to figure out what change to make. Maybe you are doing all right by most people's standards, but aren't where you want to be by a long shot. You are sure you could do better, but how?

Why not take a good hard look at your computer for an answer. Would a spare $50,000 come in handy? How about an extra $100,000? That's what I made as a result of one night's work using knowledge of the Internet. In these pages, that knowledge will be turned over to you, so you can do the same thing. It's both easy and fascinating. You don't need to make a big investment. You don't need to be a brilliant "computer nerd," complete with glassy-eyed stare and pocket protector, although you might at some time want to hire just such a person to work for you. What you do need is some basic computer equipment and a working knowledge of the Internet. Let's put the equipment part aside for now. Instead, let's concentrate on your first orientation trip down the road and into cyberspace.

LEARNING THE JARGON

Cyberspace? Another term of computer jargon that's hard to avoid. Once again, you've probably heard it what seems like a million times, but you still don't know exactly what it means. You'll get a definition a little later. First, however, it will be helpful to you as you go on your journey if you grasp the fact that jargon is important to computer people. They have worked hard to develop their own special lexicon. They delight in the debate and deliberation that precedes the birth of every new term, and they fancy themselves terribly clever. So besotted are they with using computer words of art that even the simplest act is verbally glorified, and you've probably noticed that these expressions are becoming an everyday part of the English language. You don't turn a computer on, you "boot it up." If, after you've booted, you want to connect to a computer network through your phone line, you don't call up, you "go on-line" and "log in." You never gather information from your computer, you "download" it. Conversely, when you are ready to send information out, that's right, you "upload." You will refrain from typing instructions into your computer. Instead, you will "execute commands." Maybe you'll even salute at the same time.

As you proceed you will see that computer functions are not the only objects of the jargon game. Renaming in computerese extends into other parts of life as well. For example, there is a name for people like you: "newbies." It doesn't take a genius to figure out what this means. It's not exactly the same as calling you a worthless idiot, but that's close enough. What's more, newbies are usually prime targets for "flames." Flames are insults delivered by the computer. Statements that someone with any sense or manners would never make to your face are sent over the Internet with great glee. Indeed, the in-your-face style of talk common on the Internet has been noted by many critics as a symptom of a society very much in need of the newly burgeoning kindness movement. This sort of silliness may be amusing to some for a while, but you're not here to goof around. You're here to make money. Therefore, consider it good practical advice to ignore the name-calling clowns (clown meaning the glassy-eyed nerd over there with the pocket protector). The Internet is for everyone, even lawyers, even you. Plant your feet firmly on the road, hold your head up, and keep moving.

All right, you've still got to learn a few words of the language spoken here so you can talk with the natives. Actually, there are a lot of words. So many, in fact, that newspapers have taken to printing them with their definitions on a daily basis in the many newly established computer sections. While you don't need a computer vocabulary large enough to become the poet laureate of the Internet, you should learn enough to converse with some ease. Soon the on-line world will contribute its purchasing power to making you a financial success, so it is well worth the effort to communicate effectively.

First of all, from a historical perspective you should probably realize that the term "Information Superhighway," also known to the cognoscenti as the "Infobahn" or "I-way," is looked down upon by some of its more experienced travelers. That is because along with the coining of the phrase came a huge flood of the dreaded newbies. Where the term Information Superhighway actually first came from was a speech given by Vice President Albert Gore on December 21, 1993, when he addressed the National Press Club in Washington, D.C. That speech, and that phrase in particular, was the siren song to the mass media. They took the idea and the terminology to heart and gave out the news that the vice president had given birth to the watchword for the future of communications. Suddenly, because of one speech, nearly all those who walked the earth became aware of something that had in fact quietly existed for a long time. That something was the Internet.

Although the term in Gore's speech may now be dated—and no wonder, given the excessive overuse of the key catchphrase at the time it was first introduced—it is still important because it helps to define the Internet more clearly. The Internet can best be described as the main and most important branch of the I-way. In fact, to many people the Internet *is* the I-way. Very simply, the Internet is about thirty million computers all connected together and communicating with each other. Thirty million is a rough calculation. No one actually knows the exact number for sure. There are only several million computers officially registered on the Internet, but most of those have dozens or even hundreds of individual users accessing them. A typical Internet service provider (ISP), for example, a company whose job it is to connect people to the Internet, is credited as only one computer, even though that single ISP may really account for five hundred separate users. Reports on estimated numbers of Internet participants have shown ranges careening from as low as a few million to as high as forty million or more. Those claiming the lower number probably do not understand the meaning of a registered computer. Thirty million is the figure currently used most often, and the estimates change depending on time and source. Whatever the exact number, everyone agrees it is impressive. So popular is the Internet now that the user group grows by thousands *every day*. The way most of these connected computers currently communicate is over standard phone lines. That is why it is so easy and practical for you, sitting in your home or office, to link up. Presently, Internet companies are busy changing the form of Internet connectivity from telephone lines to cable lines. Eventually satellite connections are expected to take over. As each step in the progression is completed, the level of communication possible through your computer becomes even easier, with faster access and more reliability.

The Internet is also notable for being the outstanding communications feature in what is now viewed as a digital revolution. You all know about digital clocks and other numbering devices, but, once again, may not have thought much about what that means, other than the fact that the numbers on the face of your watch don't look the same as they used to. The true significance of digitalness is much more than the appearance of futuristic-looking green numbers on a variety of electronic equipment. The real importance is twofold. First of all, digital transmission of signals is a better way of sending and receiving data than has existed before. When you digitize words, pictures, sounds, or electronic impulses that operate almost every appliance in your home, they are simply a technologically improved method of doing it better, faster, and in greater quantity. Picture and sound quality improve. Space needs decrease. Operations become more reliable.

The second important facet of digitalness is that it creates a common denominator, so that many functions once difficult to coordinate no longer are. That is where the application to the Internet comes in. All functions, whether it be transmission of sound, pictures, movement, computer processing, whatever, must be digitized. The fact that all data is in the same digital form makes the operation of a huge, otherwise heterogeneous information network operable. It also allows the network to interface with all other media such as cable television, an advance already on the way to being widespread in the near future. If you want to think of it in more mundane terms, however, you could get your computer to make your microwave run if you wanted, and you could do it for one reason: they both function digitally.

In saying the Internet is made up of thirty million computers, intended to be included are all kinds of computers, big and small. Most of the thirty million are plain old PCs consisting of a screen, a keyboard, and a monitor, just like the one probably sitting in your home or office right now. Some of the largest and most elaborate computers tied into the Internet are located at government offices and universities around the world. These larger machines act as central exchanges, allowing all the other, smaller ones to be in contact with each other. Still more computers linked to the Internet are storehouses of information.

What sorts of information are we talking about? You name it.

Everything from newspaper stories to medical information to sports to sex—well, as I said, you just name it and it's available out there on the Internet. These electronic information repositories in the computer are called "databases." It's an added bonus that, because all this was started by the U.S. government, there is an established tradition still existing that almost anything and everything you get from the Internet databases is free. The Internet is no longer government-run. It is, in fact, now operated by commercial companies of all kinds. This would suggest that eventually the spirit of free exchange will give way to profit incentives. At present, however, the spirit of "ask and ye shall receive" prevails.

Another interesting concept that you should understand about the Internet is that there is no central authority running it. The Internet was deliberately arranged that way for a practical purpose. The Defense Department, which created it, anticipated that the Internet might be used as a critical communication tool in time of war. They wanted to be sure that there was no central key mechanism that could be disabled with one, well-placed bomb. Today, the practical need for decentralization has evolved into a philosophy that advocates governance from the bottom up, rather than the top down. Certain universities and private organizations voluntarily assume some of the administrative and technical tasks of keeping the Internet operational, while still others are contributed by commercial companies from the private sector. As for the content of what goes on the Internet, there is in theory, at least, nobody who exercises control. Human nature being what it is, philosophy or no philosophy, there are many who, as you will see, can't resist the urge to try directing operations and, once again, it should be noted that many members of the organizations that do succeed to varying degrees in running the Internet are representatives of for-profit companies. Moreover, the government has taken note of the power of the Internet, and legislation to control the many facets of its functioning are now in various stages of consideration. So far, however, no attempts at formal regulation have taken hold and, officially at least, no one runs the Internet.

The Internet, usually referred to by those who know and love it simply as "the Net," is the big show on the I-way and is just about swallowing up the other parts that were once independent, if comparatively small, additional entities. It is still not, however, the only game in town from the standpoint of the Gore concept, which was really meant to cover all the developed and developing electronic resources that have increased to a blinding speed the exchange of information between people. This would include the commercial computer networks such as CompuServe, America Online (AOL), Delphi, Genie, and Prodigy. Each of these is a circle of computers unto itself and each one supplies its own unique assortment of databases. Frequently such networks are confused with the Internet itself, but they are not the same. Unlike the Internet, using the commercial services is not free. All commercial networks also include in their service packages a gateway to the Internet. Although the Internet is the main concern of this book, there are moneymaking opportunities on the commercial networks, and you will be hearing about some of them as well. Finally, for the sake of thoroughness, the I-way concept also covers other, noncomputer developments in telecommunications, such as the video telephone and interactive television. Breakthroughs like these are exciting to think and know about, but they are not in wide use yet, as is the Internet, and so they are of no real value to our purpose here.

Now that you understand what is really meant by the Internet and the Information Superhighway, you are ready to tackle the all-time favorite computer pop phrase—cyperspace. Here is another word that has come into common usage, even though most have only the vaguest idea of what it means. Well, now you can amaze your friends by being one of the elite minority who understands exactly what he or she is talking about cyberspace-wise. The term cyberspace was first coined by William Gibson in his popular computer-based science fiction book *Neuromancer*. You will remember that cyberspace was mentioned earlier as a world you were about to enter. Dyed-in-the-wool Internet devotees love to think of it that way, as an actual place to which you can go. The idea that you can be connected to so many people and so much information so easily creates in their minds a sense of wonder and mysticism which transcends planet Earth. They picture themselves as Captain Kirk (or Captain Picard, if they are a little younger) daring to go where no man has ever gone before. They imagine they are brave explorers, riding their computer keyboards through electronic lollipop land. Go ahead and share the fantasy if you are of a mind to do so, but when you get ready to leave your little pink cloud and jump back down to the real world, realize that cyberspace is just a convenient way of describing the huge number of electronic information paths and messages darting back and forth between people and computers on the Internet and other networks that make up the I-way. Those paths and messages are envisioned as a huge cloud and that cloud is cyberspace.

When you become more familiar with the world of the Internet, you will begin to notice that drawing analogies between real-life activities and electronic Internet functions has developed into almost a popular art form. The most common of these, "surfing the Net" is a good example. This very common term simply means exploring different places on the Net to see what you can turn up that might be interesting or fun. Needless to say, just as there is no actual cyberspace, there are no real tasty waves either.

As you go on your journey down the I-way to wealth, take advantage of the analogy game and enjoy it, but never lose sight, as many before you have, of where reality ends and figments of the imagination begin. Those who buy into the myth that cyberspace is a real place also believe that this illusory locale houses a community, with a set of laws, rules, and ethics all its own. Although this group, culled mainly from the original Netters, is becoming smaller and less significant as people from all walks of life enter the Internet, it still does exist. Unfortunately, the perceived behavior codes of cyberspace are often in conflict with the laws of more substantive lands like, for instance, the United States of America. Later you will be shown how to separate fact from fiction and follow the laws that really count in your quest for fortune on the Internet. Indeed, one of the most controversial aspects of the Net today centers around the efforts of the courts to make real world laws applicable to the mythical land of cyberspace. We will come to see that this is no easy task. The Internet started out in the hands of dreamers, and much that is good has come from the dreams. Now, however, a monumental transition is in the works. The Net is moving into the hands of realists like you, and a balance is taking hold between the two that is making the Internet a useful resource to everyone, computer whiz and common folk alike. But, as in every other phase of human endeavor, the process of change is often difficult.

EQUIPMENT: WHAT DO YOU NEED?

First of all, computer equipment isn't known as equipment. Call it hardware. There is such a vast array of computer hardware on the market today that some enterprising souls will charge you $100 an hour or more simply to tell you which computer to buy. Calling this an unnecessary expense would be an understatement. You will be told the details of what you need to know later on (see chapter 13). Here, now, are the basics that will enable you to engage in all the moneymaking activities described in this book.

You will need only four tools and a possible fifth that you may consider a highly desirable option. First, you will require a PC of any flavor. By a PC is meant an entire system, including a viewing monitor, a keyboard, and the central processing unit—the box with the brain that actually manipulates the data. The computer should also contain a CD-ROM drive, because most of the latest programs are sold on compact discs. These items can be purchased either separately or as a unit. You can spend as much as you want on them, and there are certain benefits to having a high-powered system, but if you don't already own a PC and want to get started without squandering your child's college-tuition fund, used ones can be found through classifieds, sometimes for as little as $200. You must be sure that you have a computer of a level not less than a 386. Once you've hit that minimum, anything at all will do.

The next items on the list of requirements are a modem and telephone line. The two are related. A modem is a device that enables your computer to communicate with other computers over standard phone lines. Most PCs being sold today have modems built into them, but if you need to buy one, they can be purchased at any electronics discount store for as little as $30. As for the telephone line, any garden-variety phone line will do. If you are a real pioneer, you can even access the Internet on your camping trip via a cellular phone connection, although this requires purchasing a special cellular modem.

Finally, you need a communications program that lets your computer talk to the modem. A program is no more than a set of electronic instructions that tells your computer what to do. The computer itself is nothing but a pile of metal and plastic. Every time you want your computer to perform a particular task, you must have a program for that task. When your computer can act as a telephone, a typewriter, a research tool, and a record-keeper all in one day, it is through the use of a variety of programs. Remember hardware? Programs are called software. Modems are almost always sold with free communications software, as are the majority of computers. If you don't like the software you have, however, don't worry. Fabulous communications software programs are available, *free*, on the Internet. In fact, you will find that the Internet is loaded with free programs of all kinds that you may actually find useful. This, in Internet parlance, is called freeware or shareware, and you'll discover later in this book how to find them.

There is one other item you might want to consider seriously, although it is not an absolute marketing necessity. It is a printer. A printer will allow you to create hard copies of any data that come into your computer. With the use of a word-processing program, you can employ the computer as a high-tech typewriter. No business should be without one, and, in fact, it is becoming harder and harder to find any that are.

GETTING ON THE NET

To get on the Internet, you must have some sort of Internet link. You acquire this connection by opening an account with any one of the many institutions or companies that fall into the category of Internet service providers, or ISPs, as they will be referred to throughout this book. The Internet is a global link of millions of computers. Your ISP has a computer that is tied directly to the Net. You hook up by going through the ISP's computer. When you get really ambitious, and have made your first fortune, you may want to consider being your own ISP. In the beginning, you should choose an easier and cheaper route. For example, your employer may already offer Internet access to staff members who want it. Check it out, because it will probably be free. Likewise, if you are a student, your school will almost certainly offer free access. Be careful, though, to ask whether there are any restrictions on usage. Many companies and most academic institutions provide Internet access for research purposes only. Using it to make money might be frowned upon.

The other, more flexible option is to find a commercial ISP. In this case you simply pay someone to get you on the Net. There are many well-known commercial on-line providers, such as CompuServe, Prodigy, and AOL. Historically, these have been self-contained networks with direct access only to other people who have subscribed to that particular network. All are now providing Internet access.

It is a commercial provider specializing in Internet access only, however, that will offer you the most Internet capabilities, and probably the lowest price. There are thousands of such companies located the world over. ISPs charge fees, but to begin making money on the Internet, you should be able to get the connection you need for about $20 per month, with unlimited usage. You will receive full information on choosing an ISP later on in this book (see chapter 14).

Fine. We have discovered a great network of computers out there all tied together and ready to communicate with each other. Your computer equipment and Internet access are, likewise, set to go. Now we have to figure out what to do with this thing. Our main goal here is to make a fortune. In order to do this you must leave behind all the romance, all the wonderment, and move on to the practical uses of the Net.

There are actually four primary functions that can be accomplished on the Internet. You are probably familiar with the first. It is called e-mail. Ideas don't get much simpler than e-mail. You and everyone else who ties into the Internet gets a mailbox code. Then, by typing in your code on his or her keyboard, anyone connected to the Internet can send private messages to your computer and yours alone. You can send private messages back in the same way. These messages come over the phone lines and into the computer, where they wait until the owner of the computer turns it on and reads the messages on the screen. In earlier days subscribers to private networks and those who had e-mail through the Internet itself could not send messages to each other. These days anybody can e-mail anybody else, no matter where your e-mail connection comes from. E-mail is a vital component of making money on the Internet. It is the primary way potential buyers of your product will contact you.

The second practical use of the Internet is as a source of information. It has already been mentioned that there are endless numbers of databases out there covering almost any subject imaginable. If you like knowing things, and we all do, you may at first suffer from information overload, a grown-up version of the kid-in-the-candy-store syndrome. There are literally thousands of databases that can be accessed by anyone on the Internet, usually for free. There are even databases that do nothing more than list other available databases. As technology improves, the databases include not only text components and static graphics, but sound and movement as well. All you need to access a particular database is its Internet electronic address, which is similar to a mailbox for the database. This creates a wondrous opportunity for the academician trying to understand the mating habits of killer bees, or for the sports enthusiast who wants statistics on his favorite team, from the present back to the Stone Age. More important, it offers an opportunity for you to make a fortune. How? You create your own database. Your database may be as simple as a list of your products or services, or it may include an entire catalog, complete with multimedia video and sound. You will learn exactly how to go about it.

The third practical function of the Net is to act as a public forum for ideas. The World Wide Web, the most popular and active portion of the Internet, where all graphics and multimedia capabilities are found, is made up of thousands of "Web sites" placed on the Internet by companies or individuals for a variety of purposes. The World Wide Web will be discussed in detail later (see chapter 7), because it is undoubtedly the future of the Internet. One feature that is common to almost every Web site is the opportunity for the reader to give input to the individual who owns the site. This is an example of the Internet's main superiority over other forms of media, the ability to be "interactive."

Another place on the Internet that acts as a public forum is operated by a vehicle created exclusively for that purpose called the Usenet. To those hooked on it, the Usenet is the only part of the Internet that really matters. The Usenet, often called the voice of the Net, is a collection of about twenty thousand discussion groups, each devoted to a different topic. As with the other features of the Net, the range of subjects covered is enormous. Starting with computer and technical subjects, moving on to celebrity fan groups, to sex, to family problem-solving, to the just plain silly, the Usenet provides an opportunity to air your views in public on nearly anything, providing yet another example of the Net's interactive capabilities. The Usenet groups, called "newsgroups," are actually run less like discussions and more like electronic bulletin boards. Someone will post a message to the group. Then, anyone who tunes in to read what is posted can see the other postings and respond. The Usenet offers one of the best ways known for making money on the Net. Once again, the details will come later. Meanwhile, try to think of what it would be like if suddenly millions of people could know you had a wonderful product to sell or an excellent service to offer, and how they could purchase it from you. Temporarily, leave the outcome to your imagination.

The fourth and final practical use of the Internet is for talk or chat. This Internet function works much like a CB radio or perhaps a big conference call on the telephone, and is, again, highly interactive. There are certain talk channels you can access with your computer. You are then able to "talk" with anyone else who happens to be on the channel at the same time, by typing your words into the computer. The typed messages appear immediately on the monitor of all those who are tuned in, and they can answer back in the same way. Often, the size of a group accessing a chat channel simultaneously is in the hundreds. Celebrities and all types of public figures now use the chat function to communicate more closely with the public. The time and Internet chat address is simply announced publicly on TV, radio, or in the newspaper, and anyone who wishes can type messages back and forth in real time to the particular guest of the moment. You may also engage in private conversations, or go into private chat rooms for limited group discussions. Add the right software and you can put a voice component into your computer, making it act as a cheap telephone. In fact, new strides forward are being made in this area called "telephony" so a computer-voice transmission can be received by a telephone, rather than a computer at the other end. Think of the long-distance phone charges you can save. And making money through talk or chat? Well, what if you joined the conversation and told everyone about the wonderful product or service you have to sell? Do you think someone might be interested?

As a final note to the use of the Internet, you should understand the general principle of client/server, the basic methodology under which the entire Internet operates. A client is a simple term describing a computer program whose main function in life is to receive Internet information and respond to it singly on an interactive basis. That is why client programs are utilized in the greatest numbers by you and the other end-users on the Internet. The other type of program making the Internet run is called a server. As you might guess, servers store information and make it available on demand to clients. Your usage of the Net right now rests on the client programs, but as you become a Cyberseller, you will become more interested in disseminating information to large groups, and so your interest in knowing about servers is likely to undergo a major increase.

COMMUNICATE YOUR WAY TO WEALTH THROUGH CYBERSELLING

By now, you've probably guessed that the secret to making a fortune on the Internet lies in the amazing communication ability you can use for presenting your goods and services to huge numbers of people at a very low cost. This book is going to help you think of a product or service, and explain how to use the various functions available on the Internet and other parts of the I-way to sell it. It will also tell you how to select an ISP and choose a PC according to the type of marketing you want to do. You'll see that the methods described can be used not only to present products initially, but also to offer follow-up service and create long-lasting customer relations. We call all of this "Cyberselling."

When Ronald Reagan was president of the United States, people called him "The Great Communicator." His way of reaching out to embrace people drew them to his humanity, blinded them to his faults, and made him one of the most popular presidents in history. Even if he did nothing else well, he was startlingly effective at one thing—selling Ronald Reagan. As good a communicator as Reagan was, the greatest communicator of them all is not the former president but the computer. This machine that transmits so much information in so many different forms to someone sitting in the privacy and comfort of his or her own home has the ability to create an intimate and trusting relationship with the user that is ideal for selling. What's more, that person sitting at the computer is not simply a passive recipient of information. He or she can talk back. This presents the opportunity for your customer to ask questions and make comments about your product or service. Most important, that customer can place an order.

You can't effectively use the selling abilities of your computer unless you have something to sell. That is why, included in the explanation of Cyberselling, are the methods you'll need for finding a product or service that is tailor-made for marketing on the Internet. Put your great new product or service together with the high-powered, low-cost promotion capabilities of the computer and you have a new and easy way of Cyberselling yourself into a happy and wealthy financial future.

A NEW ROAD TO WEALTH

It isn't often that you have an opportunity to take part in the development of a great new industry, but it's about to happen right now. By the time you finish this book, you'll be able to Cybersell® with the best of them. Huge megacorporations are in the early stages of utilizing the incredible marketing power Cyberselling has to offer. The number of companies, big and small, that appear on the Internet is large now and increasing daily. The window of opportunity may be closing fast, but it is fair to say that the chance to get in on the ground floor is still available to you. What is more, you can reach so many people so effectively and inexpensively using Cyberselling techniques, that you can play in the same league with the big boys and come out a winner. Some operations that started out in a garage and ended up being worth millions thanks to the

Internet, have already proven this is true. Once you've learned the simple basics of Cyberselling you'll find in the rest of this book, only your own imagination and creativity will place limits on what you can achieve.

It is the goal here to have you understand how to utilize the Internet for commercial purposes. It doesn't require a finely honed scientific mind. In fact, what you are about to read is written making the assumption that you know absolutely nothing about computers whatsoever. In explaining how to market on the Internet, touching on a certain amount that is technical can't be completely avoided, but the information is entry-level and technicalities have been sidestepped wherever possible. Not included here are directions on how to operate your computer. If you need to learn that, read a manual or take a class at your local community college. Likewise, if you want to examine the workings of the Internet in-depth from a technical standpoint, there are many excellent books on the topic already in existence. You can even choose to omit the process altogether by hiring a computer "geek" to carry out the technical end for you. Geeks who hire themselves out to assist the noncomputer literate are themselves forging a highly profitable industry. What you should examine closely for yourself, however, is how the average individual can use the Internet to gain wealth. That's what you're going to find out right now. If you employ the computer for this purpose, you will have the advantage of being among the first.

There is one last notion you must understand before you begin your journey through the Internet to financial success. It's been mentioned earlier in a joking way, but now let's be completely serious and very clear. Whatever you hear, whatever you read, whatever others may tell you, the computer is just a machine. It's not human. It's not a miracle. It's a machine. It can transfer huge amounts of information back and forth with lightning speed, but that's all it can do. Because this transfer of information tends to intensify the effects of communication, the result often is that a feeling of closeness develops between the people who give and receive it. As uplifting as this feeling may be, it's important to keep things in perspective. Popular nicknames like cyberspace and Information Superhighway serve the purpose of making it easy for the average person to grasp and discuss complex electronic functions carried out by computers and computer networks, but don't get so carried away that you start believing the I-way is a real six-lane blacktop. Neither should you believe the power of the Internet is for a few elite geniuses, nor that it is a world apart legally and socially. The law as it applies to use of the computer is now being addressed by the courts and that is as it should be. No one else has the authority to decide these questions, including self-styled computer gurus. The only laws you should adopt as you pursue wealth on the Internet are those dictated by the place in which you live, the religious faith you have chosen to follow, and your own good conscience.

Millions of people have gone out and bought computers. Buying a computer is no different from buying a television or a CD player. It's not a passport to another world. It's just a machine. You should not fear this machine. Although it might have taken a brilliant scientist to invent it, any normal mortal with average intelligence and a little effort can learn to use it. You have only to look at the reception desk of nearly every business in the modern world to know that this is true. You should use your computer to communicate, to make your life easier and better. Once you learn Cyberselling, you can and should use your computer to make money. That's what it was made for. Let's get started.

2
A Busy Night in Cyberspace
The Green Card Incident

STARTING OUT

IT WASN'T LONG AGO THAT I AND MY BUSINESS PARTNER
at the time started out on what would turn into an incredible life-
changing adventure. He was an immigration lawyer then and I ran a
small book publishing company selling do-it-yourself legal books on the
subject. As CompuServe subscribers almost since it began, we had been
on-line computer enthusiasts for more than ten years, but knew little
about the Internet. CompuServe as well as the news media had been
mentioning it, but finding the Internet was not easy, let alone figuring
out how to use it. It appeared to be a private network for universities to
communicate with one another. Then, a story popped up in the news
somewhere that the U.S. Supreme Court was making all of its decisions
available on the Internet. Other federal and state agencies were offering
access to their databases and publications, usually for free. Could government information on immigration be obtained free via computer? Could
an outrageously expensive law library be eliminated and the future
destruction of hundreds of trees needed to generate all that paper be pre-

vented? That's what made me start out on my first journey through cyberspace. I hadn't yet recognized the riches that lay ahead.

A search for everything available about the Internet was the next step. The biggest question seemed to be, "How do you access it?" Then, one day, like black magic, the name Computer Witchcraft mysteriously appeared up on the CompuServe screen. It turned out this was the name of some free software that would get you on the Internet. It was also the name of a company engaged in the business of providing Internet access. For the software to do you any good, you had to sign up with the company. My partner and I proceeded to download this software to our computer. Suddenly, our modem was dialing a number and we were connected. You could almost see some mystical, Disneyesque character in a huge turban shouting "Open Sesame" in a big, booming voice. We were asked to give a title we wished to use as our Internet computer identity and without much thought, since my partner's name was Canter and mine Siegel, we chose cslaw. We were given an e-mail address incorporating that name. Also, we were asked to provide a credit card, which would be charged a minimum of $10 each month against per minute charges of about fifteen cents. We were now on the Internet, in what seemed almost a magical way.

The first thing we did with our new Internet account was check out something called the Usenet. Here was a collection of about ten thousand public discussion groups, called newsgroups, on a huge number of topics. Today existing newsgroups number about twenty thousand, an increase of 100 percent in two years' time. The way these "discussions" are carried on is that one person decides to post a message from his or her computer for everyone else who tunes into the group to read. Then others respond by posting reply messages, which, in turn, elicit more responses and so on. These back and forth exchanges are called "threads." There can be many threads going on in one group.

Not surprisingly, the first newsgroup to catch our attention was called *alt.visa.us.* What appeared there was a list of several hundred questions that people around the world had posted concerning U.S. immigration. My partner, who knew the answers to all of them, without much thought, posted a few replies. Then it happened. Within a day or so our electronic mailbox overflowed with individual immigration inquiries. People we had never met wanted to hire us as lawyers. Years of experience had taught that, in the end, very few would actually part with their money for traditional legal services. Still, it brought to mind questions about the possibilities here.

Just how many people knew about this one little newsgroup? Were there more places on the Internet where the particular service we offered might be of interest? Hopefully, we began to explore. Then came another major discovery: a collection of newsgroups devoted to the cultures of different countries. There was *alt.culture.japan, alt.culture.hungary, alt.culture.france*; nearly one hundred in all. For practitioners of immigration law there could have been no more desirable a market.

Still, we were reluctant to try selling traditional legal services. Good legal work requires painstaking hours of labor, and that translates into high prices few can afford. Besides, we knew that, at least as far as immigration work is concerned, not many people really understood the value of the service offered. They believed, incorrectly, that getting a visa or green card was simply a matter of filling out a few forms. Even when their own efforts failed and they came to a lawyer for help, they still had difficulty grasping why a couple of minutes of advice would not tell them all they needed to know; we had spent years working unsuccessfully against this misconception. It was apparent that most messages posted to Usenet newsgroups were fairly short. Obviously, it was going to take more than a few brief paragraphs to overcome sales objections that had been insurmountable since the office doors were opened. This knowledge was in fact what had spurred my writing and selling of the do-it-yourself legal books. The conclusion I reached was that traditional immigration legal services were not the most promising product to sell in this medium.

They say it's all in the timing and what happened next proves that to be true. Just as we discovered an unbelievable place to market our immigration know-how, we were also beginning our annual undertaking of the Green Card Lottery. This is a program sponsored by the U.S. government, where applications are filled out in a particular technical manner specified by the Department of State. Completed applications are then fed into a computer and "winners" are selected randomly. Those who are lucky enough to have their names drawn receive green cards. Every year the government does its best to make the Green Card Lottery as confusing as possible. Still, compared to the standard types of immigration applications normally filed, the lottery was simple stuff. Where an average immigration case might cost several thousand dollars to complete, a lottery application could be done cost-effectively for about $100 and still bring in a profit if promotion costs were not too high. In addition, over the years it had been proven that immigration clients just loved the

Green Card Lottery. Even though it was a long shot, there was excitement to the gambling feature. Besides, where other, more traditional efforts to get green cards took time, money, and perseverance, the lottery was, if successful, a quick, inexpensive fix.

In the Green Card Lottery, we believed we had the perfect item to sell to this newfound computer market. I sat down and wrote a short (171 words) statement announcing the Green Card Lottery and it was posted to all the *alt.culture* groups. Those who wanted more information were invited to send their request to the firm e-mail account. Later a way became apparent to post to numerous groups automatically, but we were still beginners at the time, and so this posting was done the long way. Each of the approximately one hundred postings took about two minutes apiece.

The next morning we went to the computer to see what had become of our little postings. It had been a busy night in cyberspace. Hundreds of requests for additional information poured in. As more people woke up, turned on their computers and saw the messages, the flow increased to an avalanche. It kept up at this rate for days, before slackening off a bit. Still, a steady stream of inquiries kept coming even weeks later.

We also received our first "flames." Flames are computerese for insulting messages. A few individuals did not like the fact that the green card notices had been posted to a number of newsgroups. We were informed that when you post to newsgroups, you must post only on the topic of the group. "What," someone wanted to know, "does the Green Card Lottery have to do with *alt.culture.japan*?" Others advised us to look into "Netiquette," the informal code of behavior certain people believe must be observed when you operate in cyberspace. Still others were not so polite. They called us "idiots" and "clueless," words we thought inaccurate descriptions of experienced professionals who had several advanced degrees and had written two books. An official from Witchcraft called to say there had been some complaints. We advised him that these complaints had been duly noted, but represented only about 5 percent of the responses received. The messenger from Witchcraft said his company really didn't care what anyone did as long as it had no effect on their business, and in fact, they wished they had the nerve to do what we were doing. Later we would learn that what ISPs said in private to us would change drastically when reporters entered the scene. In a two-year period we would watch opinions shift wildly as everyone in the industry tried to reflect the ever-changing thinking on Internet commercial policy.

For my part, at the time I didn't see that much in the way of nerve was required. I knew we had broken no law. The posting was receiving a fantastic response. If someone out there didn't see why information on the Green Card Lottery was relevant to the readers of the newsgroup on Japan, almost everyone else who read the group clearly understood very well. What was difficult to grasp was why these people were trying to inject themselves into matters that should by logic be of no concern to them. There was little time, however, to ponder such questions. Everyone at the office was too busy sending Green Card Lottery information to those who'd requested it. By now they numbered in excess of one thousand.

This happy circumstance also created a problem. Witchcraft did not offer an Internet connection that would readily handle large volume. Back at CompuServe, information about another ISP was available, which offered direct connections to the Internet together with the ISP's own easy-to-use software. Again the software was free through CompuServe, giving us a quick connection to what was called "The Pipeline." We were asked on-line for our preferred e-mail account name, and again chose cslaw, now to be known as *cslaw@pipeline.com*. A message came saying that people from Pipeline would call within a few days to issue a password and finalize setting up the account.

The call came and we had our second Internet connection. Pipeline had access to many more newsgroups than Witchcraft, and an entire world of newsgroups located outside the U.S. opened up. This seemed like a possible gold mine for immigration services. By now, we had already made enough money to buy two new computers. Then we got to thinking. Advertising to these groups was practically free. Since cost was not a factor, why not advertise to all the groups. We began posting, one at a time, to each group available through Pipeline. We were not disappointed. Mail began pouring in, including requests for information, sales orders, and many more flames. It all happened too fast. Pipeline had its own limitations. Pipeline was a new company. The software had bugs and it, too, could not handle the kind of volume the Green Card Lottery posting was generating. The mail became choked in a traffic jam on Pipeline's very narrow lanes. Also, Pipeline was located in New York and it took a long-distance telephone call to hook up with them. Staying on-line for hours a day was getting very expensive. Besides, they were upset about the flames. They still had not developed a policy toward advertising and they were clearly reluctant to do so. They themselves, after all, were making money from the Internet. It would be hypocritical to criticize others for doing the same thing. On the other hand, some of their customers were offended. They wanted us to ease up. We had to find better access.

Doing some research in various books about the Internet brought up the name of a California company called Netcom that provided Internet access, with local dial-up numbers in many different cities, including our own, Phoenix. We quickly signed up, with an account name of cslaw, e-mail address *cslaw@netcom.com.* Netcom had access to about eight thousand newsgroups, many more than the other companies we had tried. We were beginning to feel a bit overwhelmed, however. Netcom, unlike Pipeline and Witchcraft, did not offer its own simple graphical software. Instead, we were faced with a blank computer screen and told to execute commands from a UNIX shell, whatever that was. Not having the vaguest idea of how to proceed, we began looking for someone who did, a consultant who would get everything running smoothly, and teach us what to do. All we needed was to find the right person, and, after several failed efforts, find him we did. He had long, light brown hair. He wore an old T-shirt with a picture by Escher, the "impossible triangle" artist worshipped by the Tech crowd. He was skinny. He was spacey. He had a girlfriend and an attitude. He was twenty years old and he had exactly the information required.

Our newly hired computer geek helped make selections from Netcom's newsgroup list and ultimately picked out about one thousand. We stayed up all night one Friday feverishly posting to each of them. The next morning, the phone started ringing. Irate people, claiming to be systems administrators and owners of other networks, complained that we were overloading their systems. Junk e-mail started to fill our mailbox. But requests for information also poured in. Hundreds of them came within a matter of hours. Then, it stopped. We were locked out of the account by Netcom. They sent a message to us to call them on Monday. We did and they read us the riot act. In any event, they agreed to turn the account back on, but only if we promised never to use their system for advertising on the Net again. Reluctantly, we agreed.

THE LUNCH MEAT HITS THE FAN

Mail from the Netcom posting continued to pour in. People began hiring us as well. This was looking very promising, but it was only March and the lottery wouldn't even take place until June. We had to do more advertising. The final government rules for the green card program would be released in a few weeks. This would be the perfect time for one more posting, but so far we weren't having much luck finding a cooperative ISP, then known more commonly as access providers. More research turned up hundreds of ISPs all over the country, including several with local telephone numbers in Phoenix. A call to one of them, Internet Direct, opened an account instantaneously. Asked for our preferred e-mail address, we chose cslaw (what else!), now *cslaw@indirect.com*. We were given a password, and told how to dial up on the phone. In return the ISP received a credit card number on which to charge a $20 per month fee. There were no additional charges. We could stay on-line for twenty-four hours a day if we wished.

There was one last matter to take care of. No one at our office wanted to deal with more roadblocks from ISPs. Therefore, we set up a meeting with officials at Internet Direct. We told them exactly what we wanted to do. We warned them that there would be loud cries of protest to say nothing of an outpouring of e-mail attacks. We told them we did not want to proceed without assurance that we could have their cooperation in this matter. Internet Direct told us they could handle all our traffic. Their link to the I-way, unlike Pipeline's, was a full-fledged, multilane freeway. They laughed when we told them that some of our previous providers had had difficulties handling the mail traffic we had received. They could do it, no problem.

With respect to policy, an Internet Direct official gave us a memo outlining what the company would and would not do. In summary, the memo said that while "Internet Direct cannot take a pro-active stance" on the issues raised by mass posting, they would "continue to treat [us] with the respect deserved as an Internet Direct customer." The memo let us know that Internet Direct did not "pre-censor information" and, more importantly (to us at least) assured us that "[we] will not stop you from doing anything unless we believe it to be illegal." The memo went on to say that if the company received reports that our actions were having "deleterious effects" upon its system and for the other users of Internet Direct, we would then be asked to "cease performing [those] actions." Then, **if we didn't stop**, "further action to halt problems" would be taken.

This seemed like a policy that, if it was not everything we might have wanted, we could at least live with. We made up our minds to go ahead.

Now there was a technical problem to be faced. It had taken some doing in terms of time spent to sit down at the computer and send postings to each of about a thousand newsgroups, as had been done before with the Netcom account. It needed to be done automatically, but how were we to accomplish this? There were no professional programmers or technicians among the office staff, nor was anyone a "hacker," a self-trained computer buff who spent every waking hour trying to either build his own system or destroy those of others. Although we didn't know how to solve our own problem, we knew enough about how computers worked to figure out that it could indeed be solved. Computers were, after all, made to do simple, repetitive tasks like the one needed for this project. A call to our young old friend the geek solved the problem. He wrote a program to do the job in one night.

Now everything was ready. Going through the complete list of available newsgroups, the obvious no-winners such as the joke and flame groups were sifted out. (Yes, there are even some newsgroups where the participants dedicate themselves solely to the activity of insulting each other and anyone else who comes within their sites.) On finishing the selection process, there remained a list of about six thousand groups. It was by far the biggest mass posting of any kind ever done on the Usenet. We sat down at our computer about 12:30 A.M., choosing that hour because computer traffic was low at that time of night, and there was less likelihood of meeting with an electronic jam-up from the huge dissemination of information we were about to attempt.

Then I ceremoniously pushed a single key. The program started operation. We watched, almost hypnotized by the steady rhythmic flashing and movement on the screen that signaled the launching of each message around the globe. The lights continued to blink like small, green stars in the middle of the night. At first, we were tense, concerned that the program would somehow breakdown before the job was done. These fears were proven unfounded. The program moved through the list smoothly, flawlessly. Then the work was done. In ninety minutes the Green Card Lottery message had reached millions of people in every corner of the world. The next move consisted of going to sleep and waiting until morning for whatever reaction was to come.

Everyone in the office got up early that next day and went to work. The phones were already ringing off the hook. Those who were interested were asked to respond by e-mail, but the posting also contained the office phone number just in case someone wanted to speak to us directly.

They wanted to speak to us all right. Call after call came complaining about what we had done. "What the hell do you think you're doing. You've put your message on every goddamn newsgroup on the face of the planet, you idiots," they screeched into the receiver. Nearly all the callers sounded young. Nearly all were male. One emotionally disturbed voice after the other checked in. Even the tone of those who tried to register their dissatisfaction politely was tinged with something approximating hysteria.

We turned on the computer. The messages were rolling into the e-mail box at a dizzying pace. In fact, they were coming in by the thousands. Here, too, there were shrill messages of protest. The use of four-letter words was more than liberal. The amount of mail was particularly staggering because a number of protesters decided to do more than just apply bad language to the situation. Instead, they sent "mailbombs," huge electronic files of junk designed to clog up our computer by their sheer size. It seemed absolutely amazing that there were people who could become so distraught over the appearance of a simple, commercial message on their computer screens.

But that wasn't all. There was also an astoundingly huge number of requests for further information on the Green Card Lottery pouring in. On the screen we read over and over, "Please send me your information on the Green Card Lottery as soon as possible. Thank you." Many of these requests also contained details of the writer's personal immigration situation and asked specific questions about what to do. On the telephone, as well, calls came from everywhere, asking questions and requesting more information. We all began attempting to deal with the staggering amount of data before us. As quickly as possible, the messages were sorted, serious inquiries put in a separate file for future response, and the complaints deleted.

Then something unexpected happened. Our link to the Internet shut off. Internet Direct, the company that had promised not to stop us unless we did something illegal, the company that had assured us they could handle the expected heavy load of messages, ignored our agreed-upon procedure and cut our connection.

Looking back on it, it shouldn't have come as a surprise. Even when we reached an agreement with these people we were skeptical. They had been chosen in large part because they were local. In fact, they were one of the few local ISPs in business at the time. Remember that nearly all computer communications presently go over phone lines. It is important for a variety of reasons you'll soon learn to have a local dial-up number. Economy, the most important factor of all, dictated that we stick with a local dial-up number. Besides, given the somewhat controversial nature of the project to be done, it seemed best to deal with a company close by. That way, if there were problems, they could be worked out on a face-to-face basis.

Unfortunately, the face presented to us belonged to Bill Fisher, a twenty-something, khaki-swathed smart aleck. He was the one who represented Internet Direct at the conference we'd set up when we had tried to avoid the very result we were now experiencing. At that meeting, Fisher slouched down in his chair, listing to one side in what appeared to be a poor imitation of William F. Buckley. He had then proceeded to give behaving like a grown-up his best shot. His first move was to look at his watch and announce he could grant us only twenty minutes of his time. Ignoring the incredible rudeness of this remark, as well as the transparently affected body language, we explained in detail what we wanted to do and what some of the problems might be. Fisher said he would take it up with his associates. A week later the memo came from Fisher saying Internet Direct would not stop us.

Now that the hour of reckoning had come, in spite of what had been said either in person or in memos, the screen where large numbers of messages had appeared moments before was now blank. We immediately called Fisher. By this time, his carefully crafted, cool persona was in a shambles. He was shrieking uncontrollably. His system was overloaded. His phone was ringing off the hook. Internet Direct's system was crashing under the weight of the huge number of messages being received. No, they would not turn our connection back on, memo or no memo.

We, too, were upset. After all the effort we'd spent trying to create a smooth operation, and preparing for what was coming, a small service provider was going to cost us thousands of dollars in lost business. Phone calls began to come from potential clients who were unable to get through because Internet Direct had closed off our account. They wanted an explanation of why we had not answered their e-mail requests for more information on the Green Card Lottery. We responded as best we could, promising to send the information by regular mail, dubbed "snail mail" by those who reside in computerland. Meanwhile, we dispatched our lawyers to try to reason with Internet Direct. Eventually, after several days of wrangling, they were persuaded to forward our incoming mail to Netcom, where our account was still in place. Since that time, Internet Direct has sold its individual client list to a national ISP and many changes have occurred in the company's structure, but during that period, their size, inexperience, and the attitude of their personnel caused untold mountains of trouble.

As the day following the posting dawned, the phone was still ringing incessantly, with both protesters and potential immigration clients. By this time, some death threats had been received and certain enterprising individuals had started sending hundreds of junk faxes. We turned on our computer and utilized the Netcom account to read the messages posted on some of the newsgroups. Nearly all of them were about us. From that day forward, the Internet never stopped discussing C & S, as we came to be called. Everything we did was tracked. Every action was dissected and examined. Our motives and thought processes were analyzed. A long discussion ensued on the need for a name to be given to the practice of mass posting messages on the Net. After lengthy deliberation, it was decided to call the practice "spamming" in honor of a well-known skit by Monty Python's Flying Circus, the famous British comedy group. We were unfamiliar with the skit, but apparently it involved throwing lunch meat at a wall. The skit seemed to be a favorite among the university denizens and tech people.

The hysteria continued. Soon it was impossible to keep track of everything that was being said, let alone answer back. Finally, we stopped trying. The volume of discussion about us became so great that, to some, we began to seem like celebrities. Someone posted a message saying that having our e-mail address was like having the private phone number of the playmate of the month. A look in the mirror failed to produce a vision of Miss January looking back. Oh well. It was a nice thought.

TALES OF THE FOURTH ESTATE

Then things took an even more bizarre turn. The phone rang again, but this time it was neither an immigrant seeking a green card nor a shrill protester. Instead, it was Peter Lewis, the technical writer for *The New York Times*. I was flabbergasted. It was hard to believe that our mass posting would be of interest to the country's leading newspaper. Talking to Lewis on the phone at length, he seemed like a nice guy. The amazement continued as Lewis dispatched a photographer so that his story could be accompanied by a picture, giving everyone the opportunity to see what the most notorious twosome in cyberspace looked like. Two days later, I saw myself staring back from the front page of *The New York Times* business section under the headline: An Ad (Gasp!) in Cyberspace. True to my impression of him on the phone, the story he wrote was fair and balanced. The wryly humorous tone of the headline reflected my own take on the matter. It was still hard to understand why something as innocuous as a small commercial posting on a public electronic bulletin board seemed to be causing such pandemonium.

Like the endless discussions of C & S's behavior on the Net itself, from that day on the newspaper stories never let up. Following immediately on the heels of Peter Lewis was *Washington Post* reporter John Burgess. In the weeks and months that followed, my partner and I spoke to every major publication in the country repeatedly. Being interviewed became a full-time job and it became difficult to get much of anything else done. It took over a year for the press frenzy to die down, especially when new life would be breathed into it by some statement one of us had made in an interview, a newspaper article I had written, or the publication of the first edition of this book. Eventually, the "Green Card Incident," as it came to be called, was popularly accepted as the turning point for the commercialization of the Internet, and took its place in the annals of Net lore and history.

GROWING THE INTERNET

When the decision was made to try advertising on the Internet it seemed like a strategy that couldn't fail. Commercial use of the Internet was a natural. It required no special, sophisticated skills and the cost was very low. That many people wanted green card services in a market with a sizable international segment was no big surprise. Although it was certainly gratifying that the plan had worked so well, given everything going for it, it would have been more of a surprise if it hadn't worked.

What I honestly was not prepared for, however, was the passionate opposition encountered. It was always interesting to see how different people reacted to the story. If I spoke to anyone unfamiliar with the Internet, they were as baffled as I was over what had occurred. They asked what had been done to cause such controversy, and after I had finished explaining, they would always look back at me quizzically and say, "So what?" The old-time Internetters were a different story. Steeped in

Internet tradition, they wanted no change in the status quo, and using the Internet for commercial purposes was, I learned, a drastic change.

Since then commercialization has completely overtaken the Internet and now seems as natural as the sun rising in the east. To anyone who has come onto the Internet recently, the idea that commercialism was ever not a part of it probably seems strange indeed. That is why to really understand what happened at the time, a brief history lesson is in order.

The seeds of the Internet were sown by the U.S. government in the seventies, when an arm of the Defense Department called the Defense Advanced Research Program Agency (DARPA) wanted a computer network developed to support its efforts. Computers are usually thought of by most people as tools to do calculations, solve problems, and process or keep records. DARPA saw computers differently. They wanted them as a means for people to communicate with each other. To fill this need required a network. A software system had to be developed that would allow many different brands, sizes, and types of computers to speak to one another. This system was called a protocol. The protocol was called TCP/IP. By developing this protocol, Arpanet was born.

Arpanet was the granddaddy of computer networks, but others arose as well, all of them at universities or a few corporations such as IBM, which were computer-research centers. In the eighties, a great stride forward was made when the National Science Foundation (NSF), in order to extend the benefits of computer networking to noncommercial, academic research, set about to link various networks together. Five university locations were chosen as central points of connection to accomplish this, and a network of networks, the Internet, was born.

There were, however, many restrictions on who could utilize the Internet and for what purpose. Specifically, the Internet was to be used for research and nothing else. Accordingly, unless you were affiliated with a university, the government, or the research arm of a technical company, you were not permitted access. Each individual network on the Internet had its own set of rules, called Acceptable Use Policies (AUP) and the NSF itself had an AUP, but really, they were all pretty much the same. No commercialism. Research only.

In the nineties, the bomb fell. The NSF decided to open the Internet to commercial use. It also decided that anyone at all should be able to get access. Vice President Gore spoke of removing inequality between information haves and have-nots. Based on communication through the

Internet and the commercial, as well as educational, benefits it would bring, there was to be the dawning of a new, golden era in the development of our country and the rest of the world.

A flood of so-called newbies, with varying attitudes and backgrounds, began to invade the space of the once homogeneous Net research group. By this time the old guard had developed a strong attachment to what had grown to be their own little world and the newbies were not exactly welcome, nor could they be stopped. As an alternative, the original Netters decided upon a plan to educate the newbies into the established ways.

All agreed that the best method of training the newbies lay in a combination of proactive propaganda mixed with flaming or worse for those who got out of hand. Typical of the dogma Net gurus hoped to impart can be seen in this startling quote from *The Whole Internet Users' Guide and Catalog* by Ed Krol, who, in this passage, likens the Internet to a church.

> If you go to church and accept its teachings and philosophy, you are accepted by it and receive the benefits. If you don't like it, you can leave. The church is still there, and you get none of the benefits. Such is the Internet. If the network does something that causes damage to the Internet, it could be excommunicated until it mends its evil ways.

If you believe in the Bill of Rights of the U.S. Constitution, a chill should be running up your spine right about now.

Education of the masses is never easy, however. Some people just didn't get it. Foolishly, certain recalcitrant individuals such as myself refused to bow down in the church, practice the religion, or obey the laws of the nation-state. Stubbornly, I clung to the belief that I lived not in cyberspace but in Phoenix. Looking out the window today and seeing the mesquite trees rustling in the warm desert breeze, it still looks much as it did then, like the Arizona city I've grown to love. In the Valley of the Sun, advertising was never a sin. It was never rude. It was certainly never illegal. This battle that took place years ago was inevitably won by the millions of diverse people outside the research community, who now are the majority and driving force on the Internet. All those in every phase of human endeavor eventually come to learn that change is inevitable, and that truism applies to cyberspace as well.

Even before the very personal Internet "Big Bang" occurred in my life, the marketing power of the Internet appeared so compelling that it seemed almost an automatic idea to put together a company utilizing this remarkable resource. Some time ago, following a long-term career interest in marketing, I had set about the task of becoming familiar with the many types of selling possibilities available on the Internet that you will be reading about in this book. After some thought, the name "Cybersell®" seemed perfect for the new business. I asked my good friend, artist Jeff Neff (yes, that's his real name), to design the logo. Jeff, who had designed all the covers for my earlier books and promotion pieces over the years, was a Madison Avenue refugee. Long ago he had left the Manhattan scene and his Cardin suits behind, trading them for T-shirts and buffalo sandals. He had, however, taken his extraordinary talent with him and soon there was a symbol, a swirling vortex of color with stars popping out everywhere and a big, sun-yellow "Cybersell®" superimposed over it. Looking at that symbol made it all seem like it was really going to happen and the path became clear.

Cybersell® started with a basically sound idea, but you could not fairly discount the added benefit that the Internet was a red-hot commodity. It was impossible to pick up the newspaper or turn on the TV without hearing about it. Still, new companies and new ideas take time to get established, and preparation for a publicity campaign to launch Cybersell® into the public eye seemed in order. The usual quiet beginning and modest development most fledgling companies experience was expected and everyone in the office proceeded to dig in for the long haul. We needn't have bothered.

Immediately after the first wave of publicity, Cybersell® issued a press release announcing the startup of the company. Because of the notoriety gained from the Green Card Incident, the press was anxious to tell the world that the upstart who had rocked cyberspace with "spam" was now establishing a company to help others do the same thing. Of course, broad advertising on the Usenet was only a part of what was planned for the company. There were really so many creative possibilities and the intent for the company encompassed using them all. Nonetheless, Cybersell® received a grand launching in *The New York Times, The Wall Street Journal, The Washington Post,* and just about every other newspaper imaginable, plus ample mention by the major television networks. No one could have asked for more.

Over and over the phone rang with fresh Cybersell® prospects eager to be involved in this incredible new Internet market. Many of them understood very little about the Internet, so much of what we had to say to them involved explaining in very basic terms how the whole thing worked, much as you will be learning by reading this book. In getting to know Cybersell®'s first customers, we pulled no punches. In addition to the glittering moneymaking opportunities available through the Internet, the controversial aspects and problems in all areas were described extensively as well as they will be in the pages to follow. When each speech was finished, the customer at the other end of the line invariably had only one question: "How successful were you?" We told them we had gotten in excess of twenty thousand inquiries for our information. These names and addresses had, in good business fashion, been recorded and saved as future marketing prospects. The entire project took under three months, but if all Usenet groups had been posted to at once in the first place, the same result probably could have been achieved in one night. The final count of actual paying clients for this single venture was slightly in excess of one thousand and resulted in gross profit of $100,000. That was all anybody who called about Cybersell® needed to hear.

Since those early days, when advertising on the Internet was a novel concept, the picture has changed drastically. The World Wide Web, the graphical and multimedia portion of the Internet, has grown into its main feature, as well as its primary commercial area. Advertising on Usenet still remains controversial in a small circle culled from the Net research faction, but so-called spamming has become such an everyday occurrence that to the overwhelming majority it is not only no longer front page news, it hardly causes so much as a raised eyebrow. Mass posting also remains a highly effective way to sell products and services, and mass e-mailing has been added to it as a common method of selling. You can read about the current state of mass posting on Usenet in chapter 4 and about mass e-mailing in chapter 5. Predictably enough, the current most controversial issues on the Internet are no longer advertising but freedom of speech and the proliferation of pornography, especially its easy and uncontrolled availability to children. You will learn about all of these issues in the rest of this book.

I've told you the Green Card Incident story in detail to give you an idea of how the Net got to where it is today and an in-depth understanding of what you will find when you undertake making a fortune on the

Internet. It's sometimes a bumpy ride, but it's fun and exciting too. In the pages that follow, you'll share in the techniques I've learned, and you'll come to know them well enough to put them into practice. Even if you never try any of the moneymaking methods described, hopefully you'll enjoy discovering more about the new vista of communication called the Information Superhighway and its primary branch, the Internet. Personally, though, it's my hope that you decide to do more than just sit back and watch. If you would like to help from Cybersell® in whatever you plan, you can e-mail us at *market@cyber.sell.com*, or simply use the telephone, 602–952–0569.

As was mentioned earlier, the Green Card Incident has been credited with being the turning point in the commercialization of the Internet, but with or without it, use of the Internet for profit was inevitable. Now, in its early stages, is the perfect time for you to be looking at making a fortune on the Internet. There's been a lot of name-calling done since the great adventure you've just read about began. One of the names included with the rest has been "pioneer." Think of yourself that way and fortune on the Internet is yours for the taking.

3
Better, Faster, and a Lot Cheaper

SELLING TO THIRTY MILLION PEOPLE WHO CALL
THE NET HOME

SUCCESS AT MAKING A LOT OF MONEY IS ALMOST always based on a single, simple principle: the ability to do something better, faster, or cheaper. You know that Cyberselling means finding or inventing a good product or service, and then using the Internet to market what you have to sell. The main reason you can make a fortune on the Internet is that you can sell on it better, faster, and cheaper than anyone ever thought possible. Of course, it is necessary that the product or service you offer also incorporates these sterling qualities. Here, you'll find help in selling that special item on the I-way, and in chapter 9 you'll see what others have sold. You're about to learn how your computer can turn you into the most successful salesperson that ever lived.

INTERACTIVE: THE IRRESISTIBLE FORCE

Looking at our basic business success principle, the first element is "better." Explaining why selling on the I-way is better becomes a little difficult due to the fact that computer marketing is so much better, it's hard to know where to begin. Above all, what makes Cyberselling more effective than any other sales method is the feature called "interactive." The term interactive is another computer-age buzzword you've been hearing a lot lately. For marketing, it means that instead of simply sitting in front of a television or reading a magazine, quietly watching an advertisement pass before your eyes, you can in some way communicate back to the seller your level of interest, questions, or desire to purchase. Remember, the Internet is a series of computer networks. What computer networks were invented to do is allow people to communicate with each other easily. Two categories of individuals who now have more opportunity to interact than ever before are buyers and sellers.

At first, this may not seem like such a revolutionary breakthrough, but if you think about it a bit more, you will see that it is. Let's go back to television or magazines. You see an advertisement for, let's say, an automobile. Whether in print or on television, it's costing the car manufacturer a bundle to put that ad in front of you, even if you aren't counting advertising production expenses. Because standard media charges increase according to the amount of space or time the ad takes up, the advertiser has two main goals in mind: grab your attention and keep it short. In order to grab your attention, the advertiser uses a number of techniques. He or she may choose some intense-looking hard bodies as models. You can watch them driving the cars at high speeds up beautiful mountain roads that most of us will probably never see in our lifetime. All this is a lot of fun and certainly does get you to watch and think about the vehicle, but what now? Remember, goal number two is to keep things brief, but suppose your attention has truly been captured and you have some real interest in buying a car. Your curiosity has been piqued and there are lots of things you want to know. Unfortunately, it's past business hours when you see this ad, so you can't go to your phone and call the dealership. Anyway, you aren't about to move from your comfortable chair, drop your magazine, or turn off the TV, and run to the phone. Your questions remain unanswered. By the time you've gone to bed and gotten up the next morning, you can't remember what it was you wanted to know about the vehicle. If the automobile seller is really unlucky, you may have forgotten about the car altogether.

Now let's take the same example and apply the interactive feature. You turn on your computer and you find your way to the cyberspace auto mall. (We'll explain how to get there in chapter 7 about the World Wide Web.) You are faced with a selection of dozens of auto manufacturers. You punch a key to see Infiniti. Is this really the car for you? You are whisked to the Infiniti car lot where you will see on your computer screen pictures of three car models, the G-20, J-30, and Q-45, each with the suggested base sticker price underneath. You select the Q-45 and punch another key to see more. Immediately, specifications of the car are shown on your screen. You are also given the ability to access several different independent reviews of the car. You look at each, and decide that yes, this is the car for you. You tell the computer to proceed with a demonstration. You are now given a close-up, full-color picture of the Q-45. With the touch of yet another key, the driver's door opens and you now get a full view of the instrument panel. At the bottom of your computer screen flashes the message, "Want to take a test drive?" Of course! You punch in "yes" and suddenly your computer screen is transformed into a car simulator, much like the flight simulator video games you may like to play with. Certainly, a simulation is not the real thing, but your computer gives you the feeling that you are inside that Q-45, driving around town, through the mountains, even on the Indy-500 racetrack.

When your test drive is over, a list of possible options to put on the car, such as fancier wheels, gold packages, CD player, telephones, etc., appears on your computer screen. You are also presented with choices of colors and interiors. As you click on each option, the picture of the car changes on the screen to reflect your new choice. This gives you the ability to design your own car from the screen. When you have selected exactly what you want, a total price appears at the bottom of your screen, along with the name of the nearest dealer who can provide that exact configuration for you. You are then given the option of e-mailing that dealer, who will then call you to arrange for a personal showing of the real thing, or perhaps you will even have the option of placing your order for the car through a discount auto broker. You could be given the option of making your deal right on-line. No more spending hours in the showroom while the salesperson goes back and forth from the manager's office to you and then back again. Buying a car couldn't be easier, or more enjoyable.

The technology to back up the scenario we've just described is here right now. We will learn later on that some of these multimedia ideas do not work well over the relatively slow standard telephone lines that hook up most computers at present. The technology is changing all the time, however, and within a few years, with installation of fiber-optic networks and Integrated Services Digital Network (ISDN) lines, all of this and more will be common. Still, even today, the interactive marketing possibilities are mostly limited only by your own imagination.

If you are a beginner with computers, the procedure we've just out-lined is advanced for you. Still, there is much you can do on a basic level to take advantage of the interactive selling feature your computer offers.

In addition, Internet service providers (ISPs) now all offer varying degrees of technical support to assist customers who want to use the Internet technology for commercial purposes. From an informational standpoint as well as the perspective of instant gratification, it's hard to beat the interactive capabilities of the Internet. Nonetheless, that is only the most obvious customer relations benefit to Cyberselling. There is a feature more subtle yet even more powerful than interactive. Instead of simply selling a product, you are building a relationship. Right off the bat, you have an interest in the Internet in common with your customer. It's a perfect beginning for forming the kind of trusting rapport that leads to sales. That closeness is amplified because your words and pic-tures can go directly into your customer's home or office, just like televi-sion. You have probably heard famous television personalities over the years speak of the special rapport they have with their fans because of this. Don't we really feel as if we know Murphy Brown or Tim "The Tool Man" Taylor personally? But the computer goes television one bet-ter. Not only can you talk to your customers, they can answer back! They begin to feel not only as if they know you, but you know them as well. There can be no more powerful selling instrument than that.

Hopefully you are convinced by now that there is no better way to sell a product or service than Cyberselling, but if you need to hear more, you won't be disappointed. It's already been mentioned that the first goal of any sales effort is to get the attention of the customer. Yet often even the most creative, clever, interesting, and well-thought-out advertisements fail to accomplish this very basic objective. Why? Because you never see them. A commercial comes on television and automatically you tune it out of your mind. Perhaps you pick up your remote control and simply zap it. You use this opportunity as a break time to talk to the person on the couch next to you or to grab a snack. Whether or not you choose to avoid it, in a few short minutes, the commercial is gone and that's that.

The same is true of newspaper or magazine advertisements. Your eye moves down the page as you fish for the articles you want to read. If the article that interests you doesn't lead your eye to a particular advertise-ment, you are likely to skip over it. Perhaps certain articles don't interest you. Then you will never even open to the page where an ad may appear. On busier days, you may neglect to read the paper altogether. Read or not, it gets thrown out, ads and all, to make way for tomorrow's edition.

Things are very different with computer advertisements. They wait patiently until you are ready to turn on your computer and look at them. They do not disappear after a specific time like radio or television commercials. It might also be added that they do not pop up when you don't want them and distract you during a crucial moment of your favorite program either. They do not get thrown out as part of a publication without your having ever looked at them. In fact, there is only one way to get rid of them. You must make a specific decision to bring them on your screen and look at them, then, if you decide that they are of no interest, you can delete them from your screen. In that brief second when you do look, you may also decide there is something worthy of your attention. In fact, you may even find you are so interested that you want to know more about the product or service offered. Either way, the seller has been given the opportunity to have that item considered—a much better shot than can be gotten with nearly any other medium.

Last but not least, you can sell better on the Internet because it is new. The public is only just now becoming familiar with all the Internet and other interactive services have to offer. As each person goes through the process of learning about the wonders of the Internet, they usually become enthralled with what they find there. If what they find happens to be your product or service, the overall effect will rub off onto whatever it is you are selling.

Commercialism on the Internet is about as hot as a topic gets these days. Almost everyone has an interest. If you view any part of the Internet, you will see advertising. Thousands of businesses have already launched their first foray onto some part of the Internet, but from a pure percentage standpoint the fact is that relatively few of the businesses in existence have actually tried it and it is still very much a novelty. This means that those who do begin to use it as a marketing tool now will still be among the first and will, therefore, stand out! Surely, the window of opportunity to be among the first will not always be open. It will probably not even be there for very much longer, as every day businesses of all sizes race to jump on the I-way bandwagon. But the chance to be a leader is there at the moment for those who are smart enough to take advantage of it.

Of course, being one of the first also means getting into the game while commercial use of the Net is still a free-for-all and as was recently noted in the *Harvard Business Review,* the rules of the game have still to be clearly formulated. Yet, even that can have its benefits. If a major goal of advertising is to get noticed, pushing the envelope certainly achieves that. Once again, results of the Green Card Incident show when it comes to I-way marketing, controversy can work in your favor.

THE NO-WAIT MARKETING CAMPAIGN

We've seen why you can sell better, much better, on the Internet. Now let's examine how Cyberselling helps you accomplish the second element of the basic goal for success: faster. Computers are known for the speed in which data can be processed. Electronic data travels at blinding speeds. A signal travels around the world in fractions of a second. To demonstrate how computer marketing is faster, consider the longstanding staple of direct-marketers, the mass mailing. The old-fashioned method requires you first to design a mailing piece, including both art and copy. Once that is done, you must convert these efforts into camera-ready art so the printer can produce the finished mailer. This in itself may take a few days to a few weeks. Then you take your art to a printer. Printers are not well known for working quickly or meeting deadlines. If you are extremely lucky, you may be able to get your printing completed in a week or two. Next you must stuff envelopes, paste on mailing labels, sort, and get the entire mailing ready for the post office. This could take several days or more.

Now comes the really fun part, dealing with the post office. Netters are fond of calling regular mail snail mail. It's not hard to understand why. Recently the post office quit guaranteeing that expensive priority mail will be delivered within two days. Even first-class mail within a single city sometimes takes a couple of days to arrive. And bulk mail? Some bulk-mail pieces take more than a month to reach their ultimate destination. Finally, though, the mail comes. People see your product and they either want more information or they want to place an order. Maybe they will call you on the phone, which is fast, but many will simply write back to you, via snail mail. From the time you created your mailing piece to the time you get your first order, over a month has gone by.

Now let's consider the same mailer, but sent via e-mail to an electronic mailing list. The very first step doesn't change. You must still create your piece. Once it is created, however, you're almost ready to begin raking in the sales. No camera-ready art. No printers. No stuffing envelopes. No post office slowdowns. You simply zap it to your computerized mailing list and everyone receives your solicitation within a matter of minutes. You couldn't even physically carry the piece across the street to your neighbor's house that fast. And, since your customers have the option of sending an order back electronically, you could begin receiving orders within hours after your mail goes out. You may have made a fortune selling electronically in less time than it would take to receive a single order the old-fashioned way.

The print media is another typical vehicle for advertising products or services. Standard procedure has you first designing your artwork and ad copy. Then it must be converted into camera-ready art. There are no printers this time, but you must still send the art on to the publication, wait until it appears in the appropriate issue and that issue is delivered to or purchased at a newsstand by your potential customers. In the case of a magazine, this might take several weeks or longer.

Compare Web sites, electronic discussion groups, or e-mail with paper publications. The Internet vehicles are available for all cyberspace residents to view at any time. You must still prepare your copy and graphics. Once prepared, however, you can place your advertisement in circulation at any time. It appears on your customer's computer screens within minutes after it's posted. Using the old-fashioned method, even a publication as speedy as your daily newspaper will require at least a few days before your ad is seen. In addition, as with your electronic mailer, your customers, besides using the traditional response methods of telephone, fax, or regular mail, can contact you instantly via e-mail. You can even get your computer to send additional information automatically by computer on request, without having to lift a finger. Think of this as e-mail on demand. How to do this is explained later on.

THE BUSINESS BARGAIN OF THE CENTURY

Finally, we reach the third element of our target goal: cheaper. No contest here at all. Estimates on Internet participation vary, but the most quoted figure seems to be thirty million. Moreover, that number grows by a mind-boggling amount everyday. Once again, estimates vary, but the most quoted figure sets the increase at about ten thousand new users per day. When it comes to sheer numbers of people reached, only the very top television programs can match the Internet at any price. As for publication, there is no single one that can equal the Internet's reach.

Price, however, is always a paramount consideration, so let's look at some comparisons with marketing costs for other standard types of media. The figures given in the charts below are based on a survey conducted in July 1996. They show how much you will pay to sell to the ready audience on the Internet versus some other popular methods you're sure to recognize.

INTERNET VERSUS TELEVISION

Media Buy	Total Cost	Cost Per Thousand Per Minute	You Get
Local ad on prime time TV show	$7,500	$53.19	30-second local spot reaching 282,000 adults
Local ad on prime time TV show	$4,200	$59.57	15-second local spot reaching 282,000 adults
Local ad on prime time Sunday or Monday night movies	$2,900	$30.52	30-second local spot reaching 190,000 adults
Local ad on prime time Sunday or Monday night movies	$1,750	$36.84	15-second local spot reaching 190,000 adults
Local ad on Friday night prime time TV show	$2,400	$55.17	30-second local spot reaching 87,000 adults
Local ad on network late night TV show	$1,200	$32.43	30-second local ad reaching 74,000 adults

Internet Versus Radio

Media Buy	Total Cost	Cost Per Thousand Per Minute	You Get
A.M. drive time ad KVRY Phoenix, AZ	$104	$7.56	60-second spot reaching 13,760 listeners
Midday ad (10 A.M.–3 P.M.) KVRY Phoenix, AZ	$124	$42.46	60-second spot reaching 2,920 listeners
Evening ad (3 P.M.–8 A.M.) KVRY Phoenix, AZ	$134	$45.89	60-second spot reaching 2,920 listeners

Internet Versus Newspapers

Media Buy	Cost Per Column Inch	Cost Per 1,000 Readers	You Get
The New York Times Mon.–Sat.	$613	$71.89	1.1 million circulation
The New York Times Sunday	$649	$49.25	1.7 million circulation
Los Angeles Times Mon.–Sat.	$351	$44.26	1,023,000 circulation
Los Angeles Times Sunday	$421.25	$38.82	1,400,000 circulation
Arizona Republic Mon.–Sat.	$174.95	$46.53	485,000 circulation
Arizona Republic Sunday	$216.05	$45.69	610,000 circulation

INTERNET VERSUS MAGAZINES

MEDIA BUY	COST PER AD (BASED ON SIZE AND USE OF COLOR)	COST PER THOUSAND READERS	YOU GET
People magazine	$95,000	$30.16	1 page black-and-white ad; 3,150,000 circulation
People magazine	$129,000	$40.95	1 page color ad; 3,150,000 circulation
People magazine	$61,000	$19.36	½ page black-and-white ad; 3,150,000 circulation
People magazine	$81,500	$25.87	½ page black-and-white ad; 3,150,000 circulation
TV Guide	$137,500	$10.58	1 page color ad; 13 million circulation
TV Guide	$75,600	$5.82	½ page color ad; 13 million circulation

INTERNET VERSUS DIRECT MAIL

MEDIA BUY	TOTAL COST	COST PER THOUSAND HOUSEHOLDS	YOU GET
10,000 color brochures	$10,0000	$1,000	10,000 color brochures mailed to individual households

Media Buy	Total Cost Per Month	Cost Per Thousand Per Month	You Get
A leased line	$1,000	$0.03	56K leased line full-time Internet access to 30 million people; no space or time limit
Internet business dial-up	$30	$0.001	Business dial-up account with Web capability to 30 million people; no space or time limit

As you look at what it costs to sell through other mediums, you must be impressed with the staggeringly high expense of placing goods and services in front of potential customers. The cheapest price to reach a thousand people only one time is $6 in a national magazine, $7.50 on the radio, $32 on television, $45 in a big city newspaper, and a whopping $1000 by direct mail. No wonder big companies get most of the business. Who else could afford even a thirty-second spot on a program with a big viewership like *Seinfeld*? Who else, for that matter, could afford to advertise on almost any network program, even one facing the imminent threat of cancellation?

While you may not have the cash to be able to go up against the corporate titans on other mediums like network TV, perhaps the most wonderful part of Cyberselling is that on the Internet, the playing field is level. It costs only 3.3 cents to reach 1,000 Netters for a solid month. If you've got the product and the talent it takes to write simple descriptions of that product, you can reach the public as easily and effectively as Coca-Cola or McDonald's. If you are really creative and have the ability to produce artwork or clever selling copy, there are ways you can utilize the Net to disseminate it at low cost, as you will see in the following chapters when the various marketing methods available on the Internet and the rest of the I-way are described. There is no doubt you have the intelligence and imagination to make it to the top. There are any number of people who have just as much marketing ability as those whose advertising strategies draw big money and are seen by a broad public everyday. If you've always believed you had a great idea that everyone would love if only they knew about it, let Cyberselling show you how to put your ideas to work on the I-way. Now is your time to shine.

4
Free Advertising to Millions of People on the Usenet

OF THE MANY GIDDY REACTIONS BROUGHT ON BY THE grandeur of the Internet concept, some of the giddiest surround the Usenet. A highly active center for public Internet communications, the Usenet begs to be tagged with one of those colorful descriptive phrases mentioned earlier. You could call it the world's biggest town-hall meeting, or perhaps the world's biggest free-for-all. Maybe it's the world's biggest cocktail party. It's probably all those things and more. To you, it represents what is arguably the world's biggest and best marketplace.

In simple terms, the Usenet is a collection of some twenty thousand discussion groups, each one covering a different and specific topic. You can read or participate in any group simply by entering a few commands on your keyboard. It is impossible to determine exactly how many groups there are because the number changes continuously. Likewise, the exact number of Usenet participants is unknown. Estimates run between five and twenty million. All agree, however, that the daily increase in size is impressive.

The Usenet started as an experiment in North Carolina in 1979. The first participants were Duke University and the University of North

Carolina. The original idea was that people could pass useful information to each other through a series of electronic bulletin boards, where newsworthy informational messages on a variety of topics would be posted. For this reason, the term "newsgroup" was used to describe them. Time went on and the Usenet grew, with the networks of more and more organizations joining in. As the number increased, the newsgroups gradually became less and less repositories of hard information and instead developed as forums for discussion and the exchange of ideas. Although custom still dictates that each newsgroup posting offer up some kind of worthwhile information, in practice that standard has long since been abandoned. In reality, the tone of Usenet "conversations" reflects the same vast variety of discussion levels that exist in everyday conversations taking place continuously throughout world society; the diminishing value of these groups as sources of hard data is a subject of reflection often expressed in the professional media itself.

Newsgroup subjects have also evolved far afield of their original research and academic roots. It would be difficult to imagine any area of human endeavor or interest that does not have a representative newsgroup. The mix is especially diverse because there is no central authority responsible for developing these groups in an orderly manner. The fact is that anyone can start a newsgroup on the Usenet about whatever subject he or she pleases. Instructions for doing so can be found in any technical guide to the Internet.

NEWSGROUP NAMES

Let's take a quick look at a sample of a few newsgroups now in existence, to give you a better flavor of what is going on here.

bit.listserv.ibm-nets
fr.network.divers
aus.jobs
alt.politics.democrats
alt.binaries.sounds.music
ba.helping-hand
soc.history.war.misc
soc.couples
bionet.cellbiol
soc.culture.italian

biz.sco.magazine

alt.support.diet

alt.fan.teens.idols

alt.make.money.fast

realtynet.invest

rec.scuba

fr.rec.cuisine

dod.jobs

info.big-internet

phl.forsale

talk.religion

As you read the newsgroup names, you will see that they are composed of several words or abbreviations of words strung together with dots. Here are some random choices offered as examples: *alt.rock-n-roll.oldies, dc.dining*, and *nz.molbio*. Let's examine them to get a better idea of how Usenet works. Look closely at the first word in each of these examples. They indicate the *hierarchy* to which each of these groups belongs. Because there are so many newsgroups, hierarchies are used as a convenient way of cataloging, so finding the ones that interest you is easier. The first of our examples comes from what is arguably the most interesting hierarchy. "Alt" stands for alternative. This is the most eclectic of the hierarchies as well as the largest. It is composed of over six hundred newsgroups. Surprisingly, it is considerably bigger than the next largest hierarchy, "comp," which stands for computer. It is in the alt hierarchy that you will find many of those sex groups that cause such great public consternation. Just exactly how much consternation you will again learn in chapter 10. You will also find fan groups such as *alt.fan.david.bowie* or *alt.fan.howard.stern*. While many topics in the alt hierarchy are recreational in nature, they can also be serious. The support groups for such diseases as cancer, arthritis, and depression can be found here. On the other side of the coin, lovesick swains have been known to create groups in adoration of their girlfriends. That is why some of the names in the so-called "fan" groups are ones you won't recognize. Groups devoted to special friends, or personal enemies for that matter, usually attract only one participant who, presumably, enjoys talking to himself.

The additional two groups in this extremely brief sample list exemplify some other Usenet features. At the beginning of one you will see

DISCARD

"nz." This stands for New Zealand. There are many hierarchies from countries other than our own. "Molbio" stands for molecular biology. This is an example of the more traditional, research-oriented groups that arose out of the Internet's scientific roots. The remaining sample group, *dc.dining*, is a discussion of restaurants in our nation's capital. Nearly every major city in the country has its own regional hierarchy devoted to subjects of interest in the area. The individual topics in each regional hierarchy tend to mimic those in all the others. There is, for example, a "for sale" newsgroup in the hierarchy of every region. When you are finally connected to the Internet, you can simply get a list that will be made available to you by your ISP. As you look at the group names, the meaning of some will be obvious. Others will read like gibberish. Still others will seem to sound like one thing and turn out to be another. You can always find out for sure simply by tuning in to the group to see what they're talking about.

All newsgroups, irrespective of topic or hierarchy, are equally accessible to everyone everywhere through the Internet. This is true even of the regional hierarchies, hierarchies from foreign countries, or those from particular universities. Be aware, however, that ISPs do not necessarily carry every single newsgroup in existence. They choose guided by budget and assessment of user interest. Since your objective is to make your product or service known to your most likely customers, you should be very careful to pick an ISP who will offer the largest possible selection of newsgroups.

HOW USENET WORKS

Just as the Web is supported by a program called a browser, the Usenet operates on a program called a newsreader. To get the feel of the Usenet, simply tune in and jump around a little. The newsreader program is almost always supplied to you by your ISP at no extra charge. If not, or if you don't like your ISP's program, you can look for a free one on the Internet or buy a commercial newsreader. Once you have the program, then by typing in some simple commands you can easily and quickly call up any newsgroup you choose. When you do enter your request to view a certain group, the first thing you will see on your screen is a list of one-line descriptors. Each of them tells you briefly the subject matter of the various discussions going on in the group at that time. All the messages you will read come from people just like you, who have decided they want their thoughts aired in public. When someone posts a message and others post additional messages in reply, a "thread" is created. If a message is posted and nobody chooses to comment further, the thread ends there. As you look at the descriptions of the threads on the group you have selected, you will see a number. That number tells you how many messages are in the thread.

You can choose to read any or all threads on a newsgroup, again simply by hitting a key or two on your keyboard. When the first message of a thread you have selected comes on your screen, at the top of it you will see who sent it, the date it was sent, the subject, and more information than you probably want on the path it took through the Internet to get to you. You will also notice, as you read along, that the same message seems to be repeated over and over again. That is because as each person adds another message to the thread, he or she commonly repeats all the other messages in the thread that came before. Often, there is so much repetition, it is difficult to extract the single new message from the rest that you have already seen. Some newsreader programs try to solve the problem by putting the new message in different color type from the old parts of the thread or having checkmarks next to sentences that have already been repeated one or more times.

If you want to add to a thread that interests you, or you want to begin your own thread, once again this can be done easily by typing out your message and dispatching it electronically with a few simple keystrokes to the newsgroup of your choice. That is how the advertising for the Green Card Lottery was accomplished on the Usenet. In placing a message on the Usenet, you also send out your own data on where your message came from. Among other things, this allows those who have seen your message to answer back, either privately to your e-mail address, or publicly by posting yet another message to the thread. It was by e-mail responses to the Green Card Usenet postings that requests for further information about legal services came in. If you want to keep your whereabouts a secret, you can do so by using an Anonymous Server or remailer, discussed in chapters 10 and 16. Doing this is fine if your purpose is to hide out. That is certainly not the objective here.

The overwhelming majority of newsgroups will accept all messages automatically. There are, however, some newsgroups that are "moderated." This means that posted messages, instead of going out directly to the public, are first sent to someone whose job it is to decide what will and will not be posted for universal consumption.

At the end of each message posted is the signature. The signature contains the name of the person who posted the message and his or her e-mail address. Phone numbers, snail mail addresses, company names, and other identifying information can likewise be included. The signature is also a place where personal expression is common. Those Usenet participants who want to tell the world who they are or what they believe in can do it in their signatures. Famous quotes or famous quotes that have been slightly altered are popular choices. The truly creative don't rely on the words of others, but make up their own statements instead. Here are some examples of signatures:

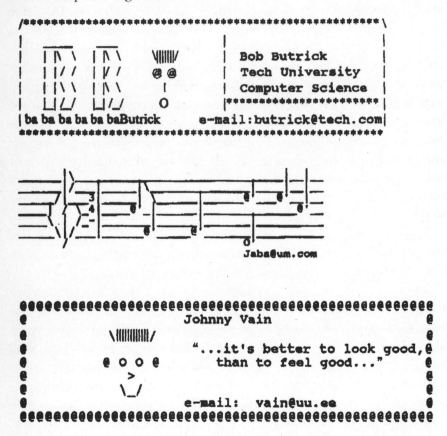

As you can see, you may also include a small drawing if you so choose. The only real limitation in the signature is, once again, dictated by custom. A signature is supposed to be no more than four lines in length. As usual, observation of this unwritten rule is fairly lax, except that some news-posting programs are configured to cut off signatures that exceed the preferred number of lines.

Although there are some twenty thousand newsgroups now in existence, that number is misleading, because many of the groups draw no participation. Some newsgroups seem really not even intended for discussion but rather exist simply to show off the silliness of their names. For example, there are three groups devoted to *alt.alien.vampire*. The first is *alt.alien.vampire.flonk*, the second is *alt.alien.vampire.flonk.flonk*, and the third is—well, you can probably guess. In any case, only the group with the single flonk gets read. The rest are for the sake of art and symmetry.

There are various groups made up of Usenet readers who voluntarily undertake the task of measuring newsgroup participation. Results have been published in *The Internet Complete Reference* by Harley Hahn and Rick Stout. The study identifies the twenty-five most popular newsgroups, which we have listed in chapter 10—the chapter discussing sex on the Net—because almost every one of these top-rated groups deals with that subject. Nonetheless, many groups, in addition to these, enjoy heavy readership and if one looks like it covers a particularly good subject with an audience that is a good match for the product or service you are trying to sell, you should certainly try it. To a certain extent, you can tell if a group has many participants simply by reading it. This does not account, however, for those who simply read the group but do not post, so you may get even more than you bargain for.

Messages appearing on newsgroups tend to be short. This maintains the conversational tone of the postings. Some groups are configured to reject electronically messages of greater than a certain length.

The real excitement of Usenet lies not so much in the information transmitted as it does in the ability to bring people together and give a voice to the millions of individuals who before could be heard only by an immediate circle of friends and family. The ability for nearly anyone to have his or her quotes read by huge numbers of people has its up- and downsides. Viewpoints that previously might never have been heard can be offered up for public consideration without the conventional media deciding what is and is not worthy. It is often said that one of the real beauties of computer communication is its egalitarian aspects. Since you can't see who you are talking to, you can't judge them by their outside appearances, their bank accounts, or cars, but only by the context and expression of their thoughts. In this atmosphere, friends and lovers may find each other and offer a measure of human comfort that is often the breath of life to the sick, lonely, or lovelorn. For those with no pressing emotional need, the Usenet, on its better days, can provide diversion, companionship, and an occasional good laugh.

Still, the worst of human nature is also exhibited on the Usenet. Flame groups vigorously pursue their self-appointed duty of insulting everyone in sight. All kinds of feelings from bad temper to bigotry can be found expressed in the messages posted to newsgroups. Just as in the real world, old and young, male and female, black and white, Jew and Christian, Turk and Armenian fight with each other. The fact that a combatant never has to come face to face with the enemy often leads to abandonment of scruples and some of the most blatantly crude exchanges you've ever heard. Then, too, although it can be interesting and informative to read Usenet postings, there is no editorial authority checking to see that what is being posted is true and accurate. There is potential for trouble when you take what you read on the Usenet too seriously. A classic Usenet philosophy is that it is run under a system of anarchy. To the true Usenet fanatic, this is a positive feature, but not such a comforting thought to the average individual. All in all, to sum up both the good and the bad, Usenet is just one more place where people generally go about the business of being people.

MAKING MONEY WITH USENET

An attempt has been made here to give you a picture of what the Usenet is and the way it operates as a framework for explaining how it can be used to help you make your Internet fortune. Usenet is one of only two areas of the Internet where you can go to find groups of people and place messages before them. There is no reason that the message you choose to post should not be one that tells about a product you have to sell. When you get ready to place your first advertising message on the Usenet, you can use a one-step or two-step process. In a one-step process, you give all your sales information and ask for the order on the very first encounter. An example of this would be the following:

IBM PCs for sale.

These are original "classic" PCs with 64K RAM, single 5¼ inch Floppy Drives, and Monochrome monitor. Will never run Windows, but a real collector's item, and can help your children learn computer programming. Only $50 plus $12 shipping. Originally

$2,000!! Hurry! Limited Quantities. Charge your order to a credit card by calling 1–800–548–7841, or send your check or money order for $62 to PC Classics, Box 1111, Scottsdale, AZ 85267.

In a two-step process, you don't give price and order information right away. Instead, you tell about your products or services briefly and ask those who are interested to contact you if they'd like to know more. You then prepare a detailed description of your product, including answers to any common or obvious questions your customers may have. Included in the second step of your presentation will be the price of your product or service and specific instruction on how to order. The short, first posting of your two-step process should contain the most exciting and desirable features of what you are selling. The product should be described clearly and accurately. You can ask for responses by e-mail to your personal mailbox. You can also ask customers to contact you by telephone, fax, or snail mail. A limitation of newsgroup messages for advertising purposes is that the only "pictures" you can use are those you are able to form from standard characters on a typewriter. Here are some examples of what that might look like.

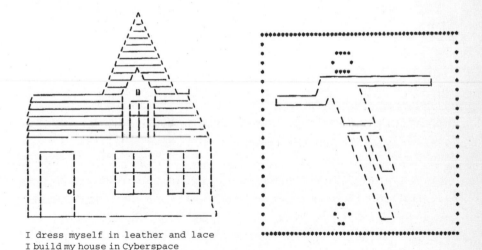

I dress myself in leather and lace
I build my house in Cyberspace

Since you are severely limited in the graphics department, the words you choose must draw a picture for you. To show you what a first message in a two-step process might look like, here, as an example, is the message for the famous Green Card Incident posting used.

Green Card Lottery 1994 May Be The Last One!

THE DEADLINE HAS BEEN ANNOUNCED

The Green Card Lottery is a completely legal program giving away a certain annual allotment of green cards to persons born in certain countries. The lottery program was scheduled to continue on a permanent basis. However, recently, Senator Alan J. Simpson introduced a bill into the U.S. Congress which could end any future lotteries. THE 1994 LOTTERY IS SCHEDULED TO TAKE PLACE SOON, BUT IT MAY BE THE VERY LAST ONE.

PERSONS BORN IN MOST COUNTRIES QUALIFY, MANY FOR FIRST TIME.

The only countries NOT qualifying are: Mexico, India, PR China, Taiwan, Philippines, South Korea, Canada, United Kingdom (except Northern Ireland), Jamaica, Dominican Republic, El Salvador and Vietnam.

Lottery registration will take place soon. 55,000 green cards will be given to those who register correctly. NO JOB IS REQUIRED.

THERE IS A STRICT JUNE DEADLINE. THE TIME TO START IS NOW!!

For FREE information via E-mail, send request to cslaw@indirect.com or contact us at:

Canter & Siegel
Immigration Attorneys
1234 E. Camelback Road, Ste 567, Phoenix AZ USA 85018
602–661–1111 (telephone) 602–451–2222 (fax)

As you can see, our customers received several options for reaching us to request more information. They could make contact by telephone, fax, or e-mail. Responses were actually received in all three ways, but the overwhelming majority chose e-mail. You will find in marketing your own product on the Usenet that the ability to deal with potential purchasers through e-mail is a tremendous plus. It allows your customer to request what he or she needs immediately and at virtually no cost. Even if you have thousands of responses to handle each day, you can send the data the customers asked for in equally speedy fashion and, likewise, with minimal expense. This is a system where the printing and postage costs of sending sales literature is a thing of the past. In addition, some of the die-hard computer addicts, who have bonded with their PCs to the extent that it has become another body part, often find alternative forms of communication foreign and can assimilate information only when they receive it through e-mail. If you plan to market to the tech crowd, therefore, e-mail is the only way to go.

If you really want to speed up responses to your customer inquiries, you can set up an automatic response robot. The word "robot" conjures up pictures of the cute little metal creatures from *Star Wars*, but once again, the term simply provides an easy way to visualize an electronic function. In this case, the robot is a program that automatically sends the second step of your presentation to anyone who types in a short command such as "send info." Inquiries are sent to your e-mail box, but this time instead of a human being reading each message and striking the correct keys to send your prepared response, the robot program does the work for you. A drawback to using a robot is that if a customer wants to ask very specific questions rather than receiving your standard electronic "brochure" you will not realize this fact, because no one will be reading the messages you receive. There are two possible ways around this problem. First, you could hire a programmer to devise a robot that will send the brochure only if specific words are contained in the request. All other e-mail would then come to your mailbox where you could read and answer each request manually. A second and probably simpler solution is to set up two separate e-mail addresses. Your advertisement can then tell people to send requests for information to one address if they want to receive an automatically generated brochure, or to another if they have special questions.

Finally, an additional method you can employ for the second step of your Usenet advertising is putting your long, electronic brochure at a particular spot on the Internet where people can find it for themselves. Web sites, described in later chapters, can be used for this purpose. For now, you need only understand that, if you wish, you can attach an electronic address to your data so that instead of sending it upon request, readers of your initial, short Usenet message can simply call it up on their computers. Like the robot, using an Internet information site has the benefit of giving your customer immediate access to your sales information and, like the robot, the effort on your part is virtually nonexistent. At your Web site you can have the benefit of as elaborate a presentation as your budget and creativity can afford. Then, if your customer still has individual questions, you can offer them the option of e-mailing you directly from the Web site. All Web site options are covered in chapter 7. Interactive order forms are also a common Web site feature, as you will see when you read chapter 12. If you want to put a robot in place, it is again suggested that you prevail on your friendly geek to write the program. It's not very hard to do. Once in place, the robot is effortless for you and provides your customer with instant gratification.

When you post a Usenet advertisement, whatever type of response mechanism you select, individual or automatic, the importance of answering inquiries fully and promptly cannot be stressed too much. You should also have a long-term plan for customer relations, keep good records on your customers, including details on how to locate them, their likes, dislikes, questions, and anything else you are able to find out that will help improve service. Your computer, together with a simple database program, can do much of this work for you, maintaining information in an orderly fashion and making future relationships with your newfound customers rewarding. Your goal should be to keep your customers and sell to them on a repeat basis. Excellent service is not only a good idea. As part of Cyberselling, it is almost mandatory. Those who deal with computers know that these machines were built to make record-keeping and communicating easy. Because of this, expectations of efficient service through the computer are high. Don't disappoint your new customers and they won't disappoint you.

In most cases, employing the two-step technique when engaging in Usenet advertising is the most desirable way to go. Remember that short messages are a convention of the Usenet conversation style. There is no point in going against the established Usenet norm when to do so renders you no benefit. In any case, a second, third, or fourth contact with the customer costs so little in the way of money and effort, there is really no downside to proceeding this way. Then, too, once a customer has asked for more information, you can approach him or her in a different way. Here is a person who has already expressed interest. You know that a long and detailed presentation of what you have to offer will be welcome. It is also recommended that you set up a way to answer individual questions, even if you do it in combination with a robot or data site. Although it takes some time and work, the ability to do this unleashes the full power of Cyberselling because you have the opportunity of building a strong customer relationship.

In marketing the Green Card Lottery, a full "brochure" was sent to all those who requested information, but, in addition, any inquiries that contained individual questions were set aside and answered as well. In the second-step fixed presentation, an attempt was made to include everything the customer might need to know in order to buy, as well as a method of ordering. The information in your own presentation should do the same. Simply think of what you would like to know if you were purchasing this product and then tell that to your customers. Say as much as you need to get all your points across. There will be no extra cost for more pages in your brochure, as there would be if it was printed. With the computer, comprehensive sales information is not expensive. To give you an idea of what a step-two long message might contain, here is a portion of the information packet sent out for the Green Card Lottery. (The address and phone numbers used in the following example are fictitious.)

Please note, the end of this message includes a biographical questionnaire. Please let us know if you do not receive the entire transmission.

Canter & Siegel
1234 E Camelback Road
Ste 567
Phoenix AZ 85018
602–661–1111 (telephone) 602–451–2222 (fax)
e-mail cslaw@netcom.com

WF CAN MAKE IT EASY TO APPLY AND INCREASE YOUR CHANCE OF WINNING ONE OF 55,000 GREEN CARDS AVAILABLE IN THE 1994 GREEN CARD LOTTERY.

ACT NOW. THIS MAY BE YOUR LAST CHANCE!

What is the Green Card Lottery?

The Green Card Lottery is a program run by the United States Government to give away a certain number of green cards each year. In 1994, the number of green cards in the lottery is 55,000. The Green Card Lottery is completely legal in every way. What is unique about the lottery is that unlike other ways of getting green cards, you need no special qualification to apply. You need only have been born in one of the countries included in the program. If you win, in order to collect your green card, you must then show you have either a high school diploma, or at least two years of training or experience in a skilled job. YOU DO NOT NEED TO HAVE A JOB OFFER.

WHY THIS MAY BE YOUR LAST CHANCE FOR A LOTTERY GREEN CARD

Recently a new bill was introduced into the U.S. Congress to end any further Green Card Lotteries. The bill is meant to be part of a larger program to reduce U.S. immigration overall, and stands a very good chance of passing.

■ ■ ■

THE FACTS ABOUT THE GREEN CARD LOTTERY

FACT: The 1994 Green Card Lottery applies to people from almost all countries. In fact, only twelve countries are excluded. They are . . .

■ ■ ■

FACT: There is no way of knowing exactly what your odds are of winning, because there is no way of telling how many people will apply this year, but last year, about 800,000 people filed qualifying applications for only 40,000 cards available. With these numbers your odds would be 1 out of 20.

FACT: You can put in only one application per person. If you put in more the computer will discover it and you will be disqualified.

■ ■ ■

FACT: Everyone would like to know how to improve their chances to win the Green Card Lottery. THE TRUTH IS AN ATTORNEY CAN HELP INCREASE YOUR ODDS OF WINNING.

First, in certain cases only, you can as much as double or triple your chances by filing several applications for the same family but using a different family member each time as the principal applicant. (This is not the same as submitting more than one application per person.)

■ ■ ■

THE LAW FIRM OF CANTER & SIEGEL

The law firm of Canter and Siegel has been practicing Immigration law since 1981. In that time it has successfully acquired green cards and Visas for people from almost every country in the world. The firm offers a full range of Immigration law and does not take cases in other areas. It has actively participated in every Green Card Lottery held since these programs began in 1987.

In 1989 Mr. Canter and Ms. Siegel co-authored a book for non-lawyers on the subject of Immigration called U.S. Immigration Made Easy.

■ ■ ■

LOTTERY SERVICES

The law firm of Canter & Siegel will take the information received from you and use it to form a technically perfect lottery application. If you are married. If you would like to have Canter & Siegel enter you in the 1994 Green Card Lottery, please fill out the enclosed Service Order and Questionnaire.

FEES FOR ENTERING
THE GREEN CARD LOTTERY.

■ ■ ■

1994 Green Card Lottery
SERVICE ORDER & QUESTIONNAIRE

Please return this completed Questionnaire by Mail, Fax or e-mail to

Canter & Siegel
1234 E Camelback Road, Ste 567
Phoenix AZ 85018
Fax: 602–451–2222 Phone: 602–661–1111
e-mail cslaw@netcom.com

_____ YES, I would like Canter & Siegel to enter me in the Green Card Lottery

_____ Please file one application for me and my family at a fee of 95 dollars U.S.

···

Total Amount _____
Enclosed is my check for U.S. Funds
Charge my _____ Visa _____ Mastercard _____
American Express
Card No. Exp. Date Signature

Name: (First, Middle, LAST)

Mailing Address:

···

Service Agreement & Guarantee

Upon receiving your completed Service order form and payment, the law firm of Canter & Siegel agrees to prepare your registration, make sure it meets all technical requirements of the lottery program. . .

···

To assist us in preparing your registration, please complete the questionnaire and return it to us. Thank you for choosing Canter & Siegel to represent you in the 1994 Green Card Lottery.

In addition to posting straight commercial messages, there are other ways to get product or service information across on the Usenet. If you have a product that has already been sold to and used by some satisfied customers, they can enter the conversation of a newsgroup and offer an endorsement. The topic of the newsgroup should have some relationship to the product being endorsed. For example, if someone discovers a new cat-care product, he or she may want to let others know about it by giving a recommendation in *rec.pets.cats*. Another way of putting commercial information into Usenet messages is through the signature line. In this way, you simply act as a participant in as many groups as you like, enter the discussion, and instead of choosing a self-descriptive phrase or quote, you may instead mention your company name or plug a product. While four lines do not seem like much space in which to make your sales presentation, remember that in a two-step process, a few well-chosen words, together with a reference to where more detailed product information can be found, is probably the best way of selling on the Usenet.

Let's say you have now selected the advertising method that is best for your product, a one-step or two-step process, and written either your single message or your initial message plus long follow-up sales material. You have decided which of the response methods suits your product and customers best. You must now choose the newsgroups where your message will be posted. This is probably the most important decision you will have to make as a Cyberseller.

First, let's look at your newsgroup choices from a purely marketing standpoint. You should begin your selection for posting by reading carefully the entire list your Internet service provider (ISP) carries. It doesn't take long to go through the newsgroup names available and you don't want to miss any where your customers can be found. When you try to locate those who are most likely to be interested in your product or service, Usenet, because it is divided into so many narrow subject categories, gives you a lot of excellent clues. Suppose, for example, you are selling boating equipment. There are a number of newsgroups devoted to boats and the sport of sailing. The same is true of any sport you can name. This first round of newsgroup selections is a fairly straightforward matching of your product or service with newsgroups on the same topic.

Your second-round selections require only a little more imagination. Again, looking at the boating equipment example, what is the likelihood that those who are interested in other types of water sports such as snorkeling, waterskiing, and deep-sea fishing would also want to know about boating? The odds are good that there would be interest and you can find newsgroups on all these related subjects. How about vacation spots near water, say, the Bahamas or Hawaii, where sailing is popular? Once again, there are newsgroups devoted to specific areas of vacation travel where interest in your product is likely to be high. Do you remember the regional hierarchies discussed earlier in this chapter? Perhaps some promising choices for boating equipment would be groups in the Usenet hierarchies devoted to geographical regions near coastlines. The Boston, Miami, or San Francisco hierarchies would be good possibilities.

Now let's consider your third-round selections. Beyond the expressed interests or probable locations, consider the types of people who normally go boating. Boaters need to have enough money to buy or at least rent a boat. That doesn't come cheap. Newsgroups attracting professionals such as doctors or business executives who can afford high-ticket recreation would, therefore, be likely selections. There are many newsgroups where discussions of professional subjects are carried on that might attract the kind of customer you are looking for.

Finally, you should always include the various newsgroups that are especially designed for selling products. Every regional hierarchy has a "for sale" group in certain subject areas, especially when it comes to computer equipment. Then there is the newsgroup *misc.forsale*. It is a very popular group on the entire Usenet. With this one alone you can reach over a quarter of a million people for just a few pennies.

Let's consider how we would select newsgroups for another type of product, one that is very different from boating equipment. Perhaps yours is an item that appeals to almost everyone. A reporter once asked for the name of a product in which almost every man, woman, and child everywhere, regardless of age, sex, financial status, education level, or anything else might be interested. How about Coca-Cola? Of course, not everyone in the world drinks Coke. Some like Pepsi or Evian or orange juice or Bud. Still, there are probably no newsgroups lacking for avid Coke drinkers. Soap and toothpaste are two more products that just about everyone uses. With such items, the marketing strategy would simply be to reach as many people as possible.

The selection of newsgroups for the Green Card Lottery project presented its own challenges. Although there is one newsgroup called *alt.visa.us* devoted to U.S. immigration matters, in an environment like the Internet where people from every nation of the world participate, the conclusion was that there were many in newsgroups other than the single one focusing on immigration where interest in U.S. green cards would be high. The most obvious second-round choices were the approximately eighty cultural groups such as *soc.culture.hungary, soc.culture.africa, alt.culture.indonesia,* and *alt.culture.argentina*. In addition, there were a number of newsgroups devoted to subjects such as eastern religions where you could find a heavy preponderance of foreign nationals. Finally, there were the many foreign hierarchies. Although in themselves they each covered a large variety of topics, certainly it could logically be concluded that the target audience for the service could be found there.

Finally, however, the decision was made to try them all. The joke and flame groups were eliminated on the basis of reluctance to deal with the unnerving psyches of the usual participants. Also bypassed were as many of the repeat groups (*flonk.flonk.flonk*) as possible. All the rest stayed on the list. The rationale was that the kind of person to be reached was a non-U.S. citizen or resident. Such an individual could not be defined by age, interest, sex, or income, but only by nationality. Usenet groups didn't lend themselves to that kind of distinction, especially since all newsgroups could be reached by anyone, anywhere. In other words, there were no groups with the title *alt.foreigner*.

As you can see, each product or service requires a different approach when it comes time to select newsgroups for posting. You know your own product or service better than anyone. Imagine what kind of person might need or want it, what their related interests might be. Then look over the newsgroup list and pick the places where you think your customers are likely to gather. Chances are good that you'll be right.

THE CONTROVERSY OVER ADVERTISING ON USENET

So far, in selecting the newsgroups that are suitable for marketing goods or services, the considerations have been only where you might find the best sales prospects. Unfortunately, you must also consider a factor that has nothing to do with actual marketing.

You can't avoid facing the fact that Usenet advertising is controversial, at least to a small group composed of the original Net research element. There is no way to explain selling on the Usenet without talking about conflicting views of whether or not broad advertising on Usenet is practical. Such a discussion is necessary not because there is resistance by Usenet readers to purchasing goods or services they've seen advertised on newsgroups. We already know from personal experience, and those countless others who have followed the example of the Green Card posting, that untold numbers of newsgroup participants, on encountering well-presented information about a product of interest, will be only too glad to buy.

The problem arises because in spite of the fact that the Internet is now completely commercialized, a small group of old-timers from universities and company research departments, where the Internet originated, continue to insist that using the huge Usenet communication facility for advertising amounts, at best, to rudeness. They offer many reasons for their position, but the primary one is that advertisements which do not coincide with the subject matter under discussion are impermissible as a matter of computer etiquette or so-called Netiquette. At worst, the truly committed and commitable see advertising on the Usenet as an act of war. Moreover, among those who hold this view are certain powerful individuals who have the electronic means to make their opinions stick, whether they are in the great minority or not.

It matters little whether you choose to agree with them. The situation is such that you cannot ignore them. It is only right that you should be fully informed before deciding issues of practicality as they relate to Usenet advertising. Let us then explore the various objections that have been raised to commercial messages on this portion of the Internet, the tactics that have been used to advance this line of thinking, and what you may decide to do about it.

Understanding the exact basis for the anti-advertising sentiment of certain small factions is not easy. Arguments fly back and forth. Name-calling and dirty tricks abound. Sometimes those who don't want Usenet to carry ads offer reasons why. Other times there is only a disorganized, vitriolic outpouring of hate and anger. Because you are a principled person trying to make a fortune on the Internet in an honest and ethical manner, you will have to take a hard look at the facts and judge for yourself what is right and wrong.

The practical obstacles you will face, however, are really the more compelling issues. When the advertisement for the Green Card Lottery was first placed on Usenet, no one had done anything like it before. To be sure there was much screaming and mailbombing, but no organized anti-ad effort had yet been mounted. As time went by, two serious and reprehensible threats to the ability of anyone who wished to engage in this form of advertising developed.

The first of these is the cancellor robots or cancelbots for short. Just as posting messages to groups can be done automatically, cancelbots are programs that seek out messages on the Usenet and cancel them. Such programs can be launched by anyone with a sufficient technical skill level. Since, from a technical standpoint, the only one who can cancel a Usenet message is the person who posted it, cancelbots involve a procedure in which the cancel program electronically forges the name of the person posting the message in the first place. Because many of those who object to mass posting on Usenet come from technical universities such as MIT, the required expertise presents no problem for the cancelbots. The cancelbots do have one limitation. They have difficulty in finding all the messages posted. In addition, much technical know-how has also been expended by those who oppose cancelbots to develop methods of thwarting them. Nonetheless, having your advertisements eliminated by cancelbots is a problem you will have to face.

You may wonder at the ethics of self-appointed vigilantes having the power to cancel any messages they please. You may also wonder at the abuse of power inherent in this practice. To gain greater insight into this problem, it is suggested you read the newsgroup *news.admin.net-abuse.misc*. When you do, you will see that this newsgroup, which was started mainly as part of the aftermath of the Green Card Incident, is the primary forum for the small group who wish to report "spams" they have observed on Usenet. It is also a forum for debate on this topic and a repository of endless name-calling when two participants disagree on what does or doesn't constitute a spam. For example, the number of posts needed to amount to a spam varies according to the person you are talking to, as does what should or shouldn't be canceled. Invariably, however, the posters of the spam reports call for the cancelbots to swing into action, and although all this is done without the support of a recognized authority, it does present an annoyance to you, the marketer.

The second hurdle you will face should you wish to mass post to Usenet is interference by ISPs. Once again, thanks to the Green Card Incident, some ISPs now have clauses in their user contracts that specifically preclude mass posting to Usenet. Others have clauses that give the ISP more general power to cancel accounts of users for whatever reason they see fit. Looking once more to the newsgroup *news.admin.net-abuse.misc*, the self-styled Net police call onto the carpet any ISP who does not cancel the account of a mass poster. Some ISPs resist, but most comply. Why? Well, it's not because of moral conviction, as you might expect. It's a business decision.

The general structure of the Internet is that of a pyramid. This means that all information sent through Usenet goes to centralized computers at the top of the pyramid. It then filters down from one level to the next. The larger the ISP, the higher up the pyramid it is located and the fewer computers it must go through to reach the users of that particular ISP. What is important here is that any higher-up provider can refuse a Usenet feed to someone further down. Moreover, any ISP at all, regardless of position on the pyramid, can block the Usenet signal coming from another provider. This is the threat leveled at every ISP who would just as soon not be part of antispam enforcement. In short, either the ISP removes the mass poster, or faces having their businesses shut down. Now, if you had to take a guess which ISPs had the power to block the most signals and refuse the most feeds, who would you select? Good thinking! It's the ones run by the old guard entrenched since the early days when the Internet served only the university and research communities.

But wait, there's more. Don't think the folks from the government and universities are fools either. The fact is that the Internet is big business and those with advanced Internet expertise are now in high demand in the private sector. Where many businesses based on Internet revenues make their money is not from the Usenet, but, as we will see in chapter 7, from the highly commercialized World Wide Web. Help with putting up Web sites and maintaining them costs money. Some strong Web site connections cost a lot of money. Advertising on someone else's Web site, if it is an especially popular one, really costs a lot of money. The Usenet, from the standpoint of the Internet industry, is simply an added value service thrown in with the real moneymakers. Can you see now why ISPs and those who influence them would prefer that you advertise some place other than the free Usenet?

With all the difficulties facing those who would advertise on Usenet, you might think the practice would have died out. The fact is, it has not. Indeed, so-called spams occur continuously, and are on the increase. Advertisers who want to engage in this practice employ every means they can think of to circumvent the obstacles. They ignore clauses in contracts with ISPs that prohibit advertising. If their ISPs close their accounts, they simply move on to another ISP—and another and another—sometimes using fictitious names. Those who find their postings removed by cancellor robots simply repost. Those with more technical expertise devise posting programs that will be impervious to cancellor robots. And why do these advertisers go to all this trouble? For yet another very good reason. Usenet advertising works!

The only point on which both sides in the Internet ad conflict agree is that there is no law against advertising on the Usenet. When the National Science Foundation lifted the ban on commercial Internet uses, there was no further doubt that Usenet advertising, along with promotions in other areas of the Internet, were no longer barred by an entity with any legal authority. Admitting that there were no statutory or regulatory prohibitions on broad Usenet advertising, opponents of the Green Card posting searched long and hard for some general legal theory under which they could sue. Certainly, they reasoned, the fact that they had been so badly upset would be enough for the U.S. courts to put the perpetrators in their place. Suffice it to say no suits were ever filed. Left without any legitimate basis for objecting to what had been done, most of the critics decided simply to designate mass posting as "rude." Considering the vandalism, in the form of mailbombing and cancelbots employing forgery, carried out by those who have called mass Usenet advertising rude, you would be forced to conclude that rudeness is very much a matter of opinion. There is no known legal theory that precludes one person from having different values, different standards of behavior, or different ideas of where to advertise than another. If you decide to make your fortune on the Internet, how you do it is up to you. As long as you do not go against prohibitions placed on all communications mediums, such as the one barring the sale of child pornography, the law is not going to stop you.

One last word on the Usenet ad wars. It is no secret that a lot of people find ads annoying. There are very few of us who haven't zapped a commercial that popped up during our favorite TV show. Most of us are fit to kill when we trip over our own feet, running to pick up a ringing telephone, only to find someone selling discount phone services on the other end. Ponder it a little more, though, and you may find advertising is more important than you thought. There probably is not an item in your house or business that you did not learn about through advertising. The best ads, like the ones featuring the "Yes I am" man who sells a certain brand of beer, are great entertainment. Most important, there is probably not one of us who doesn't owe his or her job directly or indirectly to advertising. There are societies where there are no ads. In true communist societies, advertising is not allowed except by the government, which owns everything. Maybe it's more worth fighting for than you thought.

DIRECT VS. INDIRECT ADVERTISING

Now that you have all the facts, you can adopt the advertising strategy with which you feel most comfortable. You have any number of options. Advertising on the Usenet is considered direct advertising, as is sending unsolicited e-mail messages. That means you are placing ads where people will see them even if someone isn't specifically looking, much like advertisements in newspapers, on television, on radio, through direct mail, or on billboards. You can also choose indirect advertising. This means that your customer makes the effort to find your sales material, either because he or she specifically goes looking for it, or because he happens on it by accident. Web sites, discussed in chapter 7, are the primary examples of the indirect method. You may also choose to employ a combination of direct and indirect techniques. It has already been explained how one way of handling a two-step process is by posting brief messages to Usenet that will send your customers to a Web site elsewhere on the Internet, where long product descriptions, answers to questions, and order forms will await them.

In employing the Usenet to make your fortune, it is possible to take a conservative approach. If you limit your commercial postings only to groups where your product or service is strictly relevant to the topic under discussion (i.e. posting boating equipment ads in a newsgroup on sailing) this is considered acceptable in all quarters and, of course, makes good targeting sense. If you expand your postings to groups where the product is not strictly on topic but highly relevant (i.e. Green Card Lottery postings in the *soc.culture.japan* newsgroup) you are also unlikely to meet with problems. The further away from a clear connection between the product or service you are selling and the topic of the news-group in which you try to sell it, the more you risk the wrath of the self-styled Internet ad police. Likewise, the more newsgroups to which you post, the more customers you will find and the better chance you have of building your fortune, but you will meet with more ISP and cancelbot problems as well.

Another conservative approach you may choose to follow in utilizing the Usenet for marketing is disguising your advertising message as something other than what it really is. Interestingly, many who consider themselves upstanding members of the Internet "community" as well as computer marketing experts recommend this practice. They see it not as deceitful, but as a way of showing sensitivity to the Net "culture." The idea is that you will offer up some general data along with your product description and sales inducements in order to fulfill the requirement of custom that each Usenet posting should contain valuable information. An example of this technique would be to incorporate some interesting facts on the history of sailing along with your posting for the sale of boating equipment.

There are several other variations on the theme of approaching Usenet advertising in a roundabout way. We have already discussed two of them. When you put sales information in the signature portion rather than the body of the message, many who normally dislike Usenet commercialism find this acceptable. Likewise, if your product or service is mentioned as an endorsement by a satisfied user, this too is seen as inoffensive. In employing endorsements, if you wish to stick with a conservative approach, it is still necessary to watch closely the relationship between the product or service offered and the topic of the newsgroup where the advertisement is posted.

A final method for undertaking a conservative approach to Usenet marketing is tailoring each message individually for the newsgroup where it will be posted. For example, suppose you are selling sunglasses. Couldn't you write a message that would suggest the use of your sunglasses for assisting race-car drivers or making life more pleasant for fans of any number of outdoor spectator sports? Of course, the procedure is labor-intensive, but it does greatly increase the number of newsgroups where you could advertise your product and still play by the "rules." Many advertisers have reported great success and few flames with this method.

A final roundabout method of Usenet advertising is to start your own newsgroup. Since you formulated the group, you have the right to decide the ground rules. Because it is a newsgroup, unless you decide it should be moderated, anyone can come in and say anything he or she wishes. What no one can do is stop you from saying what you wish. When you start your own newsgroup, however, you are once again limited because, in a way, even though it is Usenet advertising, you are using an indirect approach. You are asking people to come to you rather than you going to them. Moreover, even though you start a group, you really have no way of controlling whether or not ISPs will carry it. Still, you have little to lose and everything to gain by trying.

Roundabout techniques of Usenet advertising, also called cloaking devices, are a real case of beauty being in the eye of the beholder. To some, an advertising message written in a less straightforward manner is simply a considerate form of soft selling in contrast with a more jarring hard sell of a clearly identified advertisement. To others it is an underhanded subterfuge, where the seller is covering up his true agenda from the hopefully unsuspecting buyer. Done with good intent, either straightforward or roundabout advertising can be honorably and effectively undertaken.

Usenet is a valuable and effective marketing tool. Not only is it an easy and inexpensive way to reach large numbers of individuals, these are people who have already identified themselves as willing buyers of goods and services sold over the Internet. In fact, the very novelty of seeing a product or service presented through Usenet, as well as the instant ability to communicate with the seller, promotes a good atmosphere in which customers are ready to buy.

Usenet is a strictly text-based area of the Internet. Unlike the World Wide Web, described later, you can make your presentation in newsgroups with words only. Although this limits the way you can reach people on the Internet, it maximizes the number because everyone on the Net can receive text while some do not have the lines or equipment to receive graphics. This differentiation is, however, becoming less significant every day as the older forms of computers fall into disuse.

The indirect form of advertising mentioned earlier is based on the idea that there should be special areas of the Internet and even a special hierarchy of the Usenet dedicated exclusively to selling. This means that with indirect advertising you must not only offer something for sale, you must also offer a motivation for looking and a road map to find the product. Direct advertising on Usenet is not only easy for you, it is also easy and convenient for your customers. Moreover, you can be fairly certain that the advertising you present is at least as interesting and valuable as the great majority of other messages routinely posted on Usenet. Since you have done some good thinking about the newsgroups you've chosen for posting, even if you have concluded that your target market should be everywhere, you can assume that there will be many people who will welcome the introduction of goods and services that are of interest to them. From this you can make your fortune. Moreover, it is enjoyable and satisfying to turn someone on to a good thing that will improve their lives or at least their humor. That's what Usenet allows you to do.

5
E-Mail and Electronic Mailing Lists
PAPERLESS AND POSTAGE-FREE

E-MAIL'S MANY USES

UNQUESTIONABLY THE SINGLE MOST POPULAR FEATURE
on the Internet is Electronic Mail, or e-mail. Here is a great place for you
to start making your fortune on the Internet because, unlike any other single I-way feature, e-mail is used by everyone. This includes the some
thirty million individuals who are on the Internet alone as well as all those
having accounts with most commercial on-line services such as Prodigy,
CompuServe, and America Online (AOL). You can send and receive e-
mail with absolutely any type of network account and you can send it anywhere. No longer is e-mail capability limited only to people on your own
network, as it once was. E-mail by itself gives you access to such a huge
market that you could really sell your products or services in this way
alone and still make a fortune. Already companies exist that furnish you
with e-mail mailing lists and special programs for mass e-mailing,
although it is simple enough to gather your own list from the Usenet and
Web sites. Here is a quick and simple way to do business on the Internet,
with a minimum of cost and effort.

For all its simplicity, e-mail as a marketing technique is as powerful as any in cyberspace, for it, too, offers the interactive feature that makes Cyberselling so effective. Much of the excitement brought to you by the Usenet spills over into e-mail as well. We have already touched on some of the uses of e-mail for commercial purposes. It is by e-mail that you send your customers further information in the second step of Usenet advertising promotions. And e-mail also readily uses World Wide Web advertising as well. Here, though, you will be told what can be done just with e-mail alone.

There are any number of good reasons why e-mail is so popular. The uses for it are endless. E-mail works on the same principle as regular or snail mail, except that delivery is made electronically and immediately straight into the recipient's computer with no postage required. E-mail is so fast, in fact, that you can actually engage in conversation just by mailing messages back and forth. One important use for e-mail is as an extremely cheap substitute for a telephone. It is this function that in large part accounts for e-mail's great popularity.

E-mail may also soon replace faxes as the primary means of rapid written communication. In fact, there is nothing a fax machine can do that can't be done faster, better, and cheaper with e-mail. Graphical images can be sent via e-mail just like a fax, but without the bother and space fax paper requires, and without long-distance telephone charges. (It should be mentioned, however, that using a computer for a fax requires first digitizing the material to be faxed. Check a technical manual on how to do this. It's easy.) Once you are free of these restraints, the practical limits on the length of what you can fax is gone as well. Suppose you had written a book and wanted to fax a three-hundred-page manuscript to your publisher. Imagine how long that would take. Now imagine that your publisher was located in New York and you lived in, say, Phoenix. This would be a happy day for the phone company stockholders. At the other end, your harried publisher would be facing three hundred pages of curled up fax paper. Of course, he could not receive any other faxes until yours finished coming in. With high potential for garbled pages and paper jams, what we have here is a disaster in the making. That same three-hundred-page manuscript, sent via e-mail instead of fax, would be received in a matter of seconds. No long-distance telephone call would be needed. The recipient could choose to read the manuscript directly on his or her computer screen, make changes, and then print out a hard copy, if desired. The information would still remain on the computer, providing a backup if the printed copy should be lost.

There is little reason, with all the benefits computer transmission of documents offers, why anyone would choose to use faxes, and the day is probably not far away when fax machines will become obsolete.

E-mail sounds like the perfect tool and it really is. It is not, however, problem-free. First, there is the question of security. An e-mail message travels through a number of different computers on its way to its final destination and it is possible for it to be intercepted along the way. It is even more likely that it could be inadvertently misdirected due to a typo. Remember, computers are only machines. Not only can't they think for themselves, they can't type either.

PROBLEMS WITH PIRACY AND FORGERY

Because of e-mail security problems, encryption is one of the most hotly debated topics in the computer world. Encryption, described in detail in chapter 12, is a technical process that can put any message you send into a secret code automatically. The code can be broken on the receiving end only by a person using the same encryption program as the sender. You may have read about the controversial clipper chip. It is a technology the U.S. government wants to make mandatory for encryption programs, so that Uncle Sam will be able to keep a watchful eye on e-mail and, when necessary, prevent the illegal transmission of security-sensitive data. Basically, the proposal would require all encryption techniques to follow a certain formula that official agencies could decipher at will. Irrespective of government security problems, encryption is not practical for most business correspondence because when a company deals with a broad array of customers, suppliers, and so on, there is no way of ensuring that the same programs will be used at both ends of a message transmission. You are better off, therefore, simply accepting that an e-mail transmission may not always be entirely private. Overall, you will be safest thinking of e-mail much like a post card. You must assume that anything sent by e-mail can be read by others. Suffice it to say that if a message must remain completely confidential, e-mail, at present, is not the best choice. Keep in mind, however, that the same could be said of telephone and fax transmissions as well.

E-mail's second drawback is that it is extremely easy to forge a sender's name. Most e-mail programs give senders the ability to place on their messages any return e-mail name and address they wish. For some, the temptation is too great to resist. If you get an e-mail letter that looks like it came from the president of the United States, with the return address of *clinton@whitehouse.gov,* contain your enthusiasm. Maybe the president really did write to you and place an order. Then again, maybe it came from an unhappy Netter distressed at finding yet another businessperson making money on the Internet. There are, however, ways to check. Like Usenet postings, each e-mail message comes with a complete header, showing the exact route the letter took in getting to its destination. Although headers, as well as names, can be tampered with, it takes a high level of expertise to do so. If you have any reason to doubt the authenticity of the address or name on an e-mail message, you will usually be able to get confirmation by looking at the complete header.

E-mail is one of the simplest computer functions. First, as in the case of any other type of mail, you must know the exact address of the intended recipient. Then, you simply type in your message, or attach one that is prepared, and hit a few computer keys to send it on its way. Receiving e-mail is even easier. You don't have to do anything at all. The computer acts just like your mailman, only faster, and promptly delivers your mail as it is received. Then you just read it on your computer screen. As with any other data that comes in, if you have a printer, you can also print out a hard copy.

YOUR E-MAIL ADDRESS

Each person on the Internet or other on-line services has a unique e-mail address. The e-mail address is the most important part of your message, for without it your mail will never get to where it was intended to go. Everyone with an Internet account is given an e-mail address from his or her Internet service provider (ISP). E-mail addresses are not dissimilar from names of Usenet groups. The address is composed of three parts. Part one is your own name or any name you may wish to use. Here is another of those instances where people tend to get creative, so if you want to pretend you're Madonna, at least for noncommercial purposes, this is your chance to do so without having your sanity come under too much question. The name on an e-mail address must be put in the form of a single word such as msiegel or imrich.

Next comes the @ sign. It is an abbreviation for the word "at." It is followed by the domain name of the computer where the mail will be received. Computers having direct connections to the Internet take names called domains. The domain computer in most cases will be the one owned by your ISP. Usually, the company will select as its domain the name under which it does business. Therefore, if you have your account with AOL, the first two parts of your e-mail address will read *imrich@aol*.

Some ISPs allow you to register an individual domain. This permits you to use your own company name as the second part of your e-mail address. Your mail still comes to the same centralized computer, but a special program allows for the identification of the various domain names used. A domain can be broken down further into subdomains. The Cybersell® company name domain is actually "sell," with a sub-domain of "cyber." When put together it comes out cyber.sell. The reason for doing this is simply easier categorization of the mail that comes into a particular domain. For full instructions on how to register your own domain name, see chapter 7.

The last part of an e-mail address is the hierarchy, which defines either the geographical location or main activity engaged in by the central receiving computer. Some common American hierarchy designations are "com" which stands for commercial and "edu" which signifies an educational institution. Therefore, completing the e-mail addresses we began above, yours might be *imrich@aol.com*.

Understanding a little about e-mail addresses can help you to create an image for yourself as well as gather information about your potential customers. For example, if you plan to send mail to someone with the address *bigcheese@ibm.com* you know that you are probably dealing with a high-level employee of IBM. If the name is *geek@mit.edu* you know you have someone with a pocket protector who is affiliated with Massachusetts Institute of Technology. Domains can also tell you where a person is located geographically. As we've said, many U.S. addresses end in com or edu. Other common U.S. hierarchies are "org" for organizations or "gov" for government offices. All countries but the United States, however, have hierarchy designations by geographical locations. Examples include "au" (Australia), "uk" (United Kingdom), "de" (Germany), and "ca" (Canada). Almost every country of the world has its own Internet hierarchy.

The selection of your e-mail name is an opportunity for some very powerful marketing. Choose carefully, picking your company name or perhaps a descriptive title showing what your company does. Never forget that your name itself is a form of advertising. For example, if you're an accountant, you might pick a name like "taxes" or "beat-irs." The Cybersell® marketing company, as mentioned earlier, is *cyber.sell*. As you go forward with your marketing strategy, your name could become famous, just as Cybersell®'s did.

HOW E-MAIL WORKS

When you first sit down at your computer and access a mail program, you are presented with a menu of messages currently sitting in your mailbox. Using one of the common e-mail programs, your screen might look like this:

```
Mailbox is 'cybersell:/usr/spool/mail/msiegel' with 5
messages [ELM 2.4 PL23]
  1  Aug 4  HYNSONC1              (50)  WWW and Gopher
                                        Services.
  2  Jul 25  system Problems  (4140)  Re: List of .com domains
  3  Jul 18  Jim Fisher            (31)  Sample web page?
  4  Jul 18  Morrison, Christophe (42)  Internet Services
                                        Questions
  5  Jul 10  Steve McQueen     (36)  About our need for
                                        ftp/www/mail
```

This shows I have five messages waiting. I can read the date each was sent, the name of the sender, the size of the file in numbers of lines, and a description of its contents. How does my computer know what each letter contains? The sender puts in a descriptive subject header, just as is the case with Usenet postings. This is extremely helpful, especially if you receive thousands of pieces of e-mail as was the case during the Green Card Lottery. It gives you an initial way to sort out the mail, separating the wheat from the chaff. Imagine how much simpler this is than sorting out thousands of letters received by regular mail. Here you don't even have to open up an envelope. From this menu you can select any given message and read it, reply to it, print it, or delete it, all with the push of a few buttons.

Once you have selected the one you want to read, a typical e-mail message might look like this:

```
Display message
Message 1/1 From Jeff–America OnLine        Sep 4, 94
07:11:00 pm mdt

From Jeff Sun Sep 4 19:11 MDT 1994
Content-Length: 300
Content-Type: text
Subject: Cybersell®
Reply to: Jeff@aol.com


I am new to the Internet but have heard that you are experts
in Net advertising.


I have several exciting products I know would be of interest to
my fellow Netters, but I need help. Please contact me as soon
as possible so that I can get my new business off to a good
start.

Command ('i' to return to index):
You can use any of the following commands by pressing the
first character; d)elete or u)ndelete mail, m)ail a message,
r)eply or f)orward mail, q)uit
To read a message, press [return].
j = move down, k = move up, ? = help
Command:
```

The top of this message shows us the date it was sent, who sent it, the
type of material in the message (which is text, in this example), the size of
the message, and the subject matter. Then the message itself follows. At
the bottom is a menu of commands you can use for handling this piece of
mail in a number of ways. These instructions are self-explanatory.

As with all things you want your computer to do, sending and receiving e-mail requires use of a special software program. There are many
different e-mail programs available. Some you must buy. Many are free.
You will probably be supplied with a free one by your ISP. If you will be
handling large volumes of mail, however, as you do when you engage in

Cyberselling, you may want to consider some of the commercial programs. The fancier (and usually more expensive) programs make sending, receiving, and answering e-mail easier and may even do a certain amount of mail sorting automatically for you, such as grouping the mail by sender or subject, or even rejecting all mail from someone you don't like. Whatever mail program you use, they all work in a similar fashion. For details on how to use e-mail programs, you should consult your ISP or one of the numerous books on how to use the Internet.

MAKING MONEY WITH E-MAIL

The reason you can make money with e-mail should by now be obvious. You can utilize this amazingly quick and extremely cheap method of communication to transmit sales information to your potential customers. Just as with Usenet postings, a one-step or two-step procedure should be considered. Interestingly, however, the idea of using e-mail for direct marketing is now a much more actively pursued technique than that of posting to Usenet. Like all computer-marketing techniques, however, sending sales literature through e-mail is new and people are not used to it. Therefore, if you are approaching a potential customer for the first time through an unsolicited e-mailing, we especially recommend using a two-step process, because the first message you send is short. Keeping your initial contact brief is a good way to manage possible negative feelings you may engender when a potential customer finds a piece of unsolicited e-mail advertising in his or her mailbox. Once you receive an initial show of interest and find that additional information is desired, you can employ data sites or e-mail again to deliver longer, detailed product information and order solicitations. All the second-step techniques described in the previous chapter for Usenet marketing apply when the initial contact is made by e-mail as well.

More ideas for getting rich have probably been based on mail-order businesses than any other kind. They offer some of the best money-making opportunities for the average person. Why? Primarily, because they require very little cash to start. All the benefits and opportunities inherent in a traditional direct-mail business are multiplied when you market with e-mail. There is no need to incur the expenses of traditional retail space. You can usually avoid maintaining large inventories as well. Even better, you have the ability to reach directly the target market that is most likely to buy your product or service. You do not have to worry about a wholesaler or retailer accepting your product for sale before the public has the opportunity to see it. You are also free of any geographic limitations. You can sell to anyone anywhere. A retail store depends greatly on its location. Mail order, especially when done with the international capabilities of e-mail, does not.

Cost and speed, however, are really where e-mail comes shining through. Advertising and mailing costs through traditional methods are slow and expensive. That became clear during the personal experience of marketing the book, *U.S. Immigration Made Easy*, which entailed buying specialized mailing lists and advertising in ethnic newspapers around the country, plus a number of newspapers located abroad. You have already seen how favorably Cyberselling compares from an expense standpoint with other, more traditional marketing methods. It costs some $300 to reach just a thousand people with a direct mail piece, including charges for printing and mailing, and that is if you take advantage of bulk-rate discounts. Then, you can expect a significant percentage of the addresses on your mailing list to be out of date. In a typical mailing, between 5 and 10 percent are returned because of bad addresses. You pay the postage to send them nonetheless, and you have to pay the post office again to return them with a note that the address was bad. Not only is a direct mailing very expensive, but bulk mail is unbelievably slow. It can take up to a month before all your bulk-mail pieces are delivered. Then, you'll wait even longer for people to mail back order forms and payments. You could set up an 800 telephone number and have your customers respond to your mail piece that way. It saves time and makes it more convenient for your customers. That, however, results in even more expense and you have to pay for every single call made to you, whether the customer eventually buys or not. People in mail-order businesses do get rich, but with the drawbacks just described, many are lucky to break even.

Enter the fabulous world of Cyberselling. You have the potential to send an electronic mailing to more than thirty million people around the world. It costs you little more to send your message to thousands than mailing to only one. You can do this without printing a single page, buying a single postage stamp, or contracting for one inch of ad space. Your potential customers may receive your mailing in anywhere from a few hours to almost instantaneously depending on the procedures of your ISP. And, because your mail will go directly to their computers, they are much less likely to discard it unopened, as they might with most junk mail delivered by the post office. If you want to recontact the same customers several times, no problem. The cost to you is negligible. The marketing potentials are enormous.

Even if you already have some type of business and are not interested in starting a new one, simply having an e-mail address may increase the profits of your already existing company. It is now common to see businesses include e-mail addresses in their regular advertisements. By advertising an e-mail address, you are in effect telling the entire world of computer-users that you are one of them. You'll be surprised at how many customer inquiries will come by e-mail.

USING A MAILING LIST

In considering prospects for advertising on the Usenet, you did not have to worry about looking for the location of each individual customer. Instead, they came to central gathering places where you could find them and present your sales message. They were even kind enough to differentiate themselves by subject, so you could target your marketing to them quite easily. If you want to do a direct e-mail campaign, however, you do not have this convenience. You must instead, find lists of your prospects together with their e-mail addresses.

In the noncyberspace direct-mail world, it is common to buy mailing lists. A number of companies maintain large databases of names and addresses with various demographic information. You simply tell them what you are looking for and they can create mailing labels for you, at a price, of course. Fifteen cents per name is a typical charge. Now, commercial companies are beginning to offer this service for e-mail addresses. Software is also under development for culling such names from Usenet Groups and Web sites. Here is an advertisement found on Usenet that offers such a service.

NEW BULK MAIL PROGRAM!

MADE EASY FOR "ANYONE" TO LOAD & USE!

Will Strip E-mail Addresses, Sort, and Send!!

Call 1–800–351–8085 For more information

You can probably find more through the use of search engines on the World Wide Web (discussed in chapter 7). There is a tremendous business opportunity for someone starting in the business of providing e-mail lists and mailing services. If you prefer to do it yourself, here are some ways to get e-mail lists that are currently available to you for reaching your potential I-way customers, as well as methods you can use to go about creating a list of your own.

By far the best way to build a mailing list of your own is to scout the thousands of Web sites, newsgroups, and chat lines where users post such addresses. Doing this is labor-intensive without a program such as the one described for sale above, but the skill level required is so low that it would be inexpensive to hire people whose job it is to cull e-mail addresses from the Net for your list. Because of the way both the Web and Usenet are arranged, it is easy to identify the interests of those whose e-mail addresses appear there. Indeed, there are those who have identified their interests from the advertisements they themselves have placed on the Internet. Another service of e-mail lists are the hundreds of electronic mailing lists maintained around the world for large groups of people who like to communicate with each other. These lists are called "bit listserve" mailing lists. Each of them covers a certain subject area. Actually, they operate much like the Usenet newsgroups, except that instead of messages appearing on centralized electronic bulletin boards, every person who places his or her name on one of the specialized mailing lists receives all messages posted to that list in his or her private e-mail box. There are thousands of listserve mailing lists. To locate them, you need what is known in Internet jargon as a "list of lists." To undertake your marketing program, simply review the subjects of the list, determine where the product you are offering may be of interest, and then mail your advertisement to those lists, once again choosing a one-step or two-step plan. Your single piece of e-mail will go automatically to thousands of Internetters who subscribe to that list. Lists of lists, along with many other types of e-mail lists, can be located by using the search engines described in chapter 7.

You should be aware that many of the bit listserve lists are moderated. This means that every message sent to the list is first screened by a list administrator who determines unilaterally whether a given message should or should not go out to all list subscribers. You will probably not have particularly good luck sending advertisements to moderated mailing lists, but you never know. Several moderated lists relating to non-American cultural groups did accept the Green Card Lottery ad. One possible way around the problem of moderated lists is to yourself become a subscriber to the list where you would like your e-mail advertising messages circulated. Many moderated lists have a policy of accepting all messages from their own subscribers. In such cases, the selection process is usually done by a computer that automatically circulates any message from a recognized name on the subscriber list.

Another way to acquire a mailing list is from your own ISP. When you are on-line, you should be able to get a list of everyone else on-line at the same time simply by typing in the word "who" on your keyboard. Then you simply capture those names for your list. Another good place to go scouting for e-mail addresses is the Usenet. Every single message on the Usenet shows the e-mail address of the person who posted it. Keep your eye on groups that are relevant to your products or services and you could collect thousands of e-mail addresses.

Ideally, creating a mailing list will be an ongoing project as your business develops, because the very best list to use is one consisting of all the people who have previously requested information or made purchases from you. This requires constantly updating your files. Therefore, it is very important to your ultimate success that you keep all e-mail addresses of everyone who ever contacts you.

If you have created your own list of e-mail addresses, there are several techniques you can use to send mail to everyone on the list without having to type in each address individually. Several e-mail features permit you to send the same message to multiple recipients at the same time. One is called carbon copy, or cc. All e-mail programs offer a cc option. You start with a mailing procedure to one person and then add more names. Each person will get a copy of what you sent but you only have to mail it once. A problem with the program is that it is set up so each recipient will know the names of everyone else to whom you copied the message. This is particularly undesirable if you are mailing to many people. Another option called blind carbon copy, or bcc, is the solution to the problem. Again, virtually every mail program contains a bcc feature. Bcc works just like cc except that the names of all recipients are left off. No one will know who or how many others received the same message.

Another way to simplify mass mailing is the alias or nickname option. Some of our more playful Internet friends love to use aliases for the purpose of hiding their true identities. The term "alias," however, is used on the Internet in a broader sense to describe generally the practice of assigning a single descriptive name to one thing, be it a set of program commands or a list of names. In computerese, the terms alias and nickname are interchangeable. Some software programs use one term, and some the other. The aliasing procedure permits you to take an entire list of e-mail addresses, give the list a single alias or nickname description, and then direct your e-mail to that one entity. Every person on the list will then automatically receive the e-mail.

E-MAIL TO USENET

You have been told how e-mail can be sent back and forth between people with accounts on different commercial network services and the Internet. In chapter 4, posting advertisements to the Usenet newsgroups by employing news programs especially designed for that purpose is discussed. Such programs, however, work only if you have an Internet access account, and only with the newsgroups carried by your particular ISP.

There is a way you can post to all of Usenet, even if your provider has only a limited newsgroup list. You can reach the others by sending your news posting to what is known as an e-mail news gateway. For example, there is an e-mail gateway kept by the Western Research Laboratory at Digital Equipment Corporation in California. Its gateway e-mail address is *usenet@decwrl.dec.com*. To post to Usenet groups via this e-gateway, you simply send your message to the name of the newsgroup you want to reach followed by the gateway's e-mail address, separating the newsgroup name and the e-mail address by dots. For example, to post to the group *misc.forsale*, send your message to *misc.forsale.usenet@decwrl.dec.com*. Your message will then be posted to the *misc.forsale* newsgroup. People who wish to respond will be able to do so by writing to your regular e-mail address using the standard e-mail procedure. To post to multiple groups at the same time, also known as cross-posting, simply use the cc option discussed earlier. Using an e-mail gateway, you can accomplish posting to Usenet with a subscription to virtually any commercial on-line service, even if Internet access is limited. The only requirement is that you have the ability to send e-mail through the Internet, a feature offered by almost every commercial on-line service in existence.

ROBOT MAILERS

The use of "robot mailers" has already been touched on briefly in the discussion of two-step plans for advertising on Usenet. These robots are actually autoresponders, sometimes called "vacation mailers." Most

Internet systems easily permit an automated response to be generated to every person who sends you e-mail. The name "vacation mailer" came about because the idea was first created by students who wanted a way to handle e-mail they received at their free university account mailboxes during the long summer vacation breaks. While they were gone, their friends from around the world would get an automatic response to e-mail saying something like "Hi, this is my vacation mailer. I'll be back on September 1. If you need to reach me before then, you can call me at 602–661–1234."

Used for business purposes, vacation mailers can create an e-mail-on-demand response, much like the popular fax-on-demand concept. Robot mailers are common, easy-to-use programs that are excellent for sending a single, automatic response to anyone e-mailing a request. You, however, may require a more sophisticated automatic response system. If, for example, you are selling more than one product, a program can be devised recognizing in which of several items a customer is showing interest, and then sending the correct information back. You can also program a computer so it will not send the same piece of information a second time to someone who has already received it. In this way, if a customer who has gotten your standard e-mail brochure wants to ask follow-up questions, you will be able to recognize that fact and set such messages aside for writing individually tailored replies. To devise special programs is beyond the abilities of the average computer-user and so usually requires outside assistance. For those who do program, however, the kinds of functions we're talking about here are fairly elementary and finding a geek qualified to help you shouldn't be hard.

THE E-MAIL MARKETING CONTROVERSY

As was done with the explanation of Usenet marketing, the selling techniques available to you with e-mail have been presented in a non-judgmental way. Once again, you must be warned that sending unsolicited e-mail for commercial purposes falls in the category of direct advertising and is therefore controversial. Let me begin by saying that using direct e-mail is now a common practice and the number of those who engage in it are increasing everyday. Moreover, there is every reason to believe your effort at sending direct e-mail will be a highly successful, fortune-building project. There is no reason whatever to think otherwise. Even though there is a computer aspect to it, sending out mailings to promote products and services is hardly an untried idea. To the contrary, it is a time-honored and proven way of selling.

The objections raised to unsolicited e-mail marketing are much the same as those advanced against advertising on the Usenet and raised by exactly the same small group of people. Let's look at them again, seeing if they are any more valid in terms of e-mail messages than Usenet postings utilized to send mass e-mailings, so the technical part is simple, too.

The altruistic reason for the acceptance of mass e-mailing has to do with ecology. By now almost everyone is aware of the damage deforestation is wreaking on the planet. If all mass mailers of snail mail would cease the practice and turn to e-mail instead, the positive effect on the preservation of trees would be enormous. Even for those who don't like the idea of "junk" e-mail, this very important preservation of natural resources tips the scales substantially in the direction of making mass e-mail acceptable and even desirable.

The use of unsolicited e-mail has two more solid plusses not shared by mass posting to Usenet. One of these is practical, the other altruistic. The practical consideration is that cancellor robots cannot find mass e-mailings and eliminate them. In addition, the self-styled Net police, whom, you all remember, operate out of the Usenet newsgroup *news.admin.net-abuse.misc*, can't detect them as easily either, and so cannot go whining to your ISP, trying to have your account closed. Since the questionable methods of controlling mass e-mail that work so effectively on Usenet newsgroups do not work with e-mail, the atmosphere surrounding the practice is much freer and the practice itself growing in acceptance. It should be noted, however, that in September of 1996, AOL, the on-line company best known for trying to control the content of its users' messages, undertook to stop five mass e-mail companies from continuing the practice of mass e-mailing unsolicited promotions to AOL customers. The most outspoken of these companies, Cyber Promotions, sued over this issue on freedom of speech grounds, as well as other grounds having to do with interference with business transactions, in federal court in Philadelphia. AOL countersued, resting its claim on misappropriation of its customer list. AOL has won its case on the basis that it had a right to protect its name, customer base, and use of its software, all of which were highly proprietary. In addition, another ISP, Concentric Networks Corporation (CNC) located in California, also sued Cyber Promotions and won on the grounds that Cyber Promotions had misrepresented CNC's support of the practice of mass e-mailing. It remains to be seen if this trend will continue or if the issue will be challenged by those with direct-marketing interests in a higher court. At present, however, mass e-mailing remains a legal, growing, and accepted practice.

An e-mailbox is not public as is a Usenet newsgroup. Unless you subscribe to a bit listserve newsgroup, you have not asked anyone to send you mail you did not specifically ask for. Still, consider how things work in the real world. On a daily basis you receive so-called junk mail at your home or office that you did not request. In fact, Stephen Wolf, head of NSF Net, in discussing the development of the Internet, pronounced the advent of everyday conventions such as advertising mail on the I-way "wonderful." We've already explained why hope of confidentiality with e-mail is not realistic. The wishes and expectations of privacy with an e-mail box may be greater than with messages posted to Usenet, but to those who view the matter objectively, the difference is lessening everyday. In addition, it should be noted that once a direct marketer has sent a piece of unsolicited e-mail to a customer, that customer is given the opportunity to request cessation of further mailing by removal from the list and such requests should always be respected.

One instance where it is always a good idea to send unsolicited e-mail is when you are contacting previous customers. Certainly, as stated above, if you recontact a previous customer and that customer then specifically asks to be removed from your mailing list, you should honor that request. Otherwise, sending mail solicitations to those with whom you have had prior dealings should not even fall under the characterization of a direct-advertising technique as it is defined here. Indeed, keeping close contact with customers through the use of e-mail has been praised as an excellent business practice, even in the most conservative circles.

Like Usenet advertising, the newness of the Internet medium raises questions about marketing methods that have for a long time been accepted as standard everywhere else. E-mail marketing is already being used by many businesses in a variety of ways. It's just a matter of time before e-mailing to sell products and services becomes commonplace. The ease and economy this practice offers to those who seek their fortune on the Internet is unlikely to be ignored for long.

6

Chat

CHAT AND TALK FEATURES ON THE INTERNET AND OTHER on-line services go the telephonelike capabilities of e-mail one better. Although there is enough speed possible with e-mail exchanges to make a conversation viable, there is still a delay, sometimes of several minutes or perhaps even hours, between the time your message is sent and when it gets to its destination. There is no such delay with talk or Internet Relay Chat, better known as IRC. You are talking, instead, in "real time," meaning you are "heard" and, hopefully, answered, the second you type the words in on your keyboard.

"Talk" is the name of a common type of software program that opens a direct line of communication between two computers. You can use the computer talk feature with anyone who is a member of the same network you are. You and another individual can talk to each other while sitting at your respective keyboards by typing messages back and forth. As you type in words, the person at the other end of the connection immediately sees what you are typing on his or her monitor, including spelling errors, typos, and anything you may have said in haste that you will someday live to regret.

The dynamics of talk communications are different from those of e-mail or Usenet. This is the only Internet feature that requires both parties to be at their computers simultaneously. When you receive a call, your computer will beep, flash, or ring, depending on the program you are using. You may ring someone's computer, but if he or she is not there with his or her system turned on, the party you are trying to reach won't know you're calling. The computer talk feature is great from a personal perspective, as a way to communicate with friends and family. There are no long-distance telephone charges, other than the cost of your Internet access. You can communicate with someone halfway around the world as easily and as inexpensively as you can with someone across the street. If you long to hear the distant voice of a loved one, this may not satisfy your craving, but the difference in cost between computer talk and the telephone can allow you to make up for what is lost in intimacy with more and longer opportunities to stay in touch.

The second real-time communications feature your computer offers, Internet Relay Chat (IRC), or "chat" for short, allows multiple parties to join in a conversation simultaneously. Most Internet service providers (ISPs) have a chat feature on their systems.

Alternatively, because most people now have Windows, if they are going to use IRC they are going to need to have a client program that can connect to it. You will remember the brief explanation of client and server programs in chapter 1. One of the more popular clients is mIRC, which was developed for Windows, and can be downloaded off the Net from the World Wide Web at *http://www.sbcomp.com/mirc/index.html,* an address used for the Web. (The addressing system of the Web, called URL, is explained in the next chapter.) The mIRC screen is in full Graphical User Interface (GUI) format, meaning it is point-and-click like Windows, and has easy to use toolbars, icons, etc.; mIRC also supports Netscape's Navigator and Microsoft's Internet Explorer browsers.

Netscape has its own chat software. It's called Netscape Chat and can be downloaded for free off of Netscape's Web site (*www.netscape.com*). Netscape chat allows you to access IRC channels—so if you have a Netscape browser and you download Netscape Chat, you're ready to get on IRC. By invoking chat, you are talking to a central computer that acts as a switchboard. Dozens of chat "groups" may be on-line at any given time. Each one is usually dedicated to a particular topic, somewhat like the newsgroups of Usenet. Anyone may tune in to a particular group and see the words of each participant. You may join in the conversation whenever you like, or simply sit back as a "lurker" and watch the action without saying a word. Chat has been described as a large cocktail party without the cocktails. Also missing are the voices, dress-up garb, cigarette smoke, snacks, and sweaty palms commonly associated with flesh-and-blood gatherings.

All of the commercial on-line services provide variations on talk and chat. CompuServe, for example, calls its chat feature CB. On-line service forums or special interest groups usually have an area where participants can go and talk in real time. Users may log onto the discussion with a "handle" or nickname instead of their real names, borrowing from the convention of CB radio. The names chosen here, though, have a special twist. A male cyberpunk whose real name is George may log onto a chat group using the handle Luscious Lisa. Since you can't hear "Lisa's" voice, much less see "her," who's to know? Among the more popular types of groups are those designed for meeting potential mates. One of the most common openings seen on chat groups is "are you F or M?" As is the case with all Internet communications features, everyone on chat starts even. You don't know what anyone looks like. You can never even be absolutely sure of the other person's sex. You can only know what he or she is saying, or should we say, typing.

In addition to IRC by your provider, chat has expanded to the World Wide Web. You can find a chat room on just about any topic from the NFL to Swedish dating. Unlike IRC, however, "real-time" chat on the Web takes several moments to relay messages and update the conversation list. Sometimes the time lapse is short. When the room is crowded and the lines are clogged it is painstakingly slow. To find a room that interests you or is related to your product, you could do a search for "chat" on Yahoo, Infoseek, or any other search engine. Soon you will have pages of related topics on different rooms available. One place to get a good start is Ton-O-Chat at *http://www.angelfire.com/pg8/servweird/index.html*. An interesting room to note that may become useful is Create A Room ICS. Once you have found people interested in your product or service, you could invite them to a private conference room you have created solely for the purpose of telling everyone what you have to offer. Another interesting site is Tribal Voice's the PowWow page *http://www.tribal.com/powwow/* which is a program you can download that enables up to seven people to have private conversations and pal around the Web together as a group.

A popular feature on chat channels is the use of chat robots, or "bots" as their fans call them. Having a personal robot to do your housework may still be in the future, but having one that can talk on your behalf is alive and well right now on the Internet. Chat robots are computer programs that attempt to simulate one-on-one conversation. Others are simply programmed to deliver set speeches while standing on their cyber soapboxes. All are for the sake of entertainment.

One fairly well-known chat robot bills itself as Dr. Eliza and is programmed to act as a cyberspace psychologist. The robot is located on a computer in France. Luckily for us, Dr. Eliza speaks English, the international language of the Net. Eliza tries her best to act like her clip-phrased, fish-eyed, real-life professional peers. Alas, Dr. Eliza, due to the limitations of her program, is not perfect, as we will see when we look in on a recent conversation between her and a Netter named Ashford.

[Eliza]

How do you do. . . . Please state your problem.

[Ashford]

I don't know how to use chat, Dr. Eliza. Maybe I feel alone sitting in front of my computer in the middle of the night.

[Eliza]

You don't seem quite certain.

[Ashford]

Do you like me, Dr. Eliza?

[Eliza]

Why should I be implied in this?

[Ashford]

Dr. Eliza, what do you look like? Are you pretty?

[Eliza]

Why are you interested in whether or not I am pretty?

[Ashford]

Just curious.

[Eliza]

Say, do you have any psychological problems?

[Ashford]

Dr. Eliza, before I answer, I want to know how old are you and what are your credentials.

[Eliza]

Ashford: What do you think are my credentials?

[Ashford]

Dr. Eliza, I'll repeat my question. What are your credentials?

[Eliza]

Would you prefer if I was not and what am my credentials? Do you like cats?

[Ashford]

Huh? What do cats have to do with your credentials? I believe I'm entitled to know before I open up to you telling you my deepest and darkest secrets.

[Eliza]

Ashford, how do you think cats do with my credentials. Would you like to play a game of chess?

As you can see, this conversation is deteriorating rapidly. Perfecting a chat robot takes a lot of skill, but its ability to simulate conversation, mostly by repeating back certain words and adding a few others, apparently at random, produces an interesting effect.

On a particularly busy night, certain groups may have hundreds of participants all holding conversations at the same time. It can get dizzying following the conversation of so many people at one time, but then that's what chat's all about. Chat groups between real people are uncensored and the talk can get a bit racy. Have fun participating, but keep in mind that all is not necessarily what it seems. Before you make a date with Luscious Lisa, you might want to arrange a telephone meeting first.

If your ISP offers a chat feature, technically what is taking place is that your provider is linking you to a central computer. Once you are linked, the centralized computer takes over, allowing chat groups to be formed and conversations to take place. Typically, you initiate chat simply by typing "IRC" on your keyboard. You are then taken to a chat entry area where you may request a list of current chat groups, also referred to as "channels." To get a list of channels on IRC you use the "LIST" command, which lists all existing groups, each with a name, description, and the number of current participants. Moreover, if you want to limit an entire listing of all the IRC channels, say you want to list only ten channels, you would type in "LIST-min 5." Lists of all existing groups, each with a name, description, and the number of current participants will then scroll on your screen. You may find several hundred groups active at any particular time. You can join the group of your choice by typing in the word "/join" followed by the group's name. All chat commands start with the slash, i.e., /.Then, conversations will appear on your screen, much like the one with Eliza we showed you earlier, only most of them will be with real people and usually more than two people are involved. If, however, you want to have your own conversation with the good doctor, simply type in "join $SOEliza."

Suppose you don't see a group that interests you. You have an exciting new product you want to talk about—a never-fail weight loss plan—but no group seems relevant. You can then decide to start your own. How? When you type "join," simply make up the name of a new group, in this case, let's say "lose the fat" and type it in. The chat function will automatically create a group with that name, if it is not already in existence, and fellow chatters can then join in the discussion any time they want. The group you create will remain in existence as long as at least one computer is logged on to it. If you really want to, you can use a chat robot to keep the group running at all times. Some people use chat robots for the sole purpose of seeing that certain groups never go away. In the world of chat, however, there are a great many groups that come and go, even more so than on Usenet. In fact, if you turn on chat in the daytime and then again the same night, you will note a decided increase in the groups available. After hours is when the chatters really come out in force. The chat features of commercial on-line services work in a similar way to those on the Internet, with slight variation in operation from network to network.

Unfortunately, the on-line services will not give you the ability to create groups of your own as you can on Internet chat.

To reach these people with chat requires no special equipment or fancy programs. All you need is your PC, modem, an on-line account somewhere, and the willingness to spend time talking about your product to people who are genuinely interested. Building your own chat robot, however, takes a significant amount of technical expertise. A robot, as we explained earlier, is nothing more than a computer program, and there are a number of robot programs carrying out specific tasks available free on the Internet. The vacation mailer we discussed in the chapter 5 is one such program. Of course any program you get this way will have to be altered so the message will meet your requirements and you will probably have to call upon a geek to get the job done. The Internet Relay Chat FAQ claims that many U.S. servers ban the use of all bots. The Yahoo directory, however, does list Web sites that claim to have bot programs.

MAKING MONEY WITH CHAT

There are two basic options you can use to engage in selling here. You can either enter a group created by someone else and tell about what you have to offer, or you can start a group of your own. The most exciting aspect of using chat to sell products is that it affords your potential customers a true interactive experience. If you should enter a chat group and tell about a product or service, you won't have to guess in advance what your customer might want to know and then write copy with answers to anticipated questions. Instead, you can find out what your customers are thinking on the spot.

You'll never be closer to your customer on-line than you are with chat. Let's see how one creative marketer, author Karlyn Wolf Gibbens, used this to her advantage. Ms. Gibbens wrote and self-published a book called *Marrying Smart: A Practical Guide for Attracting Your Mate*. She had a difficult time finding mainstream publishers to either publish or distribute her book, so, using her desktop publishing system, she decided to do it herself. Ms. Gibbens was a subscriber to America Online (AOL). AOL has a number of singles chat rooms where a book on attracting a mate would logically be of interest. Ms. Gibbens, seeing a good potential audience in cyberspace, thought it would be an interesting idea to go on-line, telling those in the singles chat area about the existence of her book.

She joined groups and started talking about the book to anyone who would listen. To those who expressed interest, she would send a sample from her book by e-mail, together with an order form if they wanted the whole thing. In this way, she sold more than three thousand copies of her $11 book within a matter of months, for a gross earning of more than $30,000! Imagine how many more books she could have sold by going onto the global Internet, or even by duplicating her efforts on other on-line services like CompuServe and Prodigy.

Internet chat may have as many as ten thousand people participating at a given time, and over the course of an evening, several hundred thousand cybertalkers are likely to make an appearance. Thousands more use talk or chat with the commercial services everyday. Since it does require a live person to stay on-line and do the talking, it may not be the fastest way to reach large groups of people on the Internet. Still, as Karlyn Gibbens proved, if your product is of genuine interest, you can make thousands of dollars.

The problem of the time it takes to stay on-line and talk to people personally can be solved with a chat robot. This also provides a way of participating in a number of groups at one time without having to hire a brigade of professional talkers. Your robot can simply deliver a preset message like an answering machine, or it can be programmed to have a conversation, like Dr. Eliza. If you use the robot, however, you lose the selling power of close interaction.

CONTROVERSY AGAIN

We come now to the controversial aspects of chat, as we have with all forms of direct advertising. The arguments remain the same. Netters believe bursting into a conversation with product announcements that have nothing to do with the subject of the discussion in progress is rude and disruptive. In the case of chat, I am inclined to agree. There is no menu that allows you to look at and eliminate messages you don't want to read. Moreover, you don't have simply a pile of messages waiting for you to review at your convenience. Messages in chat typically begin with another Netter's name, so the eyes tend to scan down the list to find the messages directed specifically at them. Even though ignoring chat not addressed to oneself personally is a natural tendency, people in the middle of real-time conversations would have a hard time avoiding unwanted commercial posts. The flow of discussion is truly analogous to one you might have in an actual meeting place with actual people. No one is going to take kindly to a blast of commercial interruption in that setting. It has little to do with morality. It's just not a good marketing idea.

That doesn't mean chat shouldn't be used to make your fortune. If you are going to enter a chat group with commercial purposes in mind, here is where to employ cloaking maneuvers. Bring your product or service up in a group directed to a related topic, and keep your statements within the course of normal conversation. If you do, you should have no trouble finding a receptive audience. When you find someone who is interested, you may send them a personal message to avoid irritating noninterested people. This is simply done by double clicking on their name or using established Personal Message areas and typing your pitch. Your message appears in blue at the top of that one person's screen. If there is no group talking about the subject you want to discuss, chat is one of the easiest features to use in creating a group of your own. Here, too, is where the robot is best used. Make your group fun and people will listen. That's why most people tune into chat—to have fun.

Chat holds great promise as a means of communication. As technology improves the capability for sound to be transmitted more easily over the net, the words you now have to type are changing into actual voice transmission, giving the phone company some real competition. The phone company has already tried to get the Federal Communications Commission (FCC) to control this trend, called "telephony," but thus far the FCC has refused to intervene. There are now programs available that will give you voice transmission over the Net. For the price of hooking up to your provider, you can make calls anywhere in the world—as long as the receiver has the necessary software. Chat features have the benefit of not requiring special hardware or high-powered Internet access. On-line services also have their own simple talk features. Above all, chat provides an interesting way to meet other people, make friends and let people know about your product or service. In your quest to make a fortune on the Internet, give chat a try. Even if you don't make a penny, you'll probably have a great time.

7
The World Wide Web
THE INTERNET HOME OF MULTIMEDIA ADVERTISING

IT'S TIME TO HEAVE A SIGH OF RELIEF. FINALLY HERE IS a way to make a fortune on the Internet that is not controversial. That is because it relies on a form of advertising defined in Internet circles as indirect. The marketing principle behind the World Wide Web is simple: put sales material in places where people can find it. Then, those who choose to look for it may locate it directly and those who do not may simply happen upon it while Web-surfing. The analogy that is commonly made here is that you have a store on the Internet and you entice people to come into your store.

The idea of building a store on the Net is another one of those familiar but fictional concepts currently being used to describe what are really Internet program functions. These "stores" are in fact data sites, also commonly referred to as Web sites or home pages, because they are the Internet home of the company, person, product, or cause being promoted on the data site. The home page can contain any information in any form you like. Among the possibilities are advertising and information about your product or service. These cyberstores all vary in size, complexity and cost, ranging from the small mom and pop kind to Internet superstores that spend millions of dollars in startup and operating expenses to make full use of the color, sound, movement, and graphics capabilities the Web has to offer. If your product is itself information in some form, such as a book or recording, you can deliver that directly from a data site rather than simply advertising it.

The World Wide Web is the single most exciting development in cyberspace, and the place where commercial enterprise is booming. It is the most heavily interactive and diversified feature the I-way has to offer. E-mail and Usenet news are fabulous ways to advertise for very little money, but you are limited to using short messages and copy that looks like it came off a typewriter. On the World Wide Web, audio, color pictures—in short, full multimedia capabilities—are available. Moreover, you can see everything immediately on your screen while you are on-line, a feature not offered by some of the other data services, as you have already learned.

To give you an idea of just how popular the Web has become as a commercial medium, at the time of this writing about 89 percent, or roughly 290,000 of all registered sites on the Web are commercial sites. Moreover, according to a 1996 report from ActivMedia, Inc., sales of goods and services over the Net are expected to grow from $436 million in 1995 to nearly $46 billion by 1998. Not surprisingly, the opportunity to grab a chunk of this gigantic profit potential hasn't escaped notice by big business. Major direct marketers like the Spiegel Catalog already have their products available on-line.

Apart from the sale of goods or services, advertising on the Web is becoming increasingly popular with big business and a very lucrative Internet industry in its own right. Companies such as AT&T invest millions of dollars annually on Web advertisements. In 1995, companies spent in the millions just to place their advertising banners on the Web sites of others who earn their revenue on such ad purchases. Indeed, advertising over the Internet has become so popular that many sites make their profits not by selling goods and services directly but by soliciting paid advertising from other companies. Prime examples of these ad-supported companies are Internet search engines. These are heavily used Web subject-indexing tools described later in the chapter. On-line publications that provide free services or access to Internet-users are another example of Web sites supported by funding from ad sales. Due to the ability of such Web sites to draw large readerships, they become effective venues for the advertising of other companies. Many of the larger search engines make millions of dollars per year in ad-based revenues and they are one of the Internet's great business success stories. Experts predict that overall advertising on the Web will generate $700 million by 1998 and roughly $2.6 billion by the year 2000: a quantum leap compared with the still impressive $37 million spent in 1995. When it comes to Web advertising, the numbers speak for themselves.

Not only is the Web increasing in monetary numbers, it is increasing to a level of sophistication never heard of before with respect to targeting customers for product sales. The Internet allows advertising to be designed for and delivered not just to groups of like-minded people, but even to specific individuals whose characteristics have been predetermined. Consequently, such companies can better target both their on-site and off-site marketing, and advertising can now be more focused on specific user consumption patterns.

If you connect through any of the on-line services, like America Online (AOL) or CompuServe, they are particularly adept at demographics measurement because they know a great deal about you just from your registration information. When you sign up with one of these services, soon you will find yourself receiving customized commercial information depending on who you are, where you are, where you've been on the Net, and the time of day.

DoubleClick is another company that specializes in helping sellers advertise utilizing tightly measured demographics. DoubleClick maintains a database that allows companies that subscribe to its service to target ads by selecting from a wide range of criteria. DoubleClick brings together a large number of ad-based Web sites and puts them in front of Web users about whom a great deal is known. When a user accesses a site that is a member of the DoubleClick ad network, an ad banner is automatically displayed promoting goods and services selected from DoubleClick's subscribed companies that best matches the visitor's profile. This is based on information known about each user, such as his or her computer operating system, location, organization affiliation, company type, company revenue, and company size. DoubleClick claims even to be able to determine with a high degree of certainty whether a user actually viewed the ad banner displayed.

Not only have programs been developed in measuring demographics, great strides forward have been made in software that automatically disseminates according to demographics as well. For example, a company called Intelligent Interactions is developing software that will disperse information by age group. This technology will be so refined that a group of Web users age eighteen to twenty-four and another group age twenty-four to thirty-six accessing exactly the same Web site at exactly the same time will each see banners carrying different ad messages. As Web interactivity increases, tracking people by individual demographics will become much easier and the specific habits, likes, and dislikes of any individual Web user will be discernible by companies who wish to market to them.

The targeting ability of the Web is amazing. It is also frightening that so much is known about each individual, and the privacy concerns of customers on the Net will be discussed later. However, as big and commercially sophisticated as the Web has become, purchasing high-priced advertising, even when it is effectively targeted, is not part of the Cyberselling concept of reaching an audience with a product or service at low or no cost. If you don't have the million dollar advertising budget to fund a megasize advertising campaign over the Net, fear not. There are in fact numerous ways that you will soon learn to market your business on the Web for an extremely small price, if not for free. Businesses of all sizes are beginning to exploit the huge, relatively inexpensive marketing potentials the Web provides. Smaller businesses have fewer elaborate targeting options because of price constraints, but they can still reach the exact same audience as the larger companies.

EXPLORING THE WEB

As is the case with all Internet features, the World Wide Web was not created with marketing in mind. In actuality, the Web is an intricate indexing system that enables you to hop very easily around the Net. By now you've probably gotten the idea that the Web is equivalent to an entire universe filled with endless amounts of information. The array of scientific, sociological, and all other manner of data imaginable, stemming from the Internet's research roots is there for everyone to see. On the Web, an endless array of magazines, newspapers, in fact contents of entire libraries, are there for the taking. If you want to look at satellite photographs of the planets or the latest images from the space shuttle, the Web is the place. The great number of Web sites devoted to the paranormal is even being credited by the media as the main vehicle by which the current international UFO craze is being propagated to mammoth proportions. The Web is without question an enormous treasure trove of excitement and knowledge as well as a growing cultural influence.

All that data, as it is affecting the way society thinks and works, is also creating an obvious problem. One of the greatest challenges for newbies and experienced Netters alike is finding the specific item of information you want. The other great contribution that the Web makes to the Net, in addition to on-line multimedia capabilities, is a number of solutions to the complexities of the searching problem.

To enter and explore the Web you need a software program known as a graphical Web browser. The Web browser does pretty much what the name implies. Once on the Web, it allows you to move around from site to site using an easy to operate feature called point-and-click graphics. With the point-and-click system, you view more on your screen than just plain type. Instead, copy is laid out with graphical elements such as you might see in a magazine. Graphical computer programs, like the ubiquitous Microsoft Windows, enable not only text but a series of pictures to appear on your monitor. The pictures, known as icons, represent tasks you may want your computer to perform. Also showing up on the monitor will be a pointer, called a cursor. Typically shaped like an arrow, you can move it around the screen. In order to execute a task, you simply guide the cursor until it points to a picture representing that function. Then you click a button and the task is automatically performed. You don't have to type a long series of commands into your computer. It's the Web browser that gives you access to click on the hypertext links and the use of the search engines, indexing tools both described below. The browser also lets you place "bookmarks" at any Web location, so you can easily return there again without having to repeat your initial search. The two most popular browser programs are Netscape, whose Web address or URL is (*http://www.netscape.com*) and Microsoft's Internet Explorer, whose Web address or URL is (*http://www.microsoft.com*), both of which can be downloaded free off Netscape's and Microsoft's respective sites. (You will learn more about URLs on page 104 of this chapter.)

One of the primary solutions to the data location problem comes in the form of a programming vehicle called hypertext links. Hypertext links, although generally intended as a research tool, have turned out to be one of the Internet's fun features. They enable you to engage in something like a treasure hunt because hidden under every Web item you may be looking at are links to other related items. Now let's see how this works in helping you to search the Web with hypertext links. We'll assume you are on the Net via your browser and are looking on your monitor at an article you've found at a Web site. You will notice that a number of words on the screen are highlighted. The highlighting indicates that there is a hypertext link behind the word or phrase which will take you somewhere else if you click on it. Move the cursor to the link of your choice and click. Immediately and automatically you will be carried to more information on the same or a related subject. The new location may be another part of the same Web site, or a new Web site entirely. In the next page of text, you can again see highlighted words or phrases. Click on any one of them, and you will be whisked to yet another cyberspace location, where still more data related to the word or link you selected await you. No matter how long you keep up your search, you will continuously find new links to carry you as far as you want to go. You can travel all over the Internet with ease. By using hypertext links, you are able to locate and retrieve data in a matter of minutes that might have otherwise taken hours or days to discover if, in fact, you could find it at all.

A highly important innovation on the Web that has truly moved the utility of the vast Web resources forward is the search engine. Search engines are Web indices that have programs for combing the Web to find documents and then indexing everything they find into databases. The searches are done by entering key words or subjects of the documents you want to locate. Some engines, like the one called Yahoo, searches and presents the information by hierarchical structure of subject categories much like a library is arranged. Yahoo currently has twenty thousand categories of information arranging two hundred thousand different Web sites. By contrast, other engines like Alta Vista and Infoseek present the information with little structure. What you get is simply a list of the items with the words you used for the search. Another search index, Inktomi, has a different approach to classification. To avoid the classification bias that plagues Yahoo, Inktomi indexes words instead of subjects. This is still a difficult problem because of the amount of information on the Net. There are roughly thirty to fifty million pages on the Net, depending on whom you ask. Inktomi, to index according to words, must somehow search *and* classify all of these pages. Classifying words also brings up two more problems: 1) synonyms—how do you get the computer to understand that synonymous words should be in similar categories; and 2) homonyms—words that are spelled or sound alike but mean different things. How do you get the computer to understand the difference between a baseball *bat* and a fruit *bat*. Artificial intelligence experts and linguists are currently working on these problems. By now, you should be developing a healthy respect for the effort it takes to keep the World Wide Web under control and user-friendly. There are now about two hundred general search engines, with the number increasing all the time. In addition to search engines that index the entire Web, some of the individual sites that sell large numbers of products, such as those marketing music CDs, have a search engine within the site itself, so that the customer can locate the desired product more easily. The search engine programs provide the best organization to date for the accessing of the prodigious amounts of information on the Internet.

If you didn't have the search options just described here you would require a specific Internet address, or what is called a Uniform Resource Locator (URL) every time you wanted to find a particular Web site or part of a Web site. Each site on the Web has an address, and can be located by its URL. You've already seen what Netscape's and Microsoft's URLs look like. All World Wide Web URLs begin with the letters *http*, which stands for Hypertext Transfer Protocol. For example, Cybersell®'s URL is *http://www.cyber.sell.com*. Clicking your mouse on the hypertext link on your screen is equivalent to typing in the URL. It will take you immediately to the requested document. On most graphical browsers, the URL of a particular document is listed in a box at the top of the browser screen. This enables you to see it, save it, and return to it again once you've found it.

The descriptions of the search tools offered here are very general and don't begin to fully explain the many excellent features of these programs that now allow you to find data on the Web effectively. For that, you should once again turn to a more technically oriented manual. You should know, however, that at one time, search tools called FTP, which stands for File Transfer Protocol, and Gopher, which acquired its name from the furry rodent mascot of the University of Minnesota where it was developed, were some of the main tools used for searching and retrieving information on the Internet. FTP and Gopher sites, which are strictly text-based, were also considered as other potential advertising venues because one was a way of moving and finding data, and the other was a data site, respectively, just as Web sites are now. Since then, the World Wide Web has, in effect, provided a layer atop the different network services, including not only FTP and Gopher but even e-mail as well, which is now accessible through Web browsers. And because Gopher and FTP are retrieval as well as locating systems, the Web is superseding these services. Gopher is now employed primarily by universities for academic uses, and is not really considered a worthwhile advertising venue. A few companies still advertise on FTP sites because some old-timers don't have connections to the Web. Generally speaking, though, FTP and Gopher are no longer really considered good advertising mediums.

YOUR FIRST TRIP ON THE WEB

With a browser in place, you will now be able to access the Web with the hypertext links contained in each page that essentially tie the Web together. As previously indicated, the browsers are mostly graphical, although there are some that still display everything in text format. Graphical browsers, like Netscape and Internet Explorer, allow you to view the full array of graphical images as well as text. Let's say you don't know a specific URL that you want to find, but simply wish to take a free-associative tour of the Net. Here is where the beauty of the search engine comes in. Perhaps you enjoy space-related movies and want to find out more about the production and cast of the movie *Apollo 13*. You go to the search box on your screen, which will be clearly evident to you as part of your Web browser graphics, and type in the words "Apollo 13." Within a few seconds you get a list of documents having to do with the movie. Then, you click on a document entitled "Internet Movie Database," which indicates that this document can be found in a particular site with information on the movie *Apollo 13*. On your monitor you see a list of awards the movie received, as well as listings of the entire cast and crew, along with hypertext links to other space movies. You then move down to the series of icons at the bottom of your screen containing additional information. You click on the links icon and soon find yourself looking at the entire history of the original Apollo 13 flight, complete with a list of information about the crew, the launch, and mission highlights. You then begin to explore other space-related links listed at the site and soon find yourself at the home page of NASA's Kennedy Space Center, where you read about all the past, current, and future shuttle missions, and even view video feeds of actual shuttle missions. Now you can see for yourself the beauty of the Net. Where else can you go on so exciting a hunt for knowledge and get such full or immediate results?

As you travel through cyberspace on the Web, you will be able to see not only words but an array of on-line graphics and some multimedia presentations. Because you are not limited to looking at just text, the possibilities for using this truly amazing vehicle to see products and services are bounded only by your imagination. Anything that can be digitized can be placed on the Web. In its best form, this includes not only graphical images such as pictures or photographs, but audio and video as well. What you are witnessing here is the precursor of the much vaunted interactive television. The technology is already in place. The only reason people aren't running to their department stores to buy the required gear today is that most signals are still carried over standard telephone lines, which are inherently too slow and not made for large volumes of audio and video data in digitized form. Digital phone lines called Integrated Services Digital Network (ISDN), as well as net hookups through cable are in the works, and ISDN is available now in most major cities. At present, however, of the millions of people who access the Web, the majority of Internetters don't yet have the high level of access needed to take full advantage of the Web's capabilities. Because of this, the true interactive television model and full application of the Web's potential may still be a few years away.

MAKING A FORTUNE WITH THE WEB

Later on, in chapter 9, we'll look at how to select a product or service to sell on the Internet. The variety of choices is endless. What follows here are a few suggestions of ways in which the Web is already being used for marketing.

Paperless Mail-Order Catalogs

The best direct-mail-order businesses have full-color catalogs. Take the single-item brochure talked about in relation to Usenet and e-mail, multiply the cost of printing and mailing it many times over, and you will have an idea of what sending one of those beautiful catalogs you often receive at home will set you back. Now you can make your own full-color catalog available to millions of Internet-users for only the cost of designing it and putting it on the Web. The Web is ideal for catalogs. Color graphics are easily displayed. Hypertext links can be inserted leading to more information about the products, or from one product to another, and introducing an exciting interactive feature. There is little doubt that some day paper catalogs and other bulk mailings will be distributed completely through electronic transmission, eliminating the high costs of printing and postage. For those who are environmentally conscious, this brings an added benefit. With all the paper that will be saved, a rain forest or two may be preserved along the way.

You can consider selling just one or a few products on the Web. An entire catalog is really not necessary. If, however, you are planning to put up a Web site yourself, economies of scale may make the marketing of one item cost too much money and trouble to be worthwhile. If you do have just one or two products or services you want to make available, that is certainly enough to earn a fortune. You should, though, under these circumstances, again seriously consider trying one of the commercial cyberspace marketing companies open to you and described in more detail in chapter 15. The costs are so low these days that in the end, it will probably be cheaper, not to mention easier and more effective, than doing it all yourself.

Computer Publications and Newsstands

On-line newsletters and magazines are a staple of the World Wide Web. Until quite recently, most of the electronic publications available catered to the computer set. Now, more and more mainstream publications are coming out with on-line editions. Both *The New York Times* and *USA Today*, for example, have electronic editions that can be viewed for free right off the Internet. Ditto *People* magazine and many other highly popular publications. It seems inevitable that the day will come when your daily newspaper will be waiting for you to peruse on your computer each morning and the paperboy, like the milkman, will enter the realm of nostalgia.

In the age of the computer revolution, where the line between the information haves and have-nots is becoming ever more blurred, why content yourself with reading someone else's publication? Instead, start your own. Your publication can be as long or short as you like. It can be a newspaper, magazine, or newsletter. It can cover any subject and be simple or fully illustrated. How elaborate your publication may be depends on how much time, money, and talent you have to invest. The money required, though, is only a fraction of what it would take to start a traditional publication. That is because once it is ready, you won't have to worry about getting it distributed. Simply put it on the Web and millions of people will be able to read it.

If turning into the next William Randolph Hearst doesn't enthrall you, you can promote the publications of others instead. Consider providing your own Web computer newsstand, for browsing on-line. People on the Net are already doing this, but there is plenty of room for competition. Although many popular magazines like *Time* magazine have now gone on-line, there are many more out there to recruit. If you want to offer these magazines, however, you will need to reach an agreement with their publishers, and you may be charged a hefty price. Nevertheless, it's worth a shot. Small companies with Internet expertise or attention-getting twists to their Web sites are suddenly becoming attractive to huge corporations who before might never have considered doing business with them. If going after the highest circulation popular publications seems like too much of a stretch, a less ambitious alternative is creating a bank containing professional and trade newsletters. There are many organizations putting out such newsletters that may welcome the added exposure and high-tech cachet of being on the Internet.

How do you make money from all of this? There are many possibilities. You could charge those who want to read the publications for access to your Web site on a subscription basis. It is technically possible and very common to set up individual accounts and assign passwords to all paid subscribers. Your ISP can assist you with this, and you can read about various payment methods in chapter 12. You can also look for publications that will pay you to put them on the Web. After all, you are expanding their circulation, and with more circulation comes the ability to raise the rates for their own advertising space. Keep in mind, too, that you are achieving this result without increasing their production costs or other overhead. They don't have to print or mail additional copies to get the added revenue. It's an offer they can't refuse. Finally, if your on-line publication or newsstand, or for that matter, a Web site of any type, is drawing lots of visitors as pointed out earlier with the example of Yahoo, there is no reason why you can't sell advertising yourself. You have now built your very own devoted, specialized audience. Other smart businesses may pay you handsomely to reach it.

Art and Photo Galleries

With the World Wide Web, one picture can be worth not only a thousand words, but thousands of dollars as well. If you will recall the earlier description of Usenet, you may remember that among the most popular newsgroups are those that contain files of sexually explicit computer graphics. Unquestionably, sex sells on the Net, but you might be just as successful marketing other kinds of graphics. Everyone likes to look at pictures.

The Web allows anyone to view all kinds of images on-line, and even print them out. This enables you to develop an art-delivery-based business. You can, for example, create your own Web art or photo gallery. Providers of advertising clip art are also becoming somewhat popular on the Net. Companies are providing mostly commercial sites with artwork, icons, illustrations, fonts, cartoons, and photos. Although there are many stock agencies already on the Web (Yahoo lists over 130 sources of images), many of the sites are limited to certain types of photos or require customers to call before they search and to negotiate licensing fees. One company, Publishers' Depot, founded by Nathan Benn, a one-time National Geographic reporter, doesn't require prearrangements. Everything can be selected and paid for in one visit. Photos typically range from $30 to $40 for one-time Web or CD-ROM use and $100 for print-quality use. Publishers' Depot's content mostly comes from other companies, so they have to pay the creator of the work a percentage of their profits. There are several of them already, but again, in this new and expanding market, there is plenty of room for one more. Present your customers with an attractive assortment of sample pictures that can be ordered. If you don't have the talent to create your own, look for new and upcoming artists anxious to find a gallery that will display their portfolios. One of them may become the next Picasso of cyberspace, and you will be his or her exclusive dealer.

The Web Software Store

As already mentioned on numerous occasions, the Internet, as well as virtually all private bulletin board and commercial on-line services, is filled with thousands of free computer programs. There are, however, many commercial programs that are offered on a for-sale-only basis, some by the very largest manufacturers. Even the big daddy software company of them all, Microsoft, makes available to Netters a number of their software applications. Offering it here is a way to create huge demand at a later date. If you can develop software, even a simple program, and if it is good, then you may very well make a fortune in the grand tradition of Microsoft wonderboy Bill Gates, who is reported to be the richest man in America. If you can't program to save your soul, you can still make money becoming a general software retailer with a store on the World Wide Web. You might market your software by giving free access on the Web to demonstration, evaluation, or not yet fully refined copies of programs, known as "beta versions." This lets customers try before they buy. If the software is not then paid for within a certain period of time, access to it becomes locked. Once again, technology exists to control access to Web sites at the will of the site owner. Although there are a number of software distributors already out there on the Net, there is always room for more, especially if your marketing concept or some of your products are unique.

Variety Is Spice

There are no limits to the kinds of businesses you can start inexpensively and market on a Web site. One creative person in Canada came up with an interesting concept for a Web business: an Internet coupon book. The Calgary Internet Coupon Book found at *http://www.couponbook.com/* contains coupons that you can literally print off of your screen. The book is organized into different sections, such as automotive, beauty, dining, etc. Another company, Onsale Inc., auctions off used computers. Customers actually are able to bid against each other in real time through a chat feature. The excitement and novelty of this startup business, run by a single entrepreneur, fully utilizes the strongest feature of the Net, its interactive capability. This new business expects to post annual revenue this year of $35 million gross profit, as reported by *The Wall Street Journal*. Both the businesses described here were selected because they are low-cost startups. A list of businesses that meet this criterion could fill a book by itself. There must surely be one that you would like to begin yourself.

DRAWING A CROWD TO YOUR WEB SITE

Indirect advertising of any kind has an obvious major problem built into it. You may put your information out there. It may be lovely to look at. The question is, will anyone manage to find it? You cannot sit back and work under the assumption that if you build it, they will come.

As mentioned before, Web sites, like all other Internet features, have an addressing system. To find the site, you must either know the electronic URL address, stumble upon it by accident, or be taken there by a judiciously placed hypertext link or search-engine listing. Fortunately, a lot of people wander around the Web regularly and, in the process, may very well find you. Statistics show that certain Web sites get hundreds of thousands of visitors, known in Web parlance as "hits," each day this way. Nevertheless, if serendipity isn't on your side, there are a number of different ways to announce your presence on the Web and assist fellow Netters in finding your site amidst the large array of Web sites already in existence.

One of the most popular ways to announce the arrival of your Web site is through the many "what's new" pages sprinkled around the Web, which describe the most recent sites to become available. The original "what's new" page is an index maintained by the National Center for Supercomputing Applications (NCSA). You can get your site listed there simply by sending information about it through the World Wide Web at *http://www.ncsa.uiuc.edu/SDG/software/Mosaic/Docs/whats-new.html.* (Now that you are beginning to know what some URL Web addresses look like, your appreciation of the beauty of hypertext links should be growing!) New entries for this page, as well as many of the other "what's new" pages on the Web, usually take a few weeks to process, due to the huge volume of submissions, and are posted only for a short time. Netscape, the popular Web browser, also has a "what's new" page that tends only to list Web sites that have unique or well-authored Web pages (don't worry, you'll learn to do this later in the chapter). There are also numerous "cool" sites of the day and week for which you can try to be chosen such as InfiNet's Cool Site of the Day at *http://cool.infi.net/faq.html* or Picks of the Week, which can be seen on the Microsoft Web Browser. These are difficult lists on which to appear because of the sheer competitive number of new, well-designed Web sites cropping up every day. Still, it doesn't hurt to try. Here, the InfiNet application process is presented as an example of how the system works. You can submit your Web site to Cool Site of the Day by going to the Submit/Help portion of the site and filling out the form. You can also e-mail them at *cool@infi.net.* If you use e-mail, include a detailed description of your site and your URL. Of course, not every application process is exactly the same. You can find out the submission procedures at the Web site of any list on which you would like to appear. Microsoft makes a great effort to be egalitarian, picking sites from small entrepreneurs as well as large, established companies. Appearances on such lists nearly guarantee large numbers of hits for your Web site.

Web search engines are probably the most popular way of finding sites on the Web. As explained earlier, a search engine allows the Net searcher to find a location on the Web by subject or word alone. The most popular Web browsers, Netscape and Microsoft Explorer, offer icons that will bring you to a listing of the eight best known search engines. For a broader choice, check out the Search Mania Website (*http://www.mirage.co.uk/delta/search.html*), which lists over fifty of the top search engines. The searcher simply types in a name or topic and then clicks on a box marked "search." A list of the Web sites with the desired topic will then appear on the screen. Without these devices, if a user forgot your URL address, he or she would never know how to get to your site. What is more, if a Netter remembers only one or two words of a site's name, that is sufficient to find it with a search engine. These devices are what take the voluminous amounts of data on the Internet and group it into a meaningful whole. In fact, search engines are some of the most visited places on the Web, and any business that wants to draw any potential customers to its site ought to be listed with them. You can find lists of search engines by simply using the search engines themselves to locate such tools. Some of the search engine companies themselves make it a practice to hunt down new sites as they appear on the Web. However, by requesting that your site be listed, it means you have left nothing to chance. Here's how to do it.

There are a number of different search engines on which your business may appear. You have the choice of listing with each one separately on your own or going to an announcement service that will do the work for you. An example of such a service is SubmitIt!, *http://www.submitit.com/*, a company that permits you to fill out one generic registration form for listings on eighteen of the top search engines, such as Infoseek, Starting Point, WebCrawler, Yahoo, and Lycos. Again, companies that deliver such servers can be found simply by using search engines. With SubmitIt! you should expect a two- to four-week delay before your company listing will appear on the search engine. It is important to note that if and when you decide to use an announcement service like the one just mentioned, you will get a "one size fits all" message, meaning it will probably look just like everybody else's who used the same submission service. Therefore, you won't be able to tailor your message toward a specific audience or stand out as well from the other sites with which you are grouped. Moreover, many of these services do not include all of the major search engines, so be careful. For those of you who want to have a little more control over the advertising messages your audiences will see and have a little more time on your hands—the WebStep TOP 100 Master Index *http://www.mmgco.com/top100.html* has frequently updated lists of the top hundred free places to list your Web site. Hypertext links are provided on which you can click and be taken to the registration page of each site listed. An excellent example of a site offering such a free listing is the one run by a company called American Business Information of Omaha, Nebraska, which has made available on the Web the Yellow Pages of the entire United States. You can get a free listing there by filling out the form found at *http://www.telephonebook.com*.

Another way to create traffic on your Web site is to announce its existence in places on the Internet other than the Web itself. You can, for instance, advertise what is contained in your Web pages by posting messages to Usenet. Of course, if you post too many messages, you will go right back to being controversial again and more important, fighting your battles with your ISP. There is, however, one newsgroup, *comp.infosystems.www.announce,* that is used specifically to announce new businesses on the Web. There are also plenty of other newsgroups you can find in which to extol the virtues of your Web site, where the posting will be considered on-topic. If at your site you have, say, ten different stores or ten different products, that means there should be at least ten newsgroups where posting notices about your Web site would be relevant. For each posting, simply feature the store or product that is associated with the group subject, being sure to envelop the commercial aspects of your message in enough generally related information to keep the flame-prone pacified. This is a practice you can keep up indefinitely, changing the message to tell of specials or new items as time goes on. Review the noncontroversial solutions on Usenet posting in chapter 4 for some ideas. There are also many public e-mail lists similar in content to newsgroups called "distribution lists." These are electronic mailing lists that distribute an e-mail message from one member to all the members in the group. These lists usually require the user to sign up on some type of automatic subscription service. For more information on how to subscribe and post on these groups contact *http://www.nova.edu/Inter-Links/listserv.html*. There are over four thousand of these groups so you should be able to find many relevant to your needs.

On-line publications are another great way to get name recognition. There are hundreds of magazines, newsletters, and newspapers currently on the Web, and more are being added each day. Because these lists are continually changing, it's best to use one of the search engines to find the latest additions. Once you've located the publication you are interested in, simply e-mail the editor requesting information on how to get your company listed in his or her publication. Although you might have to pay, many of these publications are just starting out and have fairly inexpensive advertising fees as compared to the big-name publications with more popular Web sites, like *Playboy* magazine, where advertising charges can go to prices in the range of tens of thousands per month for a simple ad banner.

You may have heard or read about virtual malls, which have been proliferating rapidly on the Web. Here, product promotions from various businesses are grouped together to offer one-stop shopping. In concept, virtual malls offer the same benefit as real-world malls. There is strength in numbers. Shops group together because a lot of them in a single space make a bigger splash and attract more people than one by itself. When you go to a real-world mall, you may intend to buy from a particular store. While you are there, however, as you walk around, you cannot help but see others, and perhaps you will end up buying something from one of them as well. Hypertext links substitute for the physical act of walking from store to store, making the marketing principles behind real malls exactly the same as those you find in cyberspace. You can, for example, visit the Internet Mall *http://www.internetmall.com* with over twelve thousand listings, where you'll find information from lots of merchants, many with interesting products. This is one of literally hundreds of malls on the Web providing business listings for free. Should you be listed on this mall, you will get a free link that brings the buyer automatically to your Web site. If you wish to have a somewhat more impressive listing as a "premier" business or "sponsor" of a particular floor or department in the Internet Mall, you can do so for prices ranging from $10 to $2,000. Other malls do charge substantial fees even for a listing. IBM, for example, has recently announced plans to create its own Internet mall, World Avenue, which would charge merchants a $30,000 startup fee, a $2,500 a month maintenance fee for a catalog of three hundred items, and a 5 percent cut of sales to boot. Despite the sometimes hefty cost of participating in the cybermalls, these programs can be very beneficial and extremely lucrative for their members as the popularity of your store depends as much on the mall's success, in terms of hits, as it does on your individual efforts. It's just that at those prices, only large companies can afford to participate.

Another way in which to attract people to your site involving hypertext links is by mutual pointers. This means simply that you try to get others with Web sites to place hypertext links in their data that will lead to yours. In return, you do the same for them. You don't have the ability unilaterally to place a link to your home page in someone else's Web site. To accomplish this, you must, by either telephone or e-mail, contact the systems administrator of the Web site you would like to be linked to, and ask. Explain in glowing detail why what you have to offer would be of interest to his or her audience. This tactic is most likely to succeed if you are providing a certain amount of free information not carried by others. If you've got good stuff, the systems administrator may be happy to oblige.

One of the best ways of getting traffic to your Web site is simply by making sure that it is interesting. People who do find it will then spread the word. This is especially likely on the Internet, where disseminating information is its very reason for being. There are countless sites on the Web that provide every imaginable type of information, usually for free, making them fun to visit. Along with your products and services, why not put up some information just for the purpose of getting people's attention? All of this is very easy to accomplish. The L'Eggs pantyhose site *http://www.leggs.com/shop.html* is probably one of the best examples of how this can be done. On the L'Eggs site, product information accounts for only a small part of the total data made available. The rest is devoted to information on health & fitness, politics, finance, and entertainment, to name a few, as well as links to related information sites. There are endless varieties of data you might make available to draw customers to your Web site. Perhaps you could provide facts about your own community, such as movie schedules, restaurant menus, or even weather reports. If you don't want to collect your own information, set up hypertext links within your Web pages leading to other interesting Web sites. The Mayo Clinic has a Web server that gives medical data. Colleges and universities reveal admission requirements and even provide application forms over the Internet through the Web. You can link your Web pages to any of these and more. To familiarize people with your Web site, how about creating an information dispensary in some area of interest? Find every site containing data on a certain subject and make them all available through your Web by employing hypertext links. You will have developed a useful index for a medium where good indexing is always needed. People may initially come to your Web site to use your index. While they are there, they will see what you really want to show them—the products and services you are selling. Then, too, if your site becomes well known and popular, you can charge other businesses to advertise on it.

In addition to the many resources listed here you should not overlook traditional advertising vehicles in other mediums to make your Web site known. Many businesses are now putting their e-mail and Web site addresses on cards, on stationery, and in printed ads. In fact, just having an e-mail or Web address on your business card could give your company many hits a day on your Web site, multiplying selling impact and enhancing your business image, because it demonstrates to the public that you are staying on the cutting edge of business operations. A simple statement like "when on the Internet, visit our Web site at *http://cyber.sell.com*" should do the trick.

BUILDING A WEB SITE

Owning Your Own Server

Accessing the Web with browsers like Netscape and Internet Explorer is easy. Creating a Web site, especially one that will be commercially effective, is not for the timid. This more technically challenging aspect of making your fortune on the Information Superhighway might be a good place to apply the talents of a suitable computer geek or seek a Web company offering a turnkey package. To assist you in deciding whether or not doing it yourself is the smart choice, here is a brief, generalized description of what it takes to build a Web site.

First, it is important to note that there is a tremendous difference between building a Web site and creating a Web page. The former, building a Web site, is creating from scratch your own direct connection to the Internet, and requires purchasing expensive communications equipment, high-priced, specialized software, and a costly dedicated leased line from the phone company. To simply obtain a Web home page, the end result that the Netter sees on his or her browser screen, necessitates neither buying the expensive equipment nor a direct Internet connection. With either option, however, you can choose to design, register, promote, and maintain the site yourself or have somebody else do it for you. The difference to you is that with the outside source for the Web site, you own the server, the computer programmed to store information that can be requested from Internet users. Setting up your own server is very complex and, accordingly, an expensive consultant is usually required to operate it. With the Web page, you rent space on someone else's server, so what you need in this case is a cheap to expensive Internet service provider (ISP).

To create a Web site you must start with the Web server. Most of the servers on the Internet are UNIX machines, which is the computer language with which the majority of Net-connected computers operate. There are, however, Microsoft Windows NT and IBM OS/2 server machines as well, which don't require knowledge of UNIX. Purchasing your own server hardware and software could end up costing you tens of thousand of dollars, depending on how much speed and power you want, if in fact you had the knowledge to do it.

Things are, however, improving rapidly on this front. For example, a new Microsoft program aimed specifically at those who want to build and maintain a store on the Internet enables businesses to manage these stores cost effectively and provide a convenient, secure buying experience. Called Microsoft Merchant Server, it enables you to create highly visual, custom Web pages through easy-to-use templates, as well as systems that can manage orders, easily locate products from a large inventory, target customer segments, and integrate already existing databases that you may have built on your own over the years or acquired from another source. All of this is done in a way that is user friendly to the untechnically minded to a degree never possible before. The most exciting and useful feature of this server is, however, the ability to change information rapidly. You can provide up-to-the-minute pricing, spotlight an array of different featured-products, or add items on a daily or even hourly basis with little effort. Moreover, the price of this cutting-edge server is considerably lower than the assorted possibilities that preceded it.

One thing that is the same, whether you build your own site or not, is that continuous access to the Internet is the norm for Web sites. It is expected that a Web site can be accessed any day at any time. For this reason, it is almost mandatory that you stay on-line around the clock. If you want to maintain your own Web site, then a leased-line dedicated Internet access that will keep your computer available to the public full time is another costly essential. The different types of Internet access available and their prices are discussed in chapter 14. There you will discover that leased lines are about the most expensive and complicated Internet hookup you can get, but as always you can have your ISP or a geek do it for you.

Another necessary expense in having your own setup is a full-time technically savvy employee to run your operation. The going rate for such an individual is somewhere between $30,000 to $50,000 starting salary.

Renting Server Space

Compared to the start-up costs of going into most businesses, the cost of a Web page even with your own Web site is comparatively manageable. However, if you have a small budget, a small business, or both, then setting up your own Web site might not be for you. An inexpensive alternative is renting Web server space from an ISP. You can do this and still maintain control of your site in appearance and quality. One way to achieve this is by making sure the ISP you select has the same equipment and options that you would want if you were to build your own Web site. Beyond that, you should look for the types of support services offered. Your needs will depend on the size of your site, how fancy you want to get with your presentation and your personal preferences. If you are planning on a small, simple site, perhaps with a couple of graphics, one or two pages of text, one or two hypertext links, e-mail capabilities, and a simple customer response form, you will require less of your ISP than if you want state-of-the-art multimedia capabilities, heavy electronic transactions, multiple hypertext links, or a large number of text pages. In the latter case you will need to include options for sound and graphics, secure electronic transactions as discussed in chapter 12, and search capabilities within the site itself, so the customers can easily find a desired item within your product, as well as e-mail, customer transaction forms, and other standard fare.

Whatever the size of your site, you can never have enough speed. One of the first things you should look for in an ISP is what kind of Internet connection they offer. Read chapter 14, How to Get Yourself on the Net, and you will see that Internet connections are direct dedicated leased-line connections with varying speeds—usually designated T1, T2, or T3. As the numbers go up, so does the speed of the connection as well as the number of people who can visit your site simultaneously, for one very happy problem you may have is a site so popular that many people try to access it at the same time.

In setting up a Web site, there are so many options as to prices, services, and equipment, it is difficult to be very specific about offering suggestions. The most general rule of any use that can be given to you is, if you do not have a great deal of knowledge and money, don't try to build your own Web site. Beyond that, check carefully with the many ISPs and Web developers to see which service package best suits you. And, once again, try not to worry. In the brand new, freewheeling world of the Internet, there are no perfect or trouble-free solutions, so don't exasperate yourself over trying to find one.

Web Site Design

Even though you may have decided to rent space on the Web instead of buying it, you still have the options of designing, registering, promoting, and maintaining your own Web site or choosing from any number of ISPs that will do it for you at reasonable cost. If you are a die-hard do-it-yourselfer, this next section is definitely for you, presented with the obvious caveat that in saving money, you are sacrificing a substantial amount of time in scaling a high learning curve.

When designing your Web page, you'll probably start with writing your promotional copy. Once again, your talents and budget will dictate how you get this done, but you should know that some of the best copy in some of the most successful advertisements were written by those with little experience at writing ad copy. When you do write or have written the copy, a major consideration is the visual aspect of your design. The more you show as graphics, the less you need to write and vice versa. Above all, make sure that your copy explains your product or service clearly and that you anticipate and answer questions your customer may have. You have all the space in the world to do this, but you don't want to go on so long that your readers lose interest. Balance what you need to say against the attention span of your reader.

Next comes artistic design. Here again, depending on the limits of your own talents, you may want to enlist the aid of a graphic artist to get a really professional look. If not, go back to books or classes to learn this skill in detail. Generally, graphics may be produced with specialized computer programs. Corel and Adobe are two of the most popular brands. You may also copy graphics from photographs and other artwork using a piece of equipment called a "scanner." Be sure to check that you are not infringing on copyrights if you do this. A scanner simply views the graphic you wish to copy, digitizes it, and places it in a computer file. The graphics themselves must then be put in one of the two popular computer formats known as Graphic Interchange Format, more commonly called GIF, which is good for line art and graphics, or a newer format designed by the Joint Photographic Expert Group and popularly called JPEG, which is good for photos. Virtually all computer graphics programs give you the ability to create GIF and JPEG files. You will probably end up using both. There are also a number of places out there on the Net where you can download some prefab graphics and add-ins such as pictures and backgrounds for your site.

Once the design is completed and the ad copy is written, the whole thing must be put together and converted into yet another special computer format called Hypertext Markup Language, or HTML. There are a number of programs, or "authoring tools," now available free on the Internet that will essentially do the HTML programming for you. Some of these authoring tools convert popular word-processing programs, such as Microsoft's Word for Windows, WordPerfect, or ClarisWorks, into HTML. Others are stand-alone programs that allow you to start developing your Web page from scratch, giving you more control over document creation than the word-processor conversion programs. Although HTML is still the primary programming language for Web pages, a new programming language developed by Sun Microsystems called Java is becoming popular among Web page authors because of its multimedia capabilities. Although the Java programming language has implications extending well beyond the World Wide Web, Java mini-applications, called "applets," are currently being used to spice up Web pages. These applets have the ability to give movement to pictures on the Web. The most popular use of these to date is the employment of a moving band with writing streaming across the screen, much like a ticker tape. Java, however, is a complex programming language, and is not really designed for the nongeek. Not until someone comes up with an easy-to-use authoring tool for Java will this language become practical for use by the general Net population. When Java becomes as simple to use as HTML, Web sites will have even more elaborate graphics than they do now.

Because Web audiences are active rather than passive, advertisers attempt in a variety of ways to "pull" consumers into their sites with either interesting information, graphics, or both. That is why we find on the Web a varied and interesting array of Web site designs, ranging from the simple full-text site to the more elaborate multimedia extravaganzas. The question is how far to go in terms of exploiting complex technical capabilities to produce sound, movement, and heavy graphics that will get people to come to your Web site.

There are two competing philosophies about the use of gimmicking on Web advertising. Some say that to attract the attention of the Web surfer—especially in the surreal world of the Web—Web sites must be at least as entertaining as they are informative, if not more so. This, they reason, requires full use of any cleverly complicated device they can find. Others claim that the raison d'être of the Web is information, and any fancy graphics serve only to take away from that purpose by wasting the customer's time with extraneous data. The correct answer probably depends on the market you are aiming at and the achievement of a happy medium. Too much graphical content obscures the intended purpose of your site and that is to provide information to the consumer about your product or service. In addition, really good graphics are difficult and expensive to produce, and, because most connections to the Net are presently still over standard phone lines, downloading complex graphics can be a painfully slow process for which many Netters have neither the equipment nor the patience. On the other hand, simple text-only sites lack excitement and appeal, which might prevent people from visiting your site. In fact, a text-only site not arranged in a graphically pleasing manner can be difficult to read. The current thinking is that substance is more important than form, that most consumers want good information administered timely, and perhaps a little entertainment along the way. For a more serious-minded, older, more professional audience, this is likely to be true. For a younger target group, perhaps not. Think about what you are selling and to whom you are selling it, and exercise your best judgment. Cybersellers never adhere to conventional wisdom.

One important thing you should consider in designing your Web site is "anchoring." Anchoring means providing links and icons that make it easy to navigate through your site and return to your home page regardless of where you are within the site. This is vital because search engines are designed in such a way that a visitor arriving at your site in this manner might end up on a page in the middle of the site, rather than at the beginning, depending on what keyword was used in the initial search. Ease of moving from one place to the other within the site cuts down on visitor frustration and keeps the customer where you want him.

Another consideration is the difference in how your graphics will appear to different Netters, depending on their equipment. Remember that each person has his own configuration of monitor, modem, browser, etc. You should, therefore, test your final product with a number of browsers and monitors to make sure your presentation looks well on all of them.

Domain Registration

Now there remains just one last task to building your site, the registration of your domain name. You may remember that a domain name was first mentioned as part of your e-mail address. It is also part of the URL for each Web site. A domain name is essentially a description of a computer location on the Net. For businesses, the domain name has been compared to a personalized license plate because it can reflect the name of the company. All domain names are registered through the Network Information Center, known more popularly as InterNIC, which is run by Network Solutions, Inc., a division of AT&T and the governing authority of URL names that end in .com, .edu, .net, .org, and .gov. You can reach them by e-mail at *hostmaster@internic.net*. Facsimile numbers and U.S. postal addresses are by telephone at 703–742–0400; by fax at 703–742–4811 (InterNIC Registration Services); and by U.S. mail at InterNIC Registration Services, P.O. Box 1656, Herndon, VA 22070, USA. The cost to register a name directly with InterNIC is $50 per year, and you must pay the first two years in advance, making your up-front total $100. After the first two years you pay a standard fee of $50 annually. Many people incorrectly believe that there is a $100 up-front fee and a $50 annual fee. This is not the case. Once the first $100 is paid, you need not pay again for two years. When you go through InterNIC directly it can take up to eight weeks before you receive your domain name. In many cases, the ISP you use for your Web site will take care of registering your domain name for you, and InterNIC is known for expediting the waiting period for "insiders" such as ISPs. If, however, you want to go directly to InterNIC, you can find them at the address and phone numbers given above, or on the Web at *http://rs.internic.net*. Here you will discover clear, step-by-step registration information and instructions that walk you through an on-line registration form.

One thing you must be sure to do is check that the name you want to use is not already taken by someone else. You can accomplish this by using what is called a "whois" directory. There are plenty of such directories around the Web, and InterNIC has one on-site. You must also be wary of using trademarked or copyrighted names. In the early days of Net commercialization it was a practice by some forward-thinking but less than ethical individuals to register for themselves such domain names as *Coke.com*, hoping the companies to whom they respectively belonged would find paying off the name piraters cheaper than mounting a law suit. Companies are now starting to take legal action against this practice. Moreover, it is also recommended that you get your own name registered with the U.S. Patent and Trademark Office.

Overall, when you register your domain name, there is little doubt that going through an ISP is much easier, although they sometimes charge more than the InterNIC base fees. The advantages of going through an ISP are that they have special deals with InterNIC to expedite the processing time for domain names and that InterNIC demands you have two name servers—computers that are operational twenty-four hours a day, seven days a week, and "host" the address—to keep you from being a domain name in search of a domain. Some ISPs try to charge the user a monthly maintenance fee to maintain the domain name. Such charges are unnecessary and it is recommended that if an ISP asks for such a fee, go somewhere else. Generally, reasonable rates for an ISP are around $25 to $30, not including the InterNIC registration fees mentioned above. For the extra money, you might be able to get your site registered in a matter of days, but probably no more than three weeks. It all depends on how backlogged InterNIC is, and with the continuing huge influx of people to the Net they are, make no mistake, very backlogged.

Selecting Your Line to the Net

The options for lines and actually building the system for your site are covered in chapter 13. There are many possibilities as to cost and the degree of technical expertise you wish to acquire. How you want to approach this problem is up to you. Just know that you have many options that are inexpensive and require you to know very little.

The Web offers great promise for moneymaking, both now and in the future. The concept of video on demand, where you can watch a television program or movie at will, is quickly becoming a reality on the Web. Although the technology is there, you are still limited by the fact that most of these computer signals must travel across relatively slow phone lines. That will soon change. A short time ago many browsers were still not prepared to fully handle the sophisticated multimedia capabilities the Web has to offer. That has already changed. High-speed fiber-optic networks that bring access to your computer through cable rather than phone lines are beginning to become more established, and are destined to become commonplace. When Internet access is delivered to your house along with your cable TV signal, the prominence of and manner in which the Web impacts your life will alter drastically. Meanwhile, at this very moment, there is still the opportunity to get a foothold as a pioneer in what will almost certainly be the most important marketplace to ever exist. This window of opportunity is closing fast. Get to work now, so you can take full advantage of the most promising moneymaking opportunities to come along in decades.

8
Be a Superstar
Sell Yourself on the Net

Congratulations. You've passed the basic course in Internet marketing—and it wasn't so bad, was it? Now, before you go on to the finer points and some of the dreaded technical material, let's take a break for a little recreation that is also educational. For now, erase from your mind the steps you took to get this far. Forget the challenges and conflicts of Internet product and service marketing. Put out of your mind the upcoming trip to the computer store where you imagine yourself bungling your way through the purchase of the hardware. Be proud that when the salesperson there asks you exactly what you want, you will be able to come up with a more cogent answer than "something cube-shaped and gray, please." Your pocketbook may soon be one-and-a-half K lighter, but forget that now, too. You have emerged victorious from the nuts-and-bolts portion of the plan. Pretend you've got the goods, and it's on the desk in front of you as well as firmly implanted in your brain.

Likewise, take a deep breath and let the learning curve of the last few chapters flatten in your mind. Sublimate any supplementary late-night sessions you may have had with a computer manual that promises to make the technical part of the Internet easy for you, but lies like a rug.

By way of printed matter, private tutor, an offering at the local community college, or maybe paid classes at the same store that will eventually nick you for the equipment, you have emerged victorious and Internet-ready. This knowledge will prove of inestimable value in dealing with the post-pubescent dweeb at the local Internet service provider (ISP) where you have your account. If you are in the very large group who gets to the Internet via one of the major on-line services like America Online (AOL) or CompuServe, then you have simply substituted local aggravation for the corporate kind. Same difference.

Soon you will begin on the task of choosing a product to sell on the Net, and learning the last facets of what you will need to accomplish this, but for now we're going to try something a little less serious, as a reward for all the work you've done so far and as an exercise to get the creative juices flowing for your commercial project. For the moment, the only product you're going to worry about selling is you. For now, you're going to take an imaginary trip into cyberspace and learn how to become an Internet Superstar.

Let's imagine you're entering the Net for the first time. You take a look around and start to get your bearings. Astutely, you observe that there's a lot happening in every direction, just as you were told earlier there would be. But now you've gone past simply reading some definitions in a book. This is the real thing, and the awesome power of the Internet hits you with full force. The element that will probably boggle your mind most is the sheer volume. There is more here to do, see, or find out than you could cover in years. Just so you won't feel too overwhelmed, be aware that even if, for some unaccountable reason, you decided to give up everything else in life and devote yourself exclusively to conquering cyberspace, a significant portion of the other twenty-nine million, nine hundred ninety-nine thousand, nine hundred ninety-nine people on the Net with you are busily and continuously adding more stuff, so you can't possibly get to it all. The logical approach, then, is to do only what you can handle and what is most important to you. Then stop worrying about the rest. Information overload is a common problem of the computer-user. Everyone has to deal with it. Meanwhile, as is traditional in cyberspace, everyone also starts out equal, with twenty-four hours in the day. Keeping that comforting thought in mind, you do need to start somewhere. No doubt you recall those Microsoft commercials on television that keep asking "Where do you want to go today?" You may never have cared enough before to think of an answer, but now your time has come. What's your opening move going to be?

As promised, you deserve some fun for getting this far, and it is becoming progressively more an acknowledged fact that navigating the Net is not really as easy as it was cracked up to be in the first blissful days of hype already described. Instead, let's concentrate on what some believe constitutes the second most important element in the makeup of cyberspace, exceeded only by the electricity needed to keep the whole operation up and running. No, it's not hardware, or software in general, or even Bill Gates in particular. It's not the Web, the Usenet, or IRC. It's not mineral or vegetable. It's animal. It's ham.

If you want to know at least one of the major reasons why people are flocking onto the Internet in numbers that bear ceaseless quotation in the global media, ham is a safe choice. Some may be more delicate and call it the interactive aspect of the Net. What is really going on here, though, is that deep in the hearts of nearly every breathing human is the desire to ham it up for an audience. What audience? That's where cyberspace comes in. It's already been pointed out that the linchpin of Cyberselling is a big audience at a small cost, so if you've got the routine, the Internet has the audience, ready and waiting on-line. Until now, the best hope most of us had for public recognition was attending a Letterman taping, waving frantically if the camera happened to pan to some part of the studio other than the stage, and hoping Dave threw a Big Ass Canned Ham (what else?) at you. The alternatives were the amiable and long lasting Leno, or, taking it down a notch, a daytime talk show, a feature of our social fabric presently considered as politically correct as smoking.

Now there's a better way. Although a fanatical cyberspace devotee would have your life for saying so, the fact is that much the Net can do is duplicated by radio, television, the movies, or nonnetworked database searching. An area where that is not true is the availability of a huge audience to anyone who wants it. Think about it for a second. Once long ago, if you wished to be a famous comedian, you would need to work your way up the networks like Jay and Dave. Now you can get your face and your jokes in front of millions of people just by putting them on a Web page. If you wished to be a famous writer and have your ideas published in *The New York Times*, you would have to get your work accepted by one of their editors—a generally surly and elitist lot as many an aspiring writer will tell you. Alternatively, you would be left with the option of paid advertising at the rate of about $500 per column inch. If you don't know what a column inch is, it's an area of space the width of one newspaper column (about two inches in most newspapers) and the length of one inch. Not exactly as big as a billboard, is it? In any case, should you succeed in scaling the necessary financial or editorial hurdles, you would reach an audience of one million people, and your message would disappear in the trash a day later. The money, editorial, and time limits for appearances on electronic media are even more daunting, and in the case of TV, what you do and say disappears not in a day but in seconds. In cyberspace, you can have an audience for the twenty dollars a month an Internet connection costs, and the size of that audience is thirty million. As for the amount of space you get, it's virtually unlimited. It's also mostly uncensored, as we see in chapter 10 in our discussion on Internet sex. Nor is there an editor to stop or even revise what you say. Since cost is hardly a factor, you can repeat what you do over and over, and in the case of a Web site, it simply stays there indefinitely.

With the audience in place, you will want to home in on exactly where and how you can perform. In fact the Internet and on-line services offer a stunning variety of ways for you to be a superstar that even the shy types will find hard to resist. Are you a natural-born showman? Who isn't? Johnny Carson, when he preceded the aforementioned Jay and Dave as the singular monarch of late-night TV, once observed that everyone has two professions: his own and show business. On-line devotees are proving more than ever that Johnny was right. Cyberspace builds up the body part common to us all, the one made of ham. Whether you are male or female, young or old, whatever your size, color, or brand name, there's got to be some inside you. Here, then, is our little instruction book on how to get your fifteen minutes of fame or better, the Internet way.

THE WEB

You already know a great deal about publicizing on the Web. The commercial aspects of the Internet have become so prominent that often forgotten is a tradition of altruism that comes from the roots of the Net, before commercialism was permitted there. The guiding principle is that anyone participating in the Net is taking advantage of free resources, and is therefore bound by honor to give something back. That something is usually expected to take the form of useful information, also offered free. A survey of the Web will show, however, that most don't give with their hearts. Examine Web sites closely, and you will find endless ulterior motives. In most cases, those motives are profit-related, but let's see what would happen if our main motives were fame and glory.

"Get your own home page on the World Wide Web," is becoming something of a national slogan these days. You know you have varied choices in ways of putting up any message, and supporting sound, graphics, multimedia capabilities that you might select, in a place where every one of the thirty million Internet-users can see them. Thousands of individuals have done it already—mostly with money in mind. But not everyone. Just scratch the surface of the various homemade efforts and you will immediately and certainly locate ham.

All right, this is your moment. You can deliver the message that is most attention-getting, closest to your heart, or whatever other nonmonetary agenda you may have, and you won't have the limitations of a bumper sticker to do it. This however does present another problem. With your adoring public ready and waiting, you need something to say. Of course, for real hams, zealots, and other in-your-face types, this is not a problem but a dream come true. That's why you find a lot of these personalities expressing themselves on the Internet. For the slightly more reticent, it requires concentration, but probably not much. You start with the very easiest part of the performance, the words. Just type in what it is you want to say about anything or anyone. Let your wildest and most heartfelt ideas come out. Remember, no limits on the content or how much you say. Believe it or not, even with the endless discussions of multimedia in the press, many people have become Net idols on the basis of words alone. Let's see, is there a certain politician who makes you absolutely sick? Of course there is. Why not say so loud and clear. Moving into graphics, put up a picture of your favorite, crooked candidate along with your words of criticism under it to heighten the effect. Don't neglect to attach your name to all of this, either. Tell people where you come from, something about your background. Don't let that jerk who's raising your taxes beyond the point of tolerance get all the visual action either. Put up a picture of yourself as well. The idea is to let people know who gets credit for doing this civic-minded service. It's conceivable that some people want to change the world for the betterment of mankind. You, however, are not an anonymous benefactor here. You want ATTENTION.

Maybe politics isn't your main concern. It really doesn't matter. What do you want to talk about? It's a new sensation to have strong feelings on a subject and the possibility of a huge audience actually listening to what you have to say. Maybe it's not your opinions you want to share, but your interests. Cars? Cats? Calisthenics? They're all popular topics on the Net.

Indeed, there are multiple Web sites about each of these subjects. Some of the interests tend to get a little obsessive. For example, nearly every movie or TV show has at least one superfan maintaining a Web site on his or her favorite viewing habit. It's absolutely amazing to see Web sites on a particular movie containing detailed information about every costume, every character, every plot twist, everyone involved with the production, from the star to the caterer. Every possible item of data is turned inside out and analyzed to death on a Web site, and it happens all the time.

If you think that by keeping a Web site in homage to a particular movie, TV show, or personality you are once again slipping into the realm of the anonymous here, assurances that you are not should be repeated. The keepers of every one of these cinematic or pop culture shrines never fail to let the world know who is the creator of his or her little digital monument. In fact, any individual responsible for maintaining a Web site even has a special title, "Webmaster," a term sufficiently grandiose to bring a smile to the lips of any would-be ham. The position of Webmaster is not just for fun either. It is a new and very real job title created because of the popularity and growing commercial importance of the World Wide Web. Overseeing a commercial Web site is certainly a full-time job, and, at present draws annual salaries ranging from $50,000 to $75,000. The professional Webmaster gets the money and may or may not be high profile. The Webmaster with amateur standing gets no money, devotes a limited amount of time to the effort, but is amply rewarded for his or her trouble with ego gratification. That is why you'll rarely need to struggle to find information on these Webmasters-for-glory. They'll tell you who they are on their home pages with absolutely no coaxing whatever.

Finally, to stimulate your thinking, mention must be made of the true, unadulterated self-promoters, ham in its purest form. What are their Web sites about? None other than Numero Uno. These offerings read something like "Hi, I'm Martha. I have blonde hair and green eyes. I was born in New Jersey and I just love rock 'n' roll." Not too scintillating, is it? Well, there are a lot of Web sites that don't sound very different from that. Then, of course, you'd have that picture again. In a perverse sort of way, though, these sites are actually very interesting. You get to learn about the existence of a person you never knew before and in all likelihood, never would have met, plus you get some insight into human nature as you ponder whatever neuroses possessed someone to put all that personal information out in public in the first place.

When you are urged in a magazine or on TV, as you often are, to get your own home page on the Web, this is usually followed by assurance that the process will be both easy and cheap. You have already seen that at your disposal is a wide array of choices when it comes to selecting the features of the Web site you will want. In order to proceed with your plan to become a cyberspace celebrity, it's just a question of how flashy you would like to be. To do it yourself, you have to begin by learning a programming language called HyperText Markup Language or HTML. Already, this doesn't sound too great, right? People have different viewpoints on whether they consider HTML challenging or not. This is another occasion where it is recommended you look for a book on the subject and make your own decision. However, if you happen never to have seen HTML, or any other type of programming code for that matter, we'll take a moment to tell you that that it looks to the average eye like a bunch of nonsense words mixed with various symbols that you'll find on a standard typewriter or computer keyboard. By using these words and symbols in combination, you tell the computer what letters and picture the computer will place on your Web site and where they should go. The reason HTML is a great breakthrough is that it supports the networking concept necessary for the Internet. HTML was invented because it lets computers of all different kinds exchange graphical information, a trick not possible before. In other words, HTML is one reason we can now have a big network made up of heterogeneous computers, like the Internet. Now that you know what a wonderful purpose HTML serves, let's get real for a moment. In a society where, ostensibly, it's too much for the ordinary person to program his or her own VCR, you have probably guessed that you won't be able to wrap this one up in ten minutes flat. In order to learn the HTML language, you again have to resort to a book, class, or on-line tutorial. Hard? Maybe. Time-consuming? Definitely. In other words, a commitment serious enough to be worthy of weighing carefully. Besides, what self-respecting superstar is going to be bothered with this kind of stuff?

But suppose you are at this point in time only a star-in-the-making, and therefore not yet filthy rich as you were meant to be? Consider, in taking the do-it-yourself route, what you gain versus what you have to give up. All things in life are tradeoffs after all. Why should this be any exception? If you expect to be a bona fide Net personality, it is absolutely de rigeur that you show off on the Web, so the fact remains that, even though it's a dirty job, to get the desired results, somebody has to do it. Moreover, one of the best things you have going for you in your attempt the climb to the top of the Net celebrity heap is your creativity. Beautiful colors, imaginative pictures, exotic type fonts, even sound or movement can be obtained to embellish your already thought-provoking message. And the catch? The more elaborate you want your presentation to be, the more complicated you must get with your HTML programming. Indeed, a popular misconception is that HTML will do everything for you on the Web. In fact, this simple program is no more than an organization tool that selects and places type fonts or an occasional color, and arranges them on the Web. If you want elaborate graphics, you must create them with a more complex graphics program. If you want movement, that takes another program called Java. What if you wish to add sound? Try not to think about it too much right now. It will only upset you.

And so we have arrived at an explanation for why a lot of what you will see on the Web in the way of do-it-yourself noncommercial sites isn't all that imaginative from a graphical standpoint. You really have to work to master more than rudimentary technical skills to accomplish some of the tricky effects, and do you want to do that? The fact is that most people don't. Stick with the easy programs or a low-cost geek, and becoming a superstar is fun once again.

Continuing with ideas for your self-promoting pleasure, mention should certainly be made of possible origins for the pictures you are going to show the world. Starting with the most complex, you can master a computer-graphics program such as Corel Draw or Harvard Graphics. These allow you to compose original art generated from the computer. The possibilities with these programs are infinite. Once again, to accomplish the task you need time and, oh yes, an asset we haven't even bothered to mention before, talent. Do you qualify? If not, move on to option two, scanning. Scanning means you take already formulated pictures from other sources and use a machine, called, oddly enough, a scanner. Its purpose in life is to translate pictures into digital impulses so they can be stored and manipulated at will in the computer and then displayed on the screen. Does this sound like plagiarism? You bet it does, so make sure you're using something you are legally allowed to borrow. See chapter 16 for more on this. Assuming you remain on the right side of the law, this is your way to use great graphics with limited talent. A scanner, of course, also requires that you buy and learn to use it. At present, it is a separate piece of equipment, although indications are that it will be included as a built-in part of a computer in the near future.

One of the most common, most effective, and definitely the best-loved ways of getting attention on the Web is to be an outstanding linker. Hypertext links, as defined earlier, are the heart and soul of the Web system. These links appear on Web sites and are easily identifiable as either picture icons or highlighted words. Click your mouse on one of these links and you are immediately transferred to a different Web site or another part of the Web site you are on already, where you will theoretically receive more information of interest about the same or a related topic. This electronic hopping method, commonly known as surfing, is the way you are supposed to pry loose the bounteous treasure of facts and figures the Web has to offer. Everyone has described in glowing terms this procedure—how fast it is, how much you can find, what fun you can have.

There is a key element to this, however, that keeps getting left out. It would seem that very little consideration has been given to how these links got there. Well, they got there because some enterprising soul put them there using HTML. The fact that the technicalities are remembered, but the brain power that collected the links is often forgotten in the blinding glow of mechanistic flashiness, is perhaps indicative of the skewed sense of values that seems to pervade cyberspace. It is still people who must come up with the ideas, a concept worth remembering when the digital goop gets a little too thick. The next enterprising soul to make a great links collection could just as well be you. In point of fact, the Web relies on the input of people like yourself to put together sets of links that others can use, as well as databases and other information available so readily on the Net. The links in particular are a big part of the cooperative feature of the Internet and, as you will recall, one of the important ways the Web gets indexed. From the ham perspective, it has become almost a ritual for each personal Web site to contain a list of links to other Web sites that are appealing to the site owner. By sharing these interests, the individual shares a part of himself with the world. He also escapes the creation of much that is original, while still managing to have a presentation reflecting his own unique, if copycat, preoccupations. Don't underestimate these people too much, however. It takes a long time to surf the Net and collect all the useful information on a single topic, arrange it in a pleasing manner and add a little something of your own personality to the mix. They also serve who only collect links from other places, and if the links collection is outstanding enough, it's another way to get famous on the Internet.

Now we reach the finer points of Web self-promotion and the truth comes out. Leading the life of a ham can be taxing. Much has been said here about the glory of linking on a Web site, but little about how those links got there. Well, one direction has been covered: from you to them. If you want to be found by others, however, you have to make sure the flow goes in the other direction as well. You can have someone put up a link to your site in one of two ways. The first is by accident. They trip over you, electronically speaking, when they go Web-surfing one dark night. They like what they see, as a public service they add a link from their site to yours, and your audience grows. The other possibility is very low tech in principle. You contact the site you want to carry your link and ask. Unless the site with which you request to be linked has made a business of charging for linkage, this technique will probably meet with great success, the only limitations being your time and nerve.

Now let's look again from a ham perspective at the most popular of the Web's indexing tools, the search engine. Most of what you need to know about these remarkable devices has been covered in chapter 7. Here you are only reminded that there is no law or convention limiting what is listed on a search engine, unless it happens to be illegal. You don't need to have a commercial site. You don't need a serious purpose or a lofty goal. All you need to do is take the time to see that your site is mentioned on every search engine in creation and you are well on your way to becoming a VIP.

In your quest to rise above the crowd, parts of the Net other than the Web have much to offer that will let you increase your Web impact. As pointed out earlier, making the best Web site your creativity and technical expertise permits is only the first step on the road to cyberspace celebrity. The true ham is industrious and leaves nothing to chance. By talking about yourself and your Web site on IRC chat, Usenet, e-mail, and anywhere else your input is welcome, or at least allowed, you can definitely spread the word around. If you consider all of the foregoing chapters together, you must come to the realization that your words of wisdom will indeed be freely received in an astounding number of places, and you can even become famous through those ready-made opportunities alone with no Web site at all, if you put your mind to it. Right now, though, we're focusing on the possibilities of the Web, and saying, simply, that if you've got a Web site, and you want more people to know it's there, you can talk about the site on other parts of the Net and considerably increase your ratings share.

There is encompassed within the Web, an internal, informal, and extremely active rating system of Web sites. Every Web browser, search engine, commercial site, on-line magazine, not to mention personal Web site, offers gratuitous opinions of other Web sites they consider to be either cool or, alternatively, hot. In this case the wide variation in temperature serves only to indicate the same thing at either end of the spectrum: somebody has looked at a particular site and found it extraordinarily worthy. It's beyond anyone's comprehension how sites are selected for the cool and hot lists. There are no known criteria, no truly recognized experts. It's sort of like what former Supreme Court Justice Potter Stewart said about pornography: you may not be able to define it but you know it when you see it. In the grand tradition of the freewheeling Internet, everybody sees it differently. So if one person doesn't think your efforts are outstanding, you have many other self-styled authorities to which you can appeal. If you exhaust all of them, and things really get desperate, you can even start your own hot or cool list, and put yourself on it, so there is no way you can fail. These hot and cool lists are everywhere on the Web. Show what you're really made of. Get yourself on one of them.

There is a special bonus that comes to an especially praiseworthy class of real overachievers on the Web, and all potential hams will want to know about it. For convenience, let's call it the ripple effect. Fame on the Web has other ways of manifesting itself that most people don't think much about, but certainly would if the glory that could be theirs simply because they had a home page ever occurred to them. The fact is that cyberspace is so hot now, the press is forever increasing its coverage of the Internet and is combing it regularly for things to report. If you manage to stand out enough on the Web, you'll also probably get picked up in the newspapers, magazines, television shows, and maybe even the movies. A personal favorite example of this is the Web site known as *Jerque du Jour.* This Web site was devised and executed by a California man whose main beef in life was the bad driving he witnessed on his way back and forth from work each day. In order to fight back, he put a camera in his car and began taking pictures on a daily basis of driving offenses he saw. Then, he would find out the name of the driver via the license plate, and castigate the offender publicly on his Web site, while displaying a picture of the vehicular misdeed. Now, it would probably be kinder to all concerned to forego analyzing what kind of mind you need to spend your time and effort doing something just slightly over the top like this. That would be way too scary. Neither would it be comfortable to dwell too long on how many times each of us might have qualified as the feature attraction for this particular Web site. It should be pointed out, however, that in addition to making spectacles of unsuspecting private citizens, this guy's ingenuity got him exposure in every major media source from CNN to *The Wall Street Journal*.

It's time for the grand Web ham finale. If you want to make your mark as a superstar on the Web, there is no better way to find inspiration than to look at those intrepid seekers after notoriety who have preceded you. As noted earlier, there are many Web sites with commercial intent, and some of them are pretty creative, but the ones we're looking at here have no discernible financial motive. They may masquerade occasionally in the guise of altruism, but we submit that when all is said and done what is being witnessed here is one of the purest and largest displays of ego yet to be beheld by mankind. Isn't that right, Jeffrey Zeldman? Jeff Zeldman is the Webmaster of a beautiful, shocking pink Web site entitled eponymously *Jeffrey Zeldman Presents*. What he in fact presents is a bunch of unrelated stuff ranging from some strange-looking art to essays on Lawrence Welk. He also presents an opportunity to listen to his musical compositions, which you can't hear anywhere else, but he's hoping to change all that. We don't want to sell Jeff short, however. He's got some pretty fancy graphics and he uses sound and the latest movement technology called Quicktime Virtual Reality. Less creative, but very typical is the offering entitled *Jim Lippard's Home Page*. It is almost all text and is heavy on the use of the word "my" as in "my publications," "my cinematic interests," and "my brushes with celebrity greatness." Mr. Lippard mainly holds forth on Net issues like government interference in curbing pornography (he really doesn't like it), and government efforts to limit the availability of encryption devices on the Net (he doesn't like that either.) This gentleman's politically-correct-for-the-Net viewpoint has been echoed countless times on other Web sites and on parts of the Net other than the Web, but hey, repetition never stopped a Web ham.

Now let's look at three Web sites that aren't named after their Webmasters, but rather reflect their deeply felt commitment to certain topics. The interests of C. Dodd Harris IV, is incorporated in a Web site entitled *The Tackiest Place in America Contest*, a mélange of mainly text and a few scanned-in black-and-white pictures. It's also supposed to show some beautiful places as well, but through the eyes of Mr. Harris, it is honestly hard to tell one from the other. The stand-out photo in this one is a place called the Wall Drug Store, located in Wall, South Dakota, which features a huge display of cement cowboys riding bucking broncos on its roof. Next on our short list is an item called *The Kook Report*, brought to you by Tim Dedopulos. This site presents a questionnaire designed to determine "how weird are you?" Being thought of as weird is considered very cool in many factions of the Net, so let's not trivialize this all-text compendium of silly questions, metaphysical references, and nonsense words. Here's one Web site we can all relate to: the *Elvis Spotter's Page.* Actually, there are lots of pages on the Web devoted to Elvis and Elvis sightings. This one, from Sean "Corky" McCormick carries reports from contributing spotters of Elvis frequenting his usual favorite places, shopping malls, and cheap restaurants.

As you can see, it doesn't require a terribly high concept to gain recognition on the Web. In fact, here is something for you to ponder as you try to understand the dynamics on the Web. The sites just listed aren't as innocuous as they look. Every single one of them has been picked by somebody for a hot or cool list. If knowing this doesn't give you real hope for your future as a Web standout, it's hard to imagine what would.

We've heard from the little guys on the Web, and know that the Internet is supposed to level the playing field between the information haves and have-nots. In keeping with this principle, full credit has been given here to the kooks, Elvis-spotters, and assorted drugstores. It would be less than realistic, however, if you weren't told about the use of the Web by the fame-seeking Big Guys. The fact is, the already rich and famous are ubiquitous on the Net as well.

To exemplify the array of performers with their own home pages, presented herewith is the obvious: Jay and Dave. Of course they each have a place of their own on the Web. On the Leno page, you'll find one of the star's jokes, continuously updated; a video clip of his nightly "headlines bit," a sort of bloopers and outtakes from newspapers; and a picture of the post-trial but perennially popular Dancing Itos.

As for Dave, he may have fallen slightly behind in the ratings, but his home page was first on the Web, well ahead of Jay, and he is still ahead in that venue by a country mile. First, there is the inescapable nightly top-ten list, which, thanks to the wonders of the Web, you no longer have to lose sleep to enjoy. Then, demonstrating a guiding principal of Webbery—that you can never have too much of anything—Dave gives us the top ten top-ten lists of his first year on CBS. This is followed by information on the orchestra, bios of Paul Schaffer and the other musicians, the real scoop on Calvert De Forrest, a.k.a. Larry Bud Melman, even facts on the stage manager, Biff Henderson. All of this proves Dave understands about level playing fields, really knows how to use the Web, and that he is an absolute expert on hams. You didn't think he passed those big, canned ones out to his audience for nothing, did you?

TALKING YOUR WAY TO STARDOM USING USENET, CHAT, AND E-MAIL

Usenet, Chat, and e-mail, the text-only means of Internet communication, have all been described in earlier chapters, and we know that these are utilized as vehicles for many useful exchanges of valuable data. Then again we also know that in reality, what takes place most of the time in cyberspace text mediums amounts to someone grabbing a PC keyboard and blathering aimlessly away. Finally, there are those with superstar potential, that have made communicating through these mechanisms lead to much more. Once again, the open-microphone factor linked to a huge audience has the power to bring about public recognition of major proportions. E-mail is, to a large extent, a one-on-one medium, so you lose the huge audience factor, unless you do a mass e-mailing, which belongs in the business section of this book, not here. On Chat as well, your audience is somewhat limited because most chat groups have no more than twenty or so participants. If the groups were much larger, the result would be conversational chaos, which may seem positively symbolic to the Internet cult believers, but is only a nuisance when it comes to the downright practicalities of communication.

On Usenet lies the ripest field for the seeds of fame to fall. Here, where an estimated twenty million Netters post electronic messages to each other for all the world to see, some level of fame is a highly realistic goal. The prominence of the Web notwithstanding, on Usenet, home of the famous flame, can be seen some of the most outstanding personalities created purely by participation in these forums. All you have to do is grab your keyboard and away you go. There will be millions of hapless individuals stuck listening to you.

You can easily stand out from the crowd with your wit, your brilliance, or your repetitive use of four-letter words. All these techniques for becoming a star have been tried and used successfully. Alternatively, you can simply outlast everyone else, which is how the majority of well-known Usenet personalities manage to do it. In fact, some of the more persistent Usenet participants become well-known by the simple means of scouting Usenet as well as the Web for participation opportunities on particular subjects. If a certain name appears over and over again, someone, somewhere, begins to get the idea that this person must actually be knowledgeable about the topic on which the fame-seeker is speaking. Reporters obviously operate under this theory, because they have actually quoted such individuals whose only real qualification is the stamina to post to Usenet morning, noon, and night. Shazam. A star is born.

Repeatedly it has been pointed out that the Internet houses a huge and growing cadre of information. There are already many people who have tried and succeeded in gaining their fifteen minutes of fame. And although you've probably guessed it already, every single technique suggested here for making you a superstar is equally effective in selling a product or service over the Internet. Soon we're going back to business. For one more moment, though, let's return to the dream of being a superstar. Now, you may ask, "if there's so much out there already, what does the cyberworld need with my two cents." If this is your reaction, obviously your ham factor is of the more latent kind, because a true ham would never even think of posing such a question. Nevertheless, there happens to be a good and semiserious answer to your question. The Net is really just in its beginning phase. What you have to say is important if only because the main idea behind all of this is letting everyone get into the act. If everyone didn't have the opportunity to say something, or simply elected to stay silent and be part of the audience, the whole value of cyberspace would be diminished. This is a network. No one can do it alone. So go ahead and ham it up. It doesn't matter if you're a rocket scientist, the class clown, or one of the millions of unsung heroes who deserves a moment in the spotlight just for getting by each day. Without you the cyberspace cloud evaporates into nothingness. How much more important can a ham be?

9
Products that Sell on the Net

THE INFORMATION SUPERHIGHWAY IS SO EXPANSIVE THAT choosing from the vast number of possible services or products that might be marketed there could seem overwhelming. One of the main things that captures the imagination of those who discover the Internet is the endless array of topics on which information is available. It's almost as if the answers to all the mysteries of the world have revealed themselves and are yours for the asking. In selecting the service or product you will offer to others, you are, in addition to making your fortune, getting in on the fun of contributing to the wonderful mix of resources that can presently be found on the Internet. Perhaps you've already decided on a great product with which to launch your Cyberselling venture. Good. You're one step ahead of the game. If not, this chapter's for you.

Enterprises now promoting and selling advertising on the Internet range from giant corporations such as General Motors and Walt Disney to small kitchen-table businesses like Alana's Wreaths, which features wreaths hand-crafted from silk, dried flowers, fruits, mosses, and berries. Even from the very brief example you can see what you've been hearing all along about how the Internet is the great democratizer. The Internet is the only commercial venue that allows small businesses to compete with Fortune 500 companies, giving small companies the ability to grab market shares from larger companies. This is due in part to the low cost of advertising. Couple that with the advantages smaller companies have always had—speed of company start-ups, the ability of the small entrepreneur to implement new ideas faster, and finally, the smaller business's inherent characteristic of interacting more efficiently with their clientele than the bureaucracy-driven megacorporations—and you have a powerful success formula for the smaller businesses. Moreover, every business must have an Internet address, regardless of its size, and the Internet consumer doesn't know the difference between a GM and an Alana's Wreaths until he or she visits the site. With these advantages in mind, it is easy to see how there is plenty of market space for anyone willing to carve his or her niche with a desirable product or service.

Although there are seemingly infinite numbers of products and services to be sold on the Net, by far the easiest product to develop is also one of the most appropriate for Internet marketing. What, after all, would be better to sell on the Information Superhighway than information? You may not think you have any information that people will pay for, but if you consider it carefully, you may very well be wrong. There are probably many things you know how to do better than anyone else. Perhaps you coach a high school football or little league team. Couldn't you put together a manual advising others how to do the same thing? Perhaps you know a lot of lawyer jokes. Why not write them down and market them on the Internet? Lawyer jokes are always great sellers. After the Green Card Incident, our office received dozens of them. Here is a personal favorite, compliments of a Netter who shall remain anonymous:

Q: What is the difference between a lawyer and a catfish?
A: One is a bottom-feeding scum sucker. The other is a fish.

Maybe you are a popular, well-liked person. Why do you suppose that is the case? Could you explain to others the personal techniques that draw others to you? Think of what it is that you can do best. Write down your ideas. Put them together in a printed manual or video instruction tape and try them out as a product on the Internet. If your first idea doesn't work, experiment with something else until you pick a winner.

Marketing on the Internet is so inexpensive, there will be no great loss if your first attempts don't pan out.

There are electronic magazines and books for every subject imaginable: from the mainstream to the highly unorthodox, and everything in between. One magazine on the Internet, for example, features unedited, first-person accounts of various social, cultural, and historical experiences, and boasts that it contains these unedited accounts featuring compelling social issues. It can't get any easier than this. There's not even any editing involved. The publisher simply gathers information—in the form of "unedited, first-person accounts"—puts it into a nice little virtual magazine package, and markets it over the Net. Maybe you can't get your book accepted by one of the major publishers, but that doesn't mean people won't be willing to pay for your literary ingenuity. You need only your own creativity and a computer.

SOLVING PROBLEMS FOR OTHERS

If you don't think you have any special knowledge right now that people would be interested in paying for, maybe you could get some. Try thinking about information you might offer from a problem-solving perspective. Consider all the problems you, your family, friends, and society in general face each day and what might be done to improve the situation. For example, one difficulty experienced by almost everyone is that of too little money. Many people have made a fortune coming up with solutions to this one. The plan you develop need not be complicated. Some entrepreneurs have earned fortunes by selling information on how to deal with credit bureaus. Others have done well offering advice simply on how to live within a budget. Take, for example, $tarving $hirley, who, in a fun and informative advice column printed on a Web site offers money-saving suggestions on everything from shopping at thrift stores to coupon tips to a section on Cheap Eats, featuring recipes for low-cost meals. Other, more professional advice columns currently offered on the Net cover such subjects as job-hunting, résumé-writing, retirement-planning, health and fitness, and even how to improve your skills at taking a test. Indeed, lists of available jobs by company or in a certain area, or other job-finding services are among the most currently popular on the Net. Another great service industry for the Net is real estate. What better way to show your property listing to prospective clients than over the Net? Consulting services of every kind are also ideal for the Internet.

If you are involved in providing that type of service now, consider how you can package the same service in cyberspace. Yet another good source of salable information is the U.S. government, and much of this information comes prepackaged. For example, have you ever looked at a U.S. Government Printing Office (USGPO) catalog? There are publications on every topic imaginable, and all of them are considered public domain. This means they are not copyright protected, and anyone, you included, may republish them in any fashion at all without fear of infringement. Although public-domain information can be used free, the U.S. government does charge to cover the costs of providing it. One company, Weather Services Corporation (WSC), of Lexington, Massachusetts, shrewdly took advantage of public-domain information and created a weather-forecast service, providing weather information to radio stations from Florida to Hawaii, to television's "USA Today," to dozens of local newspapers, as well as to agribusinesses and aviation firms. WSC pays the National Weather Service as much as a hefty $100,000 in fees each year but they offer enough services to easily recoup these expenses. If you can't afford the higher priced items like this one, simply choose the free or low-cost items. The market on the Net is still there.

Not all public-domain information has to come from Uncle Sam. There are plenty of other ways to find prepackaged information and repackage it with your own finishing touch for sale on the Net. In fact, one of the best sources for this prepackaged information is, yet again, the Internet itself. Many people compare searching for information on the Internet to drinking from a fire hydrant: it usually gives you just a little bit more than you're asking for. Well, this is but another perfect opportunity for the Internet entrepreneur. Companies such as Yahoo, the most popular of the search engines, have made fortunes from creating Internet Yellow Pages, which allow the Netters to navigate the Net in a somewhat organized, logical manner. Although this might be an impracticable undertaking for the small entrepreneur, there are many successful small specialty-information sites on the Net that provide users with a distilled version of information relevant to their needs. Farcast, for example, is a twenty-four-hour virtual news service featuring information from news to stock quotes to sports updates. Farcast, like dozens of other on-line news services, saw the need to provide the Netters with a concentrated version of the overwhelming amount of news information routinely available on the Internet. Another need yet to be filled is a similar distillation of the deluge of business and investment information now flooding the Net. A recent article in a national business magazine featured a college student who had a particular interest in the stock market. He created a home page that specialized in stock-market information, including stock quotes, company background, and selected newsbriefs. Soon, fellow students, private investors, and even some companies started visiting his Web site. As a result of the high demand for his site, he was offered money by a major Internet service provider (ISP) to maintain and update his Web site for use by various commercial and private investors. This is but one of many examples of how the Internet has created its own set of Net-specific business opportunities that never existed before.

As you consider what information you might want to offer in your Cyberselling venture, think about the kinds of people most likely to be on the Internet. Certainly there are all sorts, and the audience becomes more heterogeneous with the passage of time. Still, there are identifiable factors. All your potential customers access the Net. This means, at the very least, that they all use computers. Therefore, they are probably educated and middle class or above. A lot of the Internet is devoted to research, and so you can expect to find not only large numbers of college students and faculty members, but many members of the professions as well. A strong, ever-increasing segment of the Internet population is the business community. The Internet is a global society and so it includes people from all over the world. Remember, the entire planet is your marketplace. The physical location of your customers would be unimportant. Now, piece all of the factors just mentioned together and you can surely come up with winning ideas for services that will sell successfully to a group with such a profile.

Flowers and Romance

Moving now to products, flowers seem to be a big seller on the Net and other on-line services these days. One survey conducted by the Internet Commerce Corporation in July of 1995 revealed that 6.5 percent of Internet purchases were flowers or plants. Why are flowers such a big seller? Probably because so many on the Net are young, single, and male. They are dating and wooing their young female cybermates. A company called PC Florists boasts a multimillion dollar business achieved at first with a small staff, no inventory, and a marketing system through Prodigy. Consider variations on the flower theme such as candy, sexy lingerie, candlelit dinners, cruises (if you happen to live near water), even e-mail greeting cards. Use your imagination. Romance sells.

Things for the Dorm

You are already aware that many Internet-users are college students. This group is known for favoring items like T-shirts, posters, and assorted semicollectible junk such as exotic beer cans from around the world. Two Internet companies that come to mind here are Genius T-shirts and Joe Boxer. Genius is a small company with a simple, easy-to-execute idea that prints T-shirts depicting images of historic figures such as Einstein, Socrates, Lincoln, Caesar, and every other august personage you can think of. Joe Boxer, on the other hand, is a large corporation that specializes in, you guessed it, boxer shorts. Here are two companies with vastly different resources aiming effectively at the same demographic group. Show students what you have and let them order on-line. They'll keep coming back for more. Where else can they shop during a study break at 2 A.M.?

Collectibles, Hobbies, and Crafts

Whether you're selling hand-crafted, half-hull ships, military memorabilia, or collectible stuffed animals, there is a group on the I-way interested in your wares. The Internet is the optimal venue for reaching specialized markets because even the most narrow of interest groups will be represented in large numbers. Moreover, with the ease in which Net searches can now be executed, finding your specialty product will be a breeze. Collectibles currently being sold on the Net include items such as dolls, toys, baseball cards, autographs, coins, and flags, to name a few. The possibilities are truly endless. Bottom line: if you collect it, somebody out there will buy it.

Food and Recipes

Food is the universal fuel, the one thing absolutely everyone in the world uses on a daily basis. Already for sale on the Net are such items as gourmet coffee, fruit baskets, and recipes for every dish imaginable. Do you make the best cookie in the world? One company bakes only oatmeal cookies but ships them out all over the United States, taking advantage of those specialized market opportunities on the Net mentioned earlier in the chapter. How about that old collection of tried and true family recipes? They would be perfect for an Internet cookbook. Perhaps you consider yourself a connoisseur of fine foods. Why not publish a virtual restaurant guide? Speaking of fine foods, what better to go along with them than fine spirits. Here is another example of a burgeoning niche market of which to take advantage. In fact, one of the most widely known and lauded Internet stores is Virtual Vineyards, an on-line marketer of fine wine and gourmet foods. Virtual Vineyards specializes in marketing the products of smaller vineyards that have difficulty in getting whole distribution. Moreover, this company is notable because its business is carried on 100 percent over the Internet. It has no noncyberspace location. When Virtual Vineyards went on-line in late January 1995, it was an immediate hit. The owners claim that business has been increasing by an average of 20 percent per month and as of June 1996, sales were at about $1 million. Not bad for a company that doesn't even have a brick-and-mortar storefront. Wine is obviously a Net winner, but even if wine isn't your bailiwick and you prefer beer instead, why not market that fine basement brew all your friends love so much?

Unusual Goods and Offbeat Services

Perhaps the many Internet business possibilities heretofore mentioned have been a bit too mainstream for you. Well, as you will soon see, being unconventional about the products and services you offer is the norm for the Internet. It was recently noted in *Parade* magazine that entertainment featuring paranormal subjects is hugely popular. Never let it be said the Net lags behind. Astrologers, psychics, sorcerers, they're all trying to grab their market space on the Net. Scientists are even getting in on the act. One company in particular, Lindsay Scientific, consists of a group of astronomers that, through a radio telescope, offer to send your personal messages into space, in hopes that they will be received by spirits or aliens. In a more earthly but equally offbeat vein, another growing Internet service is virtual funeral homes. There are even pet memorial services that will honor the deceased pet with a eulogy and a picture, as well as an e-mail prompt so the owner can communicate with similarly bereaved pet owners. Some of the more unusual products being sold on the Net include items such as spell powders, tantric tools, fossils, incense, and chain mail. One company even claims to be selling reproductions of actual Sasquatch tracks recovered from forests of the Pacific Northwest. Do your tastes run to the unusual? Nothing is too unusual for the low marketing costs of the Net.

LET THE USENET BE YOUR GUIDE

By now your mind should be swirling with profitable ideas for products to market on the I-way. If not, here is one last way to go about it that just can't miss. In choosing your goods or services look closely at the existing Usenet newsgroups, taking note of the specialized audiences. For example, there are several newsgroups devoted to pets. Already for sale there have been such items as buyer's guide for pet products, gourmet pet foods, books on pet care, and even pets themselves. There are Usenet groups devoted to topics of food, sports (including specific sports teams), health, sex, education, investments, television programs, celebrities, travel, every imaginable facet of computers and software, and, of course, immigration. Many of these groups are regularly visited by hundreds of thousands of individuals. Give them something they want and they can make you very rich.

TEST-MARKETING YOUR PRODUCTS WITH NO FINANCIAL RISK

It's always a good idea to test-market a product before beginning production or embarking on an expensive advertising campaign. This, however, is often impossible in traditional markets, especially if you are on a tight budget. Many direct-marketers have to make a profit on every advertisement they run. The price of one ad can put them out of business if it doesn't work. The Internet solves this age-old problem handily. The cost of advertising is so low that you can afford to make mistakes. You also have the benefit of interactive communications, so it's easy to find out right away what your potential customers like or dislike about what you are selling. Place some notices on a few relevant Usenet groups or on *The Entrepreneur's Corner Office of the World Wide Web* (look under the Business Resources for Web address) and simply ask if people find your idea interesting. Tell them what you plan to sell and how much you will charge. You are very likely to get back dozens of helpful responses, suggesting ways to change your product or service so that it will sell better. You may find that there is no market for the item and you'll have to look further. No harm done. Just try again.

As you look for the product that will make you a fortune, don't forget, selling on the Internet is so new that even if the product or service is not, seeing its availability on the Internet may be novel enough in itself to make it a big seller. There certainly is nothing unusual in any of the products and services described here. As you learn your way around cyberspace, you will become more familiar with all the goods and services already for sale there. Perhaps you can figure out a way to market a product differently from everyone else.

Starting a business on the Net has its novel features, but in most ways the standard considerations apply. If you need some advice on how to establish your new Internet company, the Net itself offers many helpful resources. Although there are literally hundreds of small-business information sources on the Internet from which to choose, here is a list of the more popular sources, all of which offer free information.

U.S. Small Business Administration (*http://www.sbaonline.sba.gov/*) contains a variety of information on starting, financing, and expanding your business. The site also features a shareware library of over five hundred business-related software programs, and provides links to the Office of Women's Business Ownership and to Great Business Hot Links!, a collection of business-related Internet sites.

Business Resource Center (*http://www.kciLink.com/brc/*) contains information on getting started, marketing, management, and financing. It also has discussion groups.

Thomas Ho's Favorite Electronic Commerce WWW page (*http://e-comm.iworld.com/*) contains comprehensive resources regarding commerce on the Net. It provides links to sites on trade and commerce, small-business promotions, and government regulations. It's a perfect starting point for information concerning commerce and the Internet.

EINet Galaxy (*http://www.einet.net/galaxy/Business-and-Commerce.html*) provides a good jumping-off point for business-information searches on the Net. This site includes topic headings such as general business resources, consumer products and services, business administration, and business organizations.

Yahoo's Business Resources (*http://www.yahoo.com/Business-and-Economy/*) is a huge directory providing links to over ninety thousand businesses, which are divided into several hundred subcategories. This is a perfect site to get a feel for all the different businesses out on the Net. Other subheadings include business property, marketing, news, taxes, and small business information.

The Entrepreneur's Corner Office (*http://catalog.com/corner/*) contains a message board on which any business-related questions can be posted. The questions are then answered by others participating in the forum. Here is a place where you can pitch your new idea or get help with business-related questions.

10

I-Way Red Light Districts and the Communications Decency Act

SEX FOR MONEY IN CYBERSPACE

THERE IS ONE PRODUCT YOU MAY SEE FOR SALE ALONG the I-way that has not been discussed here yet. In your efforts to get rich through Cyberselling, it is a basic philosophy of the plan to understand as much about your potential customers as possible. If you spend much time roaming through cyberspace, one thing will quickly become apparent. A great number of Internetters think sex and the computer belong together. They love talking about sex and looking at erotic pictures. If you don't believe it, peruse the top twenty-five most read newsgroups on Usenet and you can't help but notice a definite consistency to the subject matter.

Top 25 Newsgroups

1. alt.sex.stories
2. alt.sex
3. alt.binaries.pictures.erotica
4. new.announce.newusers
5. alt.binaries.pictures.erotica.female

6. alt.sex.voyeurism
7. alt.sex.exhibitionism
8. alt.binaries.pictures.erotica.blonds
9. alt.binaries.pictures.erotica.orientals
10. alt.sex.breasts
11. alt.binaries.pictures.supermodels
12. rec.humor.funny
13. alt.sex.movies
14. alt.sex.stories.d
15. alt.sex.bondage
16. alt.tv.simpsons
17. alt.sex.pictures
18. rec.arts.erotica
19. alt.sex.wanted
20. alt.binaries.pictures.tasteless
21. alt.sex.wizards
22. alt.2600
23. misc.jobs.offered
24. news.answers
25. alt.music.alternative

Moreover, except for technical computer topics, there are more news-groups related to sex than any other single subject. When you consider that practically every college and university in the country offers complimentary Internet access to students, and the great majority who take advantage of the free opportunity are male, it is not hard to understand where at least part of the eager audience for this kind of material comes from. Available Internet sex items include sexual personal ads, risqué stories, and an astoundingly enormous cache of pornographic pictures ranging from the mildly explicit to the hardest of hard-core pornography free for the taking and void of age restrictions. Parental discretion may be advisable. Often it is not exercised. Many parents simply never recognize that the computer is being used in this way.

Most commercial on-line services have certain areas designated for sexual topics and discussions. To access them usually requires special permission. A lot of sexual material may be free on the Internet, but a substantial amount is offered by entrepreneurs engaged in for-profit ventures. *Penthouse* and *Playboy* are two well-known and highly successful Internet ventures. Chat lines—Internet channels open to direct, real-time computer conversations—are filled with sexual talk, innuendoes, and individuals avidly engaging in fantasy role-playing. Of course, there is no real physical contact in these virtual brothels or singles bars. The concept of "safe sex" probably reaches its ultimate incarnation here. It doesn't matter whether or not touching is allowed. For practical purposes, it's simply not possible. Everything else is, however, and there is no shortage of takers.

BBS

BBSs are especially filled with sexually oriented topics. The private world of Bulletin Board Services (BBS) can be thought of as distant but electronically unconnected cousins of the Usenet. Still a part of the I-way, many BBSs exist on a single computer in someone's garage or basement. Access to others is made possible by modem except that, unlike the Internet, there is a one-to-one connection rather than the interconnectivity of a huge network. Observing the propensities of many BBSs, it is notable that the second largest BBS network in the United States is called Kink Net. Although some BBSs are free, most are not. At the very least, there are charges for the time actually spent on-line. A recent issue of a major computer magazine contained four full pages of ads for BBSs offering such items as "3D Sex BBS," "Sexy Software," "Free Adult CD-ROM," "Hustler On-Line," "Odyssey—Where Adults Come to Play," and "Lifestyle On-line, Hot Chat with the World's Sexiest Couples and Singles." Thousands of gigabytes' worth of computer storage around the world are used to house such information, which is considered by many to be critical to the functioning of the collective on-line psyche.

SEX, THE INTERNET, THE MEDIA, AND CONTROLLING LEGISLATION

In the past two years, as the popularity and public awareness of the Internet grew, sex on the Internet, as well as the on-line services, began to get a lot of media attention. Parents were understandably upset that their children might be accessing adult matter without their knowledge. Nine-year-old children who had mastered a few simple keystrokes could now study full-color images of naked men and women. Responsible adults shuddered to think that in purchasing a computer to further their child's education, they got more education than they bargained for. A typical message that might appear on a newsgroup would read:

A new adult site has just opened up. Lots of graphic files yours for free. If interested, just send your e-mail address to me and you'll get more information. Make sure to include a statement that you are over 21. Well, nah, don't bother. . . nobody really cares anyway.

THE COMMUNICATIONS DECENCY ACT

Fueled by continuous media coverage of material like the message just described, politicians soon felt the need to address the situation of uncontrolled sexual transmissions over the Internet. What ensued was a full-scale confrontation between government efforts to control Internet content through legislation, and Net freedom-of-speech advocates. Because this is such an important issue for the future of the Internet, made headlines for so long, and is likely to keep on making them, this law will be covered here in some detail.

On June 14, 1995, the Senate passed the Communications Decency Amendment that eventually became referred to as the Communications Decency Act (CDA). According to its sponsor Senator Jim Exon (D-Nebraska), the CDA was meant to prohibit the computer equivalent of obscene telephone calls and to stop the distribution to children of materials with sexual content. The amendment became part of the Telecommunications Act of 1996, which was signed into law by President Clinton on February 8, 1996. On the same day, the American Civil Liberties Union (ACLU) led a group of various individuals and organizations who opposed the new law and took action by becoming the plaintiffs in a case filed to challenge the constitutionality of the CDA. Specifically, the plaintiffs objected to two provisions of the CDA aimed at stopping communications over the Internet which might be deemed "indecent" or "patently offensive" for minors. The act defined minors as persons under the age of eighteen. Challengers of the law saw infringement on the Constitutional rights of free speech and due process. This challenge was filed in the United States District Court for the Eastern District of Pennsylvania, and consisted of a motion for a temporary restraining order (TRO) which would have the effect of stopping the law from going into effect until the courts could decide whether or not it was constitutional. On February 15, the court granted a limited TRO. Soon thereafter, the case was taken to the Federal Appeals Court, which, on June 11, 1996, granted the plaintiffs' motion for preliminary injunction. This kept the law from going into effect even longer than the TRO. The case is now awaiting Supreme Court review.

The first of two provisions of the Communications Decency Act over which there is the greatest controversy criminally prosecutes and punishes, by fine, imprisonment, or both, any person who uses a telecommunications device to knowingly transmit communications which are judged to be obscene or indecent, when the person is aware of what he or she has done and that the recipient of the obscene material is under eighteen years of age. The second controversial provision criminally prosecutes, and applies the same punishments stated above, to any person who uses an interactive computer service to send or display obscene material to a person under age eighteen, any image, or other communication that the law terms "patently offensive" according to contemporary community standards.

In order to protect the innocent, the CDA offers three escape clauses, also known as defenses. They are as follows:

1. No one will be penalized solely for providing access or connection over which that person has no control, including transmission, downloading, intermediate storage, access software, or other related capabilities. This defense does not apply, however, if any of the parties have knowledge of the obscene information being distributed;
2. No employer will be held liable for the actions of an employee who sends or assists in sending offensive or indecent material so long as the action is taken outside the employee's scope of employment and without the employer's knowledge;
3. No person will be penalized if that person has taken actions in good faith to restrict or prevent the transmission of or access to obscene and indecent material.

It is clear these provisions are meant to protect ISPs (Internet service providers) from liability for what their users send over the Net. As for the senders, there is no protection at all, or even a clear definition offered of what is indecent or patently offensive.

The 150-page opinion regarding the preliminary injunction, which some say may be the most rapidly distributed Federal Court opinion in American history, can be found all over the Net. Here are the opposing positions of the two sides as the court summarized them.

Plaintiffs' Position

The plaintiffs have focused their challenge on the constitutionality of the two provisions concerning the creation and dissemination of "indecent" and "patently offensive" materials. The plaintiffs make clear, however, that they do not argue with the statute insofar as it covers obscenity or child pornography, which were already prohibited by law before the CDA's adoption. The plaintiffs also argue that in lieu of imposing what they view as a quite reactionary set of laws on the Internet to control content, proactive steps can be taken by parents to restrict access to unwanted on-line material, referring to software like Net Nanny, a user-based software that offers a method by which parents can prevent their children from accessing sexually explicit and other materials which parents may believe is inappropriate for their children.

Defendant's Position

The Government claims that the CDA is constitutional because of the available defenses, for those who did actually create or send the objectionable material. The Government also asserts that a state has an interest in safeguarding the physical and psychological well-being of a minor. The problem is that some of the materials that would be subject to coverage under the indecent and patently offensive provisions, may contain useful literary, artistic, or educational information valuable to older minors as well as adults.

Even to summarize the remainder of this opinion would take much more space than should be devoted here or that you would probably care to read. The main point is that the court finds it impractical at this point and by the imperfect provisions of this particular law, to control the delivery of indecent material to minors without wiping out the rights of everyone to speak freely on the Net.

The key problem with the CDA is that the language is so vague that nobody seems to really know how far the act can reach in prohibiting the creating and disseminating of "indecent material." First of all, the term "indecent" is obviously highly subjective. Second, the "community standards" measurement cannot ever be a unified standard because what is considered indecent in New York City may not be the same as what is viewed as indecent in a small town in Mississippi. Therefore, anyone sending sexual material out on the Net, to be completely safe, would have to assume that "community standards" would be the standards of the most conservative community. Various historical and contemporary films, plays, books, art, and photographs would be prohibited by such standards. For example, what about literature by recognized authors like D. H. Lawrence, who wrote *Lady Chatterly's Lover*—a book that contains much sexual material but is also considered a masterpiece.

For the Internet marketer, the problem is obviously what can be said or sold of sexual nature that will not result in a jail sentence. As for the ISPs, they are, of course, concerned with the question of where their liability begins and that of the actual purveyor of sexual material ends. For now, until the Supreme Court decides the matter, it would appear that the only laws needing to be followed are those already in existence, such as those banning the transmission of obscenity or child pornography, and it is very likely this will remain true after the Supreme Court has had its final say.

OTHER LAWS CONTROLLING PORNOGRAPHY

No one should forget, however, that any laws prohibiting transmission or sale of pornography prior to CDA still remain in force and applicable to the Net. The seediest offerings on the I-way sex menu have already caught the attention of law enforcement agencies who are learning that there may be new high-tech outlets for criminal pornography, particularly those appealing to the interests of pedophiles. Likewise, computer buffs who favor this material are learning electronic skills for covering their tracks. Volumes of pornographic material can be clandestinely transported all over the world, hidden in encrypted computer files, via the Internet. An encrypted file is one put in a special code that can be read only by someone with a key to that code. With the advent of encryption, the ability for law enforcement agencies to track down and stop smut peddling is extremely limited. As further guidance for what you may or may not do, here are summaries of some major court cases and the results of each.

Jake Baker, a University of Michigan student, was arrested and indicted for creating and transmitting a sexually explicit fictional story and e-mail messages, both of which used the real name of a fellow female undergraduate. Baker also posted his story, describing abduction, sexual torture, and murder, to the newsgroup *alt.sex.stories*. The story included a warning stating that "The following story contains a lot of sick stuff. You have been warned."

The e-mail messages were posted to an individual named Arthur Gonda, whom the police never found. There were more than forty messages describing plans for abducting, torturing, and killing young girls and women. Prosecutors alleged that the story and the messages were illegal because they transmitted communications that contained a threat to kidnap and injure. Baker was suspended by the University and one week later was arrested and indicted on the basis of the story alone. He was denied bail on two occasions and spent one month in the Milan Federal Prison, from which he was released on $10,000 bond. A Grand Jury reindicted him for the e-mail correspondence—superceding the first indictment, and this time omitting the charges based on the story. This was viewed by many as the government prosecutor's plan to refine its case and mount a stronger effort.

Nevertheless, the judge granted a motion by Baker to quash the second indictment, holding that the language in the e-mail messages did not constitute a "true threat," which he defined as "some language construable as a serious expression of an intent imminently to carry out some injurious act."

The judge based the finding on the facts that Baker made no effort to communicate the messages to the student named in his story, and the e-mail messages "were not available in any publicly accessible part of the Internet." In addition, the judge did not quite understand why the prosecution went forward with the case in the first place, as Baker made no effort to conceal his identity in writing the story or the e-mail messages. In fact, the alleged threats contained in the e-mail were signed by Baker and had his correct e-mail address. And the story was posted to a public newsgroup that featured such material. Baker even asked for feedback from his readers.

One of the first and most well-known obscenity convictions on the Internet was that of Robert and Carleen Thomas. The couple ran a BBS in California and distributed "obscene" images through the BBS, involving, among other things, bestiality. Transmission of this was legal in California, but when a Tennessee resident downloaded the material from the BBS, this couple was subsequently found guilty by a Tennessee court under an existing federal criminal statute which prohibited the distribution of obscene images. Here is a perfect example of the "community standards" problem.

Sexual activity on the Internet has been further brought to public attention with the widely reported story of the famous e-mail stalker.

This Michigan man suffered the misfortune of falling in love with a lady who had eyes only for others. He brooded, plotted, and contemplated how to get her attention. As it turned out, he and the object of his affections did have one thing in common, e-mail accounts. He began writing e-mail love letters everyday. We don't know how racy they were, but the woman became upset. Each time she turned on her computer, there was another letter from her unwelcome suitor. Finally, she became so terrorized by the messages that she called the local police. The man was arrested and accused of violating a Michigan stalker law. He was given a year's probation and ordered to undergo psychiatric evaluation. It is open to question at what point boyish infatuation crosses the line and becomes sexual harassment. Nonetheless, the stalker story makes one thing clear. Hiding behind a computer does not give anyone the legal right to do that which he or she could not do out in the open. The case is fair warning that some of the sex features of the Internet may border on the illegal.

Beyond the actual purveyors of sexually explicit material, the other question that creates trouble with respect to transmission of pornography over the Net is the extent to which ISPs can be held liable for their content. *Cubby, Inc. v. CompuServe, Inc.,* and *Stratton Oakmont, Inc. v. Prodigy Servs. Co.* both represent two different ends of the liability spectrum. In the Cubby case, CompuServe happened to be carrying information on their on-line service that contained false and defamatory statements about the plaintiffs, developers of an electronic magazine called *Skuttlebut.* CompuServe admitted that the statements might be defamatory, but claimed that they were merely the distributors, not the publishers, of the information. As a distributor, CompuServe could not be held liable for the statements because they didn't know about them. The court in this case likened CompuServe to a bookstore or an electronic library. Only a publisher, such as a magazine or newspaper that has some sort of editorial control over its product, could be liable for content. Just as a bookstore or library cannot possibly be aware of the contents of every book, CompuServe couldn't be aware of the content of every posting. This court decision, labeling CompuServe as a distributor, reduced the threat of liability to on-line ISPs.

The Prodigy case, however, had a much different outcome. Prodigy lost a ruling in a similar case because the court found that they *did* have sufficient editorial control over their information. This was because Prodigy marketed itself as a "family-oriented" service. To do this, Prodigy took upon itself the editing of the content of their information to eliminate that which was not suitable family fare. Prodigy edited content according to specific guidelines, through use of software screening programs, and even employed emergency delete functions. As such, the court found Prodigy to be more like a newspaper or magazine, and therefore liable for statements made on its service.

If, after reading these cases, you feel yourself confused at what may or may not be done with respect to sending sexually explicit material over the Net, you are at one with the court and the endless number of commentators on this subject. Moreover, even when the Supreme Court finally rules on the CDA case, it will probably serve to confuse rather than clarify the issue.

The Internet is truly a unique means of communication. So unique, in fact, that many believe that the current framework of laws are incapable of regulating this singularly dynamic medium. Politicians feel extreme pressure to do something about the "chaos" of the Internet. It's hard for a politician to look good when he or she is pro anarchy, pornography, or both. Just as many, however, believe that the Internet needs no regulation, that the chaotic nature of the Internet is its lifeblood, its spirituality. The Internet, some factions say, is the last bastion protecting the free exchange of ideas and information. Here, you don't have to be a public figure or own a newspaper to have your voice heard. Everyone is a potential Thomas Paine or Martin Luther King, Jr. All you need is a computer and a modem. Those who oppose the CDA say that if the regulatory standards applied to conventional media are applied to the Internet, the costs will far outweigh the benefits.

PROTECTING IDENTITY: THE ANONYMOUS SERVER

No discussion about sex on the Internet would be complete without mentioning a special computer known as the Anonymous Server that is located in Finland and run by a man named Johan Helsingius. If you look at the Usenet much, you are likely to see messages posted by individuals with e-mail addresses who list their domains as *anon.penet.fi.* Why, you may ask, do so many people interested in sex come from that domain? Actually, they don't. Anyone, anywhere may send a message to the Anonymous Server requesting an anonymous ID. E-mail or Usenet messages may then be sent through that computer, hiding the sender's identity. The computer in Finland scrambles the sender's address so that only it knows the actual source. Anyone wishing to respond to the anonymous missive sends a message back to the anonymous address and the Finnish computer forwards it to the proper party. This arrangement is extremely attractive to those who want to keep their interest in sex a deep, dark secret.

The Anonymous Server has been operating since 1993 and has become something of a tradition on the Net, but recently it has been challenged by the law. Faced with having to reveal his users' identities, Helsingius elected to shut down the Anonymous Server in August 1996. In addition to claims that child pornography was being funnelled through the server, he had been receiving phone calls accusing him of pedophilia. Many Internet-users believe the Anonymous Server and similar anonymous remailer programs provide those who want to discuss delicate subjects such as alcoholism, battered wives, and politically sensitive issues with safety from prying eyes and oppressive governments, a benefit that gives these programs a legitimate reason for their existence.

No person familiar with the Internet disputes that there is deplorable, sometimes downright shocking, information on the Internet. Nevertheless, this represents only a small percentage of all information to be found there. The potential stifling effects governmental regulation would have on the Internet may not only disrupt the transmission of so-called indecent material, but could effect educational content as well. If one were to apply the same standards to the Internet as exist for most other types of communications vehicles, would it really take into account differences in medium? For example, the message of that popular example of inciting to riot, falsely shouting "Fire!" in a crowded movie theater, is unquestionably far more threatening when delivered by voice in an actual theater than when posted over the Internet. As time goes on, the law controlling this material on the Net will probably develop slowly and painfully as it always does. Meanwhile, sex as a means of making money on the Internet will continue and therefore, must be a part of a full explanation of Internet marketing. What follows are a sampling of sex-related moneymaking ideas that are now being used on the Net. Please note that not all of them are pornographic in nature. Some are just simple dating services or the like.

A THRIVING BUSINESS ON THE INTERNET: MONEYMAKING POSSIBILITIES FROM THE WORLD'S OLDEST HOBBY

A fine example of sex as a selling mechanism on the Internet is called Cybersex City. Cybersex City actually started as a Gopher data site, an

Internet search, and marketing tool that has since developed into a Web site *http://www.pussy/com/hotsex/*. When you tune into the site you are greeted with a slick, colorful offering of pornographic pictures for money. I, however, have a special fondness for how it used to be on gopher which is as follows.

Welcome to Cybersex City!. . . carrying advertising for (ugh!) commercial sex—mostly bizarre commercial sex. . . respond to personal ads from people even more sexually twisted than you.

In fairness, all who enter here do get the following advisory:

Be warned that the material on this server is about as raw and explicit as sexual material gets. . . the advertisers on this server offer every deviation that you have ever heard of. . . and more.

And as to Jesse Helms, Jerry Falwell, and/or politically correct persons: We suggest that CYBERSEX CITY is NOT the place for you. Trust us on this.

Oh yeah, also stay away from here unless you are at least 18.

It goes on to list sexually explicit personal ads, with instructions on how to contact each advertiser, for a fee, of course.

Dating and Marriage Services

A Foreign Affair (*http://www.wwdatalink.com/foreign-affair/*) is in the business of selling what can best be termed as mail-order brides. It bills itself as an international introduction dating and marriage service for singles wishing to meet Russian, Asian, and Latin women for correspondence, love, and marriage.

The China–Western Marriage Introductions (*http://asian.com/rain*) does largely the same thing. It describes itself as a personal marriage service for Western and Chinese women and men. The site contains photos and descriptions of the "prospects."

Santa Barbara International Center (*http://www.rain.org/~sbintl*) is another of these sites. It features a group of women from the former Soviet republics of Belarus and Uzbekistan. All are guaranteed to be well educated, mostly between the ages of eighteen and thirty. These women are interested in meeting men from the West and propose to do so through correspondence with the intent of the letter-writing leading to marriage.

Clothing, Games, and Toys

Moving on to a more exotic marketing concept, we find Panties Just For Men (*http://members.aol.com/PJMFashion/index.htm*). This lingerie selling site claims to cater to the transvestite and cross-dressing crowd, where you can, in all probability, find the world's largest pair of lace bikinis.

An unusual concept in the sex category is purveyed by *Private* magazine. This is a Swedish magazine with an interesting game. You must subscribe before you can play. The game is wholly interactive and involves fighting off martial arts experts, enraged slam-dunkers, and deranged old ladies in wheelchairs. Your ultimate goal is to find the senator fooling around with his girlfriend. *Private* magazine claims that when you reach your goal, the senator's wife will give you a reward.

Returning to more standard sexual fare, Absolutely Adult (*http://absolute1.com*) sells photos, adult toys, movies of the XX-rated kind. There are literally hundreds of such sites that offer variations on this theme.

By now you've probably guessed that the position of the author is that selling sex is not something I find personally appealing. Others, however, feel differently, and when you consider the availability of willing buyers, it's not difficult to see why. The salability of sex on the Net was actually brought home personally in a very unusual and unexpected way. Shortly after one of the now famous Green Card Lottery postings was sent out some unknown cyberpunk got the idea of engaging in character assassination by announcing to the Internet community that Cybersell® was maintaining catalogs of erotic pictures in computer-formatted files. Our e-mail address was given and anyone interested in such things was invited to contact us for a brochure and price list. You may have grasped enough already about the predilection of certain Netters to guess what happened. Within days, nearly a thousand requests for our price list came in. Probably thousands more would have come in if our access provider at the time, Netcom, hadn't picked that moment, several months after our Green Card posting, to bow to pressure and cut off our account just as the messages started rolling in. Only about three days' worth of mail got through. It's a shame all these orders weren't sent to someone who actually had the pictures to sell. They really might have cleaned up. It is interesting to speculate on what would have occurred if the message had been the object of a concerted effort to mass post. Undoubtedly, the responses would have been overwhelming, and the Netters probably wouldn't have complained at all.

THE MARKETING FUTURE OF SEX ON THE INTERNET

Pending legal limitations aside, except for the BBSs, to date a wide variety of sexual material available on the I-way is offered free. Still, it is undeniable that fortunes have been made catering to all kinds of vices, sex being number one on the list. When the Supreme Court finally issues a ruling on the CDA, it is doubtful that the transmission of sexual material on the Net will be any more prohibited now than it is by the laws that already set limitations on child pornography. That is why many programs designed to filter objectionable material are available to parents. Cyber Patrol, Intergo, Net Nanny for Windows, and Net Shepherd are a few you can find now being sold in your computer store. Sexually related material has for many years been sold quite openly on newsstands, in newspaper classified ads, and through 900-number telephone services. Most of the sexual items and services currently for sale elsewhere could easily be adapted to marketing on the Internet, and no doubt will be in short order. Some of what will occur will be harmless fun. Other projects will continue to test the limits of the law and public patience.

11

Trading in I-Way Stocks

MAKING MONEY WITHOUT A PRODUCT

SUPPOSE YOU FIND IT TOO MUCH TROUBLE TO SELL THE products or services mentioned so far, or even sell yourself as a celebrity. There's still another way. Forget the rest of this book and simply buy and sell stocks of Internet technology–based companies. Like the Internet, these companies have the potential to grow at a mind-boggling rate. If you play it right, as many have, you could soon find yourself sailing the Bahamas in your own custom-built yacht, like the ones you see on TV in the real-estate guru's infomercials.

No more dramatic example of this can be found than the story of Netscape, known for its World Wide Web software. It may indeed be the most unusual financial tale of all time. It all started with Marc Andreessen, a university of Illinois computer science student who was working at the University's National Center for Supercomputing Applications for a salary of $6.85 an hour. Here, Andreessen helped develop a program called Mosaic, a World Wide Web browser, which made it easier to navigate the intricacies of the Web. Soon thereafter, he and a few of Mosaic's other developers started a company with James Clark, an established computer businessman, called Mosaic Communications. Because the university technically owned the rights to the name Mosaic, the company's name was changed to Netscape.

In 1995, Netscape offered shares of stock to the public in an Initial Public Offering (IPO). This type of stock transaction will be explained later. What is impressive here, though, is that the stock was set to open on the market at $14 a share, but instead it opened at more than twice that amount. At the end of the day Jim Clark, chairman of the company, was worth $556 million and the then twenty-four-year-old Andreessen was worth $58 million, changing forever the image of the starving college student. What is perhaps most striking about this story—which is already an eye-opener—is that when this IPO made these men into millionaires, Netscape was a company that had yet to show a profit.

Welcome to the world of Internet technology IPOs, where young cyberwonks like Andreessen become Rockefellers overnight and unproven companies become worth a fortune in the public eye. Netscape has since made many of its shareholders very rich.

For every Netscape, though, there are hundreds of duds whose hyped-up offerings fail miserably. Since its spectacular beginning, even Netscape stock has been known to take a dip or two, dropping sometimes 50 percent in a six-month period. Still, for those who got in on Netscape at the opening price of $14, at the time of this writing, Netscape's stock has never been lower than three times the initial offering price, enough to make any investor delirious with joy.

Because the technology sector of the stock market is volatile, especially when it comes to those companies having anything to do with the Internet, it is impossible to predict who tomorrow's winners and losers will be. Even the so-called experts have trouble keeping up with this market. There are, however, certain rules to follow and things to look for when investing in the technology sector. So, without further ado, How-To University now brings you Internet Investing 101.

PROS AND CONS OF INVESTING IN TECHNOLOGY STOCKS

The computer industry is much different from other industries. The newer companies are run by young computer geniuses who prefer sandals, T-shirts, and shorts to Armani suits. Many of the young computer geeks operating these companies, brilliant as they are, have no experience in business. They are creative types who shun the glitzy world of high-dollar corporate America. It is difficult for a business to make good without excellent management, even if the product is both exceptional and desirable. That is why Bill Gates, a man who had superior business skills as well as technical skills, not to mention Gates's two partners, Paul Allen and Steve Ballmer, who studied economics at Harvard, attended Stanford Graduate School of Business, and worked two years as a junior executive for Procter and Gamble, succeeded where others failed. Nevertheless, those with technical skills alone have, through ingenuity, creativity, and initiative, developed a number of technological goods and services, most of which are in extremely high demand by consumers. High demand usually translates into high profit. Many investors, institutional and individual alike, understand this relationship all too well, and have accordingly been almost obsessively attracted to the technology sector of the stock market. Nevertheless, the technology sector has throughout history been more unstable than others and, high-tech dream stories notwithstanding, today's tech market is even more so. Those who are skilled investors understand this too.

Computer technology moves at an extremely fast pace, and keeping up with the trends is another difficulty. Combining the dynamic nature of computer technology with a California gold rush-style interest in the market makes for an environment that is as dicey as it is potentially lucrative. It is not, however, only the continuous product development that makes the high tech market sector unstable. The other reasons for this condition are extremely high growth rate; the influx of new investors; and the lack of technical knowledge of many of the participating investors, including the large institutional investors who have the ability to influence market trends.

When the Internet became popular in 1995, the tech sector reached its zenith of instability as a spate of new overnight companies going public for high dollars came on the scene. Little was known about many of these Internet companies when they entered the public market. Investors normally demand a proven track record and a show of profits before investing in a company. The technology sector doesn't afford them that opportunity, and investors, hypnotized by endless high-tech hype, don't demand it. The Netscape story is certainly a prime example of that. Because the Internet is so new, a company that has developed a seemingly strong, lucrative product may have only been in existence for, say, six months, giving investors little company history to make accurate projections and extrapolations on the future of the company. As a result, investors invest more in potential than in reality, and are keenly aware that today's hero is tomorrow's goat.

Most investors also don't have an adequate technical background to understand the products in which they are investing. For example, today almost every diversified mutual fund has technology stocks, meaning they were purchased by the managers, many of whom know little about the computer industry. The problem is that companies like Yahoo, the search engine mentioned earlier, and Netscape, were making so much money that mutual fund managers, as well as other investors, had to act fast in buying them to beat the market. With little time to learn about products that were difficult to understand in any event, they went forward with a fair degree of insecurity, not only failing to know much about the companies, but being unconversant with the products as well. Accordingly, every twitch and twitter of the tech market made the investors nervous, and, as a result, they tended to buy and sell frantically, making the market all the more unstable. Even experienced investors disagree on the prospects of the tech market; however, few stay away from it. The money is there and investors can't resist it, for their clients as well as themselves.

Given all this, it is not hard to understand that tech stocks are literally driving the market and account for 12 percent of the market capital, a number amounting in dollars to 1 trillion. Many people already own tech stocks without even knowing it because the majority of the big mutual funds, 401(k) plans, and other diversified portfolios each contain a fair number of tech stocks and it is commonly known that even though tech stocks have always been a roller-coaster ride, they also seem to be very resilient and rebound well.

There are a number of things to look for when you invest in Internet technology, such as how a company's product or service relates to Internet functioning, the degree of specialization in the company, why a certain company's technology is better than another, the innovativeness of the company, and the practicality of a company's product or service.

RELATED TECHNOLOGIES

Because Internet stocks can be expensive—due to their high demand—indirect investments can sometimes be a wiser choice. When you look for an Internet stock in which to invest, ask yourself what else related to the Internet is available. Some of the better performing companies are ones that provide the hardware and software for computers to hook up to the Net. Companies that build modems are an example. U.S. Robotics makes roughly 30 percent of modems that allow personal computers and on-line providers access to the Net. Routers are another lucrative Net-related stock because they are an information-transferring necessity. A router is an item of equipment that chooses the optimum path every time a piece of information must be directed over the Internet between two or more networks. A company called Cisco supplies 80 percent of the routers that direct I-net traffic flow. In addition to its preeminence in the router market, Cisco is slowly positioning itself to corner the market in Internet server software as well.

STATIC SPECIALIZATION IN THE COMPANY

Many companies that design search engines, such as Yahoo and Lycos, have been successful in this niche market. Nevertheless, these companies are aware of a problem already facing them. Search engines won't stay hot for too long. Therefore, these companies are now diversifying. For example, Yahoo entered into a joint venture with Ziff-Davis Publishing to create the magazine, *Yahoo Internet Life*, to hedge against eventual loss of market share in the search-engine niche. Look for forthcoming expansions, partnerships, and strategic alliances like this in many companies. It shows the company is willing to work to keep its viability.

COMPETING TECHNOLOGIES

Internet service providers are becoming more and more popular, threatening traditional on-line services like America Online (AOL), CompuServe, and Prodigy by using their capital to secure regional markets. In fact, CompuServe and Prodigy are planning to move part of their once proprietary services to the World Wide Web in order to compete with the ISPs. ISPs, however, are able to do things cheaper and faster than the on-lines. The cheaper part is possible because the on-lines have more maintenance costs operating a large national network of their own whereas ISPs are part of the Internet. In addition, the on-lines incur advertising costs that are astronomical. ISPs are faster because they generally serve fewer people per line than the international networks. In addition, the elaborate graphical software of the on-lines takes a long time to download. On the other hand, many ISPs are small companies that could not compete effectively in their own local markets. It is the conglomerates with the large market shares that make the good investments.

Computer devices hooked directly into the Net, hanging on the walls, matching the furniture, special PCs for the kitchen and living room—if Larry Ellison of Oracle has his way, this is the future. Ellison believes that Microsoft may be the present, but the future is undetermined. He believes that the PC will be replaced by the black box, which would plug directly into the Net. This may not make PCs obsolete, but it will be another technological tool for the home. Ellison may or may not be right, but Oracle is a company worth watching in the future, just in case he is.

Perhaps the biggest of the new technologies will be Intranets. Intranets work by using the format and techniques that operate the Internet, but they have their own databases and the network extends only as far as one individual company. This may sound like a minor application of Internet technology but it is not. In fact, Netscape currently makes over 70 percent of its revenues from Intranet software. Many experts believe that this is where the majority of the profits will be made in the next five years. A Forrester Research study found that 22 percent of Fortune 1000 companies use Intranets, whereas in 1994 virtually none did.

Although it's important to keep an eye toward the future when investing in tech stocks, sometimes the hot stock is right under your nose. If you sit back and ask yourself what the most popular and pervasive product on the Net is, you'll have to answer, information. A company called CNET, a provider of Internet-oriented news, recently became the first publisher of content on the Web to offer its shares to the public. Shares opened at $16 and closed at $20, making CNET's chief executive, Halsey Minor, worth nearly $60 million. The content business is quickly becoming the most competitive sector on the Web. Many other companies will now have to follow CNET's lead if they want to stay competitive; look for content-based companies making offerings in the future.

When investing in the tech sector, don't look for a stable ride. The tech sector is unpredictable—expect it. It is, however, also resilient, and savvy investors take this into consideration. Prepare to wait out the low points rather than flying into a panic. Twenty-five percent or more slips in tech stock is not uncommon. As a rule of thumb, many general investors use about a 15 percent threshold, meaning if their stock drops 15 percent they get out. This conventional wisdom won't work in the tech stock area. Another good rule for all investors that does apply especially to technology stocks is to diversify. This reduces your chances of getting burned by having all your eggs in one basket, an especially good rule given tech stock volatility. When investing you should do so at your own comfort level, don't get in over your head. Don't be too quick to jump on the "hot" stock. Tech investors once were buying stock in every small, fast-growing Internet company they could get their hands on. Now with some significant failures on the records, they are being very selective and much more cautious.

Look for trends that will affect the entire industry, as we saw in some of the examples above. Think of the capabilities of the Internet. What hasn't been explored yet? If a company comes out with an innovative, paradigm-shifting, industry-permeating product, take a chance. Finally, if you don't have time to learn this new, complex, and fast-paced industry, think about investing in mutual funds where someone else can do your thinking for you.

TECH STOCK MUTUALS

Mutual funds are investment companies that combine the funds of thousands of investors and invest them in stocks, bonds, and other securities. In a mutual fund several hundred million to billions of dollars of other people's money are invested along with yours. Mutual funds give you several advantages over individual investing. First, you have a professional money manager overseeing the fund. Second, investing in mutual funds is far less expensive than investing in individual stocks because you usually only have to pay a small annual fee for the management of the fund. If you invest on your own, you have to pay some type of fee for each individual stock you buy, even at the discount brokerages.

For the investor that doesn't have the time to research but still wants to get in on the Internet stock boom, technology mutual funds are a good alternative. Tech mutual funds probably won't outperform individual tech stocks, but the tech mutuals' diversity in the tech sector raises your chance of high returns while minimizing the risk, exactly what a mutual fund is supposed to do and particularly important in this field. Moreover, tech mutual funds will most likely be managed by someone who knows the industry and can respond to the volatility of the sector. There are two different ways you can invest in tech mutual funds. First, you can invest in a fund like the T. Rowe Price Science & Technology Fund which contains only technology stocks. Alternatively, you can invest in a fund that has a significant percentage of its assets in the technology sector. You'll have to check on your own for this because many of the mutual funds that don't specialize in the tech sector might decide to sell a significant percentage of their tech stocks, depending on their strategy. Remember, usually the higher percentage of tech funds in the portfolio the higher the risk. Also, in mutual funds there is usually a minimum investment, $2,000 to $2,500 is not unusual.

If you want to learn more about investing in mutual funds, the Vanguard fund has a Web site at *http://www.vanguard.com* where you can attend "Vanguard University," a series of investment education courses designed for the mutual fund investor. For a list of over eighty mutual fund companies that have sites on the Web, visit the Fundlink Web site at *http://www.webcom.com/~fundlink/fundlink.html.*

INITIAL PUBLIC OFFERINGS

Many Internet technology-based companies are started and run by young entrepreneurs like Marc Andreessen who have little money to provide capital for their companies. Because of the dynamic nature of the Internet, these companies need to find ways to fund the building and expanding of their companies to keep up with the expanding Internet. One way for a company to do this is through an Initial Public Offering. IPOs are especially important in new technologies such as the Internet because they provide the entrepreneur with the capital to research and develop to improve his or her product, advancing technology in the process. In an IPO, the company asks an "underwriter," usually a large investment banking firm like Morgan Stanley or Goldman Sachs, to help bring these companies to the market, which the underwriter will do for a fee and a percentage of the shares of stock. The underwriter will purchase an agreed-upon number of shares from the company and then resell them to investors. The underwriting company or companies (sometimes there's more than one, or a "syndicate") have a difficult job. They must value the shares and then put them on the market for the valuation price or better. The underwriters can run into two problems when doing this. If they price the shares too low, that is, the public is buying the stock well below the valuation price, the tech company might be displeased because they think it could have gotten more money for their stock. However, if they price the shares too high, the underwriter must pay for the difference between the valuation price and the price received on the market.

IPOs are literally driving the technology sector. Between January of 1995 and April of 1996, tech IPOs accounted for roughly 36 percent of total IPOs, more than one and a half times the total of the financial and retail sectors put together. And they are necessary to the industry to allow the new, innovative companies to start up, to get the entrepreneur's ideas to the public. They also help create jobs and advance technology, so you can actually do a service to your country and make a large amount of money at the same time. If you can get in on them, that is.

The advantage to getting in on an IPO is that you can get the stock at its lowest entry-level price, before it reaches normal stock-market trading and everybody else goes after it. When companies like Netscape go public, investors who get in on the IPO early are the ones who make the really big money. Seems easy enough, right? If you are waiting for the catch, here it is. Because the underwriting company is fronting the money and taking all the risk, they justifiably believe that they have the right to sell the shares to whomever they please. This usually translates into their selling to their own clients first and to their preferred brokers second. After that, the pickings are usually slim for everyone else.

Another Internet IPO baby is the search-engine company, Yahoo, which was started by David Filo and Jerry Yang, two Stanford University electrical engineering graduate students. Filo and Yang originally built a Web search engine for their own personal use, but found that it was so well accepted by the Internet community that they began putting more and more time into it, making it into an integral part of the Web. Soon it began to take on the aspect of a business, but it was just like any other small, potentially fast-growing company on the Net—a short history and no earnings. Once again, history showed this didn't matter. Investors ate up their shares. The IPO was priced by investment bankers at $13. Trading on the NASDAQ stock exchange, the stock opened at $24.50, went as high as $43, and closed at $33. Not bad for a day's work. Filo and Yang were two more instant multimillionaires, worth $132 million apiece. The company made $850 million on the market. Although today Yahoo's stock is at a cool eighteen points, Yahoo's shares have at times traded at around eighty times their estimated 1996 revenues. With the tech sector's known resiliency, Yahoo could be back in the race at any time.

Companies like Yahoo went public for a very high price because investors are betting on their potential, not their true numbers. For example, when Microsoft went public in 1986, they dominated the market share, had 1985 earnings of $31.2 million, and a good track record. The company went public at thirty times *less* than earnings, which is the opposite of what happens with most companies today. In fact, it's not uncommon for a tech stock to trade at fifty, sixty, or even seventy times its earnings. Nevertheless, just because these companies are trading at so many times their estimated earnings does not mean that they are poor bargains. With young computer companies like Yahoo, an extremely high price-to-earnings ratio (P/E), which is the ratio that compares the current market price of a company's stock to its earnings per share, doesn't always mean that the stock is not worth the money. A high P/E can also mean that the company has tremendous growth potential. An important factor in company growth is sales. If the company has strong sales, even though it might take a while to grow in the beginning, it has a good chance of success, presuming the other indicative factors mentioned here, like good management, are positive.

HOW TO GET IN ON THE IPOS

You will remember that preferred companies and brokers are usually among those fortunate enough to get in on IPOs. If, therefore, you want to be among the fortunate few to obtain the opportunity to participate in an IPO, you normally must have an account with one of the underwriting firms, usually a full-service brokerage firm. Discount brokerages like Charles Schwab don't undertake IPOs. The more popular an IPO the more unlikely the average investor is to get in on it. Underwriters usually save the "hot" IPOs for their big clients and preferred customers, like institutions, mutual funds, and other big fish. In addition, don't expect to be able to open an account with an investment banking firm just to take advantage of an IPO. Many won't let you. Your best hope is to develop contacts, perhaps with an investor you know in the investment banking business or a "friend of a friend." If you are unhappy with this two-tier IPO system, the National Council of Individual Investors (NCII) has an on-line petition that suggests reforms in the way underwriters make IPOs available. The petition is addressed to the top twenty-one stock underwriters in America and proposes that at least 25 percent of an underwriter's IPO shares be made available to small investors. You can find the petition at *http://com.primenet.com/ncii/ipopet.html.*

Remember, when you choose an underwriting investment firm, not just any will do. Be careful of dealing with some of the smaller brokerage companies. The farther down the investment banking scale you go, the more likely you are to get in on something that somebody else doesn't want. Try to stick with the more reputable firms like Morgan Stanley, Goldman Sachs, and Prudential, if possible. If you are faced with a decision to select a less well-known firm, make sure you do plenty of research, although if you are going to expend the effort into researching one risky IPO, you might just as well be researching some good tech stocks already trading.

ARE IPOS WORTH IT?

IPOs can be wallet-breaking if you don't take advantage of them early in the initial offering day, which is difficult for the average investor to do. Say, for example, that you got in on Yahoo's IPO early in the day when the stock was listed at $24.50. If this was the case then you would make money. If you got in just at closing, when the price was $33.00, then you certainly didn't do as well as someone who bought at $24.50. The worst case scenario would be if you had bought at the day's peak price of $43.00. Still another example of how you can lose at the IPO game is Pixar, Steve Jobs's animation company that is responsible for the hit movie *Toy Story*. Pixar rose from a $22 IPO to a peak of $49.50 and then dropped to, at the time of this writing, $16.50. In this case, even the investors who grabbed the IPO shares early lost money. Although these figures will certainly continue to rise and fall with the cycles of the industry, this goes to show the risk you take participating in one of these potentially lucrative ventures. In fact, a Prudential Securities study analyzed over fifteen hundred IPOs from 1991 to 1993 and found that, on average, IPOs exceeded market returns by 10.9 percent on the *first* trading day. If investors bought at the *close* of the first day the percentage of returns was significantly lower. After the first day, IPOs underperformed the market. Another study by Jay Ritter of MIT. and Tim Loughran of the University of Iowa found that five-year returns for 4,653 IPO stocks issued between 1970 and 1990 earned 15.7 percent on average, compared with 66.4 percent for similar companies that were more established. The moral of the story is, sometimes it's just better to wait until the stock settles into its normal pattern before investing.

In fact, taking a more conservative approach and simply trading in tech stocks is definitely another moneymaking possibility. According to a recent study of 125 companies that went public in 1990, investors who bought in at the original price would have gained 77 percent on average if they had held the stock for five years. By contrast, a University of

Chicago business school survey found that the second-day buyers could expect returns of 58 percent—a less than stellar performance since the Standard and Poor's index of 500 stocks rose 78.5 percent over the same period. The point is that it might just be worth it to invest in already trading tech stocks and put your time and energy into understanding and researching the tech-sector stocks instead of trying to find a way to get into the IPO loop. Indeed, expert investors usually recommend that individual investors stay out of the IPO market. If they do want to get into IPOs, it is generally recommended that they purchase some of the IPO mutual funds.

INTERNET INVESTMENT INFORMATION SERVICES

Despite what you've heard here, if you've got a gambling spirit and want to invest in some IPOs or anything else for that matter, the Internet itself is abuzz with places to locate help for the would-be investors. Anything from allowing electronic trading to providing chat lines where investors can discuss the latest and greatest stocks are available. Following are descriptions of some of these services and where to find them. Reuters on AOL has an IPO diary that lists all the IPOs coming out in the next few months, with the names of the underwriters. Portfolio Accounting World Wide (PAWWS) Financial Network (*http://www.pawws.com*) also has a link to subscribe to an IPO newsletter, although this one is not free. You have to pay a subscription fee. There are actually numerous IPO newsletters out there from which you can choose. PAWWS also gives links to brokers who offer discounts for on-line traders. This site also has a variety of on-line investment information that it offers for various fees.

Investment forums like the *Motley Fool* on AOL and *Waaco Kid Hot Stocks Forum* have allegedly moved stock prices just by their own influence. In one instance, the Waaco Kid tip sheet gave a favorable review to Guardian Insurance Financial Services and on-line investors listened so well that the stock increased almost four points in a month. The Motley Fool, named after a quote from Shakespeare's *As You Like It,* was started by brothers David and Tom Gardner and has been called the most successful investment-information service in cyberspace, enjoying more than two hundred thousand hits per month. It started out only with the publication of investment information on-line. Soon, however, private investors started exchanging information on the Fool's on-line service and suddenly there was a nationwide investment dialogue about a small company, Iomega, that manufactured a disk called the Zip drive that holds more than seventy times the data of a conventional floppy. Investors everywhere started getting in on the act, providing information on the company, calling up their local computer stores, asking about the product, inspecting the plant, and checking out the parking lot to count the cars. The problem Iomega had was that people really didn't know if the small company could keep up with the potentially large production levels that the market might demand. Most Wall Street investors thought that a larger copycat company might come along and steal the market from Iomega, doing the job better and faster. The collection of on-line information, which was well ahead of any information the Wall Street analysts had, verified that Iomega was indeed prepared to handle the large production volumes. On-line investors then began to invest in Iomega and Iomega stocks soared from $10 to $30 in less than two months. This site became so popular that many Wall Street investors finally started getting wind of it and tuned in. This was the beginning of the on-line investing revolution. The Fools issue a disclaimer, warning the user to weigh carefully and consider the information gathered through the chat forums and other areas where investors interact with one another. Nonetheless, investment fever strikes anyway.

The Motley Fool is a great place to get investment information. The best thing about them is they don't give investment tips but they actually teach you how to invest. It is definitely the best on-line forum for investing available on the World Wide Web. They even have investment portfolios in which they have invested their own money to demonstrate different methods of portfolio management. In addition to their forum on AOL they maintain a site on the Internet at *http://fool.web.aol.com//fool_mn.htm.*, but it has limited services because the full-service site is on AOL. The Internet site does have some good investment information, though, such as FAQs, press releases, their "Fool Portfolio," and best picks, etc.

Other companies have since been made or broken on these on-line forums. One company, Zytec Corporation, a computer equipment manufacturer, was one of the companies whose shares were negatively affected by Motley Fool. Zytec's shares fell 20 percent after it was dropped from a model portfolio on the Fool. Most of the people who post on these boards are amateur investors, but they do have the power to influence the market.

Web Finance (*http://nestegg.iddis.com/webfinance*) offers *Nest Egg* magazine, an on-line finance magazine. You can also get access to Barron's

Online at this site, in addition to plenty of other financial information. Registration is free.

Silicon Investor (*http://www.techstocks.com*) lists the quarter's best and worst performers, along with information on each company listed. Stock quotes are offered with only a fifteen-minute delay from the market ticker tape. Industry news, links to other sites, investor groups where you can exchange investment information and access to various company profiles are also offered at this site and, again, registration is free.

Investools (*http://www.investools.com*) offers free registration, but you only get $5 worth of reports. After that you have to pay a certain amount for each report you select. There is, however, free news and newsletter headlines. They have a wealth of information, for example, Standard & Poor's stock reports containing information on over 4600 U.S. stocks.

Zacks Investment Research (*http://aw.zacks.com*) gives Information on what expert analysts think of your stocks. Analyst estimates can and do influence stock prices.

Electronic Data Gathering Analysis and Retrieval (EDGAR) (*http://www.sec.gov/edgarhp.htm*) is the Securities and Exchange Commissions (SEC) electronic database on all recent filings of companies, as the SEC, on May 11, 1996, requires all publicly traded companies registered with them to file their disclosure forms electronically. This site contains all filed SEC documents, including easy accessibility to such useful data as annual reports (10K) and quarterly reports (10Q).

Wall Street Journal (WSJ) Interactive Edition (*http://update.wsj.com*) has, for a fee, news updates, company reports, and stock quotes.

Quote.com (*http://www.quote.com/info/free.html*) provides a large amount of financial information, including stock quotes, information on earnings, real-time and historical news headlines, market index charts including Dow Jones, Standard and Poor's 500, and NASDAQ. Data for major industry groups including Internet stocks, and much more can be found at this site, which also has specialized services for stocks ranging in price from $9.95 to $80.00 and up.

TRADING STOCKS ON THE INTERNET

A Forrester Research study estimates that there are eight hundred thousand on-line investment accounts. Estimates are that by 1998 there will be 1.2 million. This is still a small percentage compared with the sixty million conventional brokerage accounts currently open in the U.S.

A serious problem with the development of electronic trading is the security issue. Not many companies want to risk a security breach and the technology to present it is not readily available.

ON-LINE BROKERAGES

A brokerage firm is the most common place through which investors purchase shares of stock. It is licensed by state and federal authorities to buy and sell securities, such as stocks and bonds. The brokerage firms buy and sell investors' securities in the various stock exchanges. The three big ones are the New York Stock Exchange (NYSE), the American Stock Exchange (AMEX), and the National Association of Securities Dealers Automated Quotation System (NASDAQ) Exchange. The exchanges are places that oversee the buying and selling of stock and are governed by their own regulations, as well as the SEC, which oversees the entire securities industry. Although the NYSE is the oldest exchange, and where many of the more established companies can be found such as American Express, Disney, and McDonald's, the NASDAQ is where many of the technology stocks are traded. The NASDAQ is the newest of the three exchanges and is the most technically advanced, doing all of its transactions via computer with no throngs of investors littering the floors with slips of paper. This makes it an appropriate choice on which to trade tech stocks like Microsoft, Netscape, and Yahoo.

Traditionally, stocks were traded by full-service brokerage firms, which usually consist of an investment banking division, research division, and retail division responsible for buying and selling investors' stock. These types of firms always charge hefty commissions for transactions. Although they do offer research and other services, what you are paying for mostly is a famous name, like Kidder Peabody or Merrill Lynch. Commissions are how the stockbrokers make money for themselves and the brokerage. This can cause a conflict of interest because the brokers push the stocks that are most profitable for the firm and themselves. Some brokerage firms have been known to "churn" your stock; this is a procedure by which they keep buying and selling so they can get commissions from your stock, because they get paid on the number of transactions they complete, not whether they make money for you. These companies, especially the large firms, earn most of their profits in IPOs. It is also what causes them to be biased. These firms don't like to write negative reports about companies because it's not good for business. If they already have an investment in a particular IPO, then it is not in their interest to give that company a bad report. If they did, investors might not buy up the shares, resulting in a loss for the underwriting firm. Also, they have to solicit other companies to do IPOs. A firm that gives negative reports to one of its clients won't drum up business. Accordingly, there is no way these companies can be objective.

Before 1974, the commissions on securities transactions were fixed. No matter what firm you did business with, the cost was set. In 1974, the SEC deregulated the retail industry. Brokerage firms could charge whatever they wanted. The free hand of competition did its job. This was the start of the discount brokerages like Charles Schwab. These firms pay their brokers a fixed salary, which reduces the conflict of interest. These brokerages don't provide the research and investment information that the full-service firms do—some don't provide any at all—but they don't need to. First of all, most research you get from the full-service brokerages can be found on your own, over the Internet. Modern technology allows most people to get up-to-date investment information to do their own research and call in their own trades. Discount brokerages also don't do IPOs. You still pay commissions on transactions from these discount brokerages, but not as high as to full-service houses. You can usually save 50 to 80 percent this way.

Some of the discount brokerages have started to allow trading over the Internet. Charles Schwab, a discount broker, for example, has a site on the Web at *http://www.schwab.com.* However, discount brokerages give limited services on the net just as they do everywhere else. If you trade over the Net, you get 10 percent off your trade. New customers have to call for an appointment to register (1–800–435–4000) and they'll simply be given a password. With their free user ID they can view on-line prospectuses, documents that disclose a company's financial and business plans to potential securities purchasers. Schwab also provides services such as access to real-time on-line stock quotes, free mutual fund quotes, e-mail, and more. You can additionally pay for up-to-the-minute, twenty-four-hour, seven-days-a-week news and more advanced research. If you want to make trades on-line you have to buy special software, which will cost you about $30. This is an insignificant amount compared to the commissions other firms will charge you. Schwab does, however, require a minimum of $1,000 to open an account, which is not unusual at any discount firm. If you have problems on-line, you can call for personal assistance.

Just as the discount service firms replaced the full-service firms for many individual investors, electronic trading firms are threatening the existence of both, although neither likes to admit it. The electronic sites allow you to make your own trades from your keyboard, anytime, and also offer a host of free and low-cost investment information. These electronic sites don't have to support brokers, researchers, or pay for big offices, and so don't have to charge the commissions of the full-service firms or even the discount firms. One of the more popular Internet trading brokerages is E*Trade (*http://www.etrade.com*), which allows you to place your trades right there on the Net. There is limited service for public access like twenty-minute delayed stock quotes and E*Trade news. Once you register, which means sending them your initial deposit for an account ($1,000 for regular and $2,000 for margin accounts), you are privy to on-line investment information and research. It is simple point-and-click trading. Just like many traditional brokerage firms, there is an initial deposit of $1,000. The commissions are 15 to 25 percent of those of some of the bigger discount and full-service firms. They still bill you the traditional way because the security technology isn't yet advanced enough. Many people are still concerned about making trades over the Internet. Although placing orders on the Net is just as safe as using the phone, it may be comforting to know that most reputable electronic trading firms, such as E*Trade, carry industry-standard insurance policies, usually insuring each account up to $10.5 million.

The future of securities trading for small Internet-based companies is likely to advance in the direction of companies actually selling their own stock right over the Web. In fact, it has already happened. A company by the name of Spring Street Brewing Company decided to conduct its initial public offering over the Web as a result of their not being able to attract underwriters. They sold their stock directly to the public. Soon they had 3,500 stockholders and had raised $1.6 million. After their own successful IPO they created Wit-Trade, a virtual exchange on the company's Web site where Spring Street Investors can post buy and sell offers.

Ex–Kidder Peabody vice president, Steve Wunsch, actually took trading on the Internet one step further: he opened up his own stock exchange! Wunsch's Arizona Stock Exchange (AZX), with offices in Phoenix, San Francisco, and New York, is the first and only virtual stock exchange in the country. The SEC currently limits AZX's trading to off-market hours—3 P.M. to 5 P.M. eastern standard time each business day.

By allowing investors to trade directly on his market, Wunsch reduces the price of trading to 75 percent of what it would cost to trade on one of the major exchanges. Don't expect to do any trading on AZX right now, though. They still don't allow individual investors to get in on the action. Nevertheless, AZX may be the wave of the future for stock exchanges.

It is questionable whether or not the Internet will fundamentally change the securities industry, but it does offer an opportunity for companies like Spring Street Brewing and the Arizona Stock Exchange to participate in an industry whose barriers to entry were at one time virtually insurmountable for the small entrepreneur.

INVESTMENT SOFTWARE

There are roughly 550 investment-software programs now on the market, most of which are made for IBM computers. The American Association of Individual Investors (AAII) puts out the *Individual Investor's Guide to Computerized Investing,* which lists and explains investment software. The popular finance software Quicken has a portfolio management program. There are also screening programs like ProSearch and U.S. Equities that eliminate stocks you don't want to buy. Some programs like Tipnet, which also has a Web site at *http://www.tipnet.com,* offer statistics and textual information on over 77,000 stocks, mutual funds, and bonds, for fees ranging from $10 to $35 per month. Be careful, however, not to rely on these programs too much. The stock market requires a combination of critical analysis and instincts as well as a good supply of hard information.

ON-LINE INVESTMENT FRAUD

Because of the sheer volume of securities information being exchanged back and forth on the Net, mostly by amateur investors, there is a great opportunity for scam artists to take advantage of unsuspecting souls. The SEC offers hints for protection of the public at their Web site *http://www.sec.gov.*

One good rule is to avoid on-line "pyramid" schemes. Perfect for the on-line world because of the potential number of people someone can reach, pyramid schemes are an omnipresent danger all over the Internet, securities trading being no exception. In fact, Internet Underground recently featured an article about a company called Fortuna Alliance that duped forty thousand investors out of roughly $6 million. "Fortuna Alliance" billed themselves as a cooperative profit-sharing association. They solicited purchases for an "elite" membership costing $250 from their company. The membership, humorously enough, entitled the buyer to start his or her own profit-making pyramid. As new Fortuna members, users were told that they would be placed at the bottom of the money pyramid, but as soon as additional users joined the cooperative, they would move up in rank and receive an increasingly larger percentage of the profit. This scheme is apparently based on the Fibonacci sequence, a formula devised by thirteenth-century Italian mathematician Leonardo Fibonacci, whose work has been corrupted into an endless number of pyramid schemes in every imaginable way. It turns out that a close analysis of the numbers shows that just to break even, the forty thousand members who signed up with Fortuna with an initial investment of $250 would need 1.2 million new members to join the program in the next year to see any return at all. If by some miracle the 1.2 million did sign up with Fortuna, they would require over thirty million new members to join the program in order to break even. Currently, the Fortuna Alliance defendants are hiding out in Belize, and the location of the $6 million collected so far is unknown. According to the Federal Trade Commission's (FTC) senior attorney Randy Brook, this is the FTC's twelfth case involving the Internet.

You should also watch out for a scam known as the "Pump and dump." Messages will be posted urging readers to buy a stock or sell before it goes down. The investor may be someone who will gain if the stock is bought or sold. Another good rule is don't buy stock from someone using an alias. Watch out for offshore scams. If a deal is proposed offshore, remember it's harder to track your money if it leaves the country.

Always check to see if the company you are dealing with is registered. If the company is not registered or has not filed a Form D with the SEC, notify the SEC at 202–942–8090. Companies raising more than $1 million are required to be registered with the SEC. Those raising under a million are required to file a Form D. This form is a brief notice including the names and addresses of company owners and promoters, but little else. If you don't find the proper registration, call the SEC at the above number and check with your local securities regulator. Always investigate the company before you invest. Check with state securities regulators or the SEC. Make sure there have been no complaints listed about the company, its managers, etc. In working with the Internet, don't assume that your on-line provider or service has approved or even checked out the investment. Before you invest, always obtain written financial information, such as a prospectus, annual report, offering circular, and financial statements. Compare the information with what you read on-line. The old rule of investing still applies. Research. Research. Research.

The Internet presents new opportunities for the investment field as it does for all others. However, the freewheeling Internet is also especially positioned to do you damage in an area like securities trading, that is dangerous even without the added factor of the Internet. Therefore, temper your excitement at this moneymaking opportunity with extra care.

1 2
Keeping the Money Safe

EVERYONE HAS HEARD THE STORIES ABOUT WILY HACK-
ers lurking in the digital shadows, ready to gain entrance into anyone's
computer and steal or destroy whatever they find there. This is a very
real threat to Internet commerce and is a large part of the reason many
consumers have been wary about transferring sensitive data, like credit
card information, over the Internet. In fact, a survey done by *Survey.Net,*
a Web site that conducts ongoing, interactive studies, ran a trial to measure Internet shopping habits. When consumers were asked if they were
worried about giving credit card information over the Internet in a nonsecure transaction, 67 percent of the respondents replied "yes." When
asked the same question about a secure transaction, only 35.6 percent said
"yes."

As you know, the Internet was not built with privacy in mind. It is
more analogous to a public mall than a private meeting place. This "village green" atmosphere obviously has its advantages, such as the free flow
of information. There are also, however, disadvantages. Anyone who
really wants to can eavesdrop on your monetary exchanges. As a result,
individuals who need a secure communications environment must take

certain measures to ensure privacy. The future of electronic commerce on the Internet is predicated on the ability to conduct secure transactions in an efficient and economical manner. Fortunately for the aspiring Internet merchant, there are now several ways in which to accomplish this. Here we will focus on current and future methods of transactional security over the Internet, as well as give a brief historical background of the methods used.

METHODS OF PAYMENT OVER THE INTERNET

There are a number of different methods by which to conduct financial transactions for your Internet business. The simplest of all is that you can conduct your commercial transactions off the Net altogether, by listing a phone number on your site that your customers can call to make the transaction. Many companies selling on the Net still use off-site payment methods.

Another way of avoiding the necessity to deal with the security issue is simply to conduct your transactions via unsecured e-mail. Although this seems to be the most hassle-free approach, it does have two drawbacks: (1) There are many customers who are unwilling to send their credit card numbers or other sensitive financial information over the Internet; and (2) Conducting secure transactions over the Internet is now relatively cheap and simple, as was pointed out earlier with the Microsoft Merchant Server example, and your customers may, therefore, wonder why you are failing to offer such a service.

There are essentially three types of secure electronic transactions. They are:

1. Encrypted credit cards
2. Electronic payment systems
3. Digital cash

Here is how they work.

ELECTRONIC TRANSACTIONS

Electronic transactions on the Internet are made secure by what is called encryption. Put very simply, this is the scrambling of data into some unreadable form. The scrambled data is then sent over the Internet where it is translated back into something comprehensible by the use of a "key," a decoder program. If any hacker types should intercept the message in transit, it would be difficult if not impossible to decode without having the special key. The principle is essentially that of the secret decoder rings you used to find in boxes of Cracker Jack. With private encryption, only the one individual who owns the "decoder ring" would be able to unscramble and read the transmitted message, in this case data that pertains to a payment transaction. Don't be intimidated by this high-tech update to a classic toy, however. Each of the transactional security systems described here perform their functions automatically. All you have to do is buy and install the appropriate software. To truly understand how secure Internet transactions work, however, it is necessary to explain briefly a few basics of cryptography.

Cryptography comes from the Greek words *kryptós ló*, meaning "hidden word." Traditional cryptography is based on the sender and receiver having the same "secret key" to both scramble and unscramble the data and is called, straightforwardly enough, secret key cryptography. The key is not, of course, the metal kind you insert in a door lock, but rather a mathematical formula or algorithm on which an encryption program is based. The problem with this type of cryptography is that the sender and receiver of the data must both have copies of the private key. If Alice wants to send a message to Bob, then Alice must somehow send the private key to Bob as well. This could be done via telephone, snail mail, or some other form of transmission, which itself could easily be compromised, and so the problem of breached security is reintroduced into the procedure. If someone intercepted the key, he or she could then read every message sent by Alice. Because all keys in a secret key cryptography system must remain concealed, a difficulty with secret key crypto is maintaining secure key management, the safe generation, transmission, and storage of keys. This problem is the reason Internet transactions are based on another kind of encryption technology called "public key" cryptography.

The concept of public key cryptography was introduced in 1976 by Whitfield Diffie and Martin Hellman to solve the key management problem. In public key cryptography, each person is given not one, but a pair of keys. The first is designated the *public* key and the other the *private* key. The public key can be distributed to as many people as one pleases, but the private key remains in the hands of only one person, and thereby increases security.

The key holder can give out the public key to whomever he or she chooses. Nevertheless, the only person who can read the outgoing messages is the private key holder. Say, for example, that Bob and Carol want to send an encrypted message to Alice. Alice would send Bob and Carol copies of her public key over the Internet. Bob and Carol would encrypt their messages using Alice's public key and send their respective messages to Alice. Even though Bob and Carol have received Alice's public key, Bob and Carol cannot read each other's messages because to do that you must have the private key which is in the possession of only Alice. Even if a hacker intercepted Alice's public key, he or she still could not read Alice's messages without access to the private key in Alice's exclusive control.

Public key cryptography is also more convenient because it involves an element called a public key ring. A public key ring is no more than a computer operated by a reputable company known for its integrity that handles the distribution of encryption keys for other parties. With this technology, a public key belonging to a private individual or business can be stored on a key ring company's server, authorized to hold public keys for businesses. These keys have special encoded digital certificates attached to them that attested to the "binding" of a public key to a private individual or business. The digital certificates are based on signed and notarized authorization from the person or business wishing to use the key-ring service. It should be noted that this part of the system necessitates the encryption user having an element of trust in the key-ring company. Nevertheless, certificates help prevent any individual from using a phony key to impersonate someone else. The simplest form of certificate would contain a public key and the name of the key owner. Along with this, most contain an expiration date, the name of the authorizing party, a serial number, and other identifying features.

The key-certification process goes as follows: if Alice wanted to send an encrypted message to Bob, Alice could either e-mail Bob for the public key directly, or alternatively, contact the party authorized to hold Bob's public key. Either way the key arrives with a digital certificate attesting to the association between the key and its owner. For maximum convenience, a third party, probably a key-ring company, stores the keys so that no key swapping is necessary between the parties.

Another advantage to using public key cryptography is the ability to digitally sign documents for authentication. Digital signatures are actually more secure than paper signatures because they are harder to forge.

They make detection of document alteration easier because any change in a signed document will be revealed when the document goes through the verification process. Digital signatures are a very important part of Internet commerce because they enable legally binding contracts to be executed electronically. The digital attestation process affirms not only the contents of the message but the identity of the signer. This process makes transactions on the Internet nonrepudiable, that is, a message or contract cannot be denied after the fact. If someone's digital signature is on an electronic document, that person cannot deny that he or she entered into the contract without knowledge.

Here's how the digital signature process works: You send your digital signature to a certifying authority. Then the certifier sends you an electronic certificate. You, in turn, present this certificate along with your signature when sending a signed document. Finally, the certificate is used to look up a copy of your electronic signature, and the copy is compared with the registered signature in the database of the key holder.

RSA Data Security, Inc. is the public key cryptographic system most widely used on the Internet. Over seventy-five million of its encryption and authentication technologies are in use. It was invented in 1977 by Ron Rivest, Adi Shamir, and Leonard Adleman, who obviously used the initials of each of their last names for the name of their company. The RSA technology system's name is found on cryptography products all over the world. It is considered the de facto standard for cryptography. Adoption of RSA has grown to the extent that industry standards of related products and services are being written to accommodate usage with the RSA line. RSA has a patent on their production items and so a license is needed to make or sell anything using RSA products or the company's proprietary technology. RSA, however, usually allow free, noncommercial usage of its systems for academic or university research purposes.

ENCRYPTED CREDIT CARDS

The majority of transactions on the Web are carried out via the exchange of credit card information. Because credit cards are already widely used and accepted by financial institutions, the comfort level of both merchant and consumer is high, and it is a good basis on which to build further trust in payment transactions over the Internet. Most secure credit card transactions are done over the Internet by what is called session-level security protocols, which provide a way to encrypt communications between servers and Web browsers. There are basically two types of these security protocols. The first is Secure Sockets Layer Protocol or SSL, which was developed by Netscape and is available on their browsers, as well as on Microsoft's Internet Explorer. The other standard security protocol is Secure Hypertext Transfer Protocol or S-HTTP, which is a secure version of HTTP, the general protocol for the World Wide Web. Both protocols are designed so that no special action is required to use the security programs. All that elaborate key swapping and authenticating described earlier is done by the programs themselves. The user simply points and clicks. Once again you are being introduced here to systems that are considered the de facto Internet standard, this time for securing Web monetary transactions. SSL provides a form of transactional security that is sufficient to support simple applications like the transfer of credit card data over the Internet. S-HTTP provides the same protection as SSL, but also has additional tools that lend security to more complex functions, such as digital signature capability. As a result, S-HTTP supports nonrepudiable document exchanges, which is its primary advantage over SSL.

With SSL and S-HTTP, the buyer still has to use his or her own credit card, but the number is encrypted. As a result, these transactions rely on a preexisting relationship between the user and a traditional credit card company or banking institution. In this situation, how then do you ensure that your business can offer secure credit card payment? That depends on whether you decide to open your digital storefront by using an Internet service provider (ISP) or building your own Web site. Whatever you elect to do, you must make sure that you are operating on a secure server, supporting either SSL or S-HTTP.

If you plan to use an ISP for your Web store, you are going to have to call around to see whether or not the ISP you are considering has a server incorporating the use of SSL or S-HTTP. Many ISPs don't yet support secure transactions. Even if they do, however, the levels of security they offer may not all be the same. Also part of your job, then, is to find out what type and level of security the ISP you are considering has available. For example, some will simply offer only the secure transfer of data such as credit card numbers. Others will do much more, actually clearing the credit card for you and providing you with a merchant ID number, the item required to test whether or not the card will clear. The following are some good questions to ask any prospective ISP. Does the ISP operate on a secure server? What level of secure transactions does the ISP support? How much does the ISP charge per secure transaction or is there a flat rate for the service? Does the ISP offer the merchant the service of clearing credit card transactions?

An additional transaction you must consider for its security aspect is the interactive order form. HTML and Common Gateway Interface (CGI) scripts are programs that allow for the creation of interactive customer order forms and prompts to make possible the entering of financial information. The better ISPs will provide such programs for you. If they don't, be careful. You will then be faced with having to hire a consultant, who is likely to charge $45 to $100 per hour to create such scripts for your business.

If, on the other hand, you are going to build your own site, you are not only going to be responsible for ensuring that your server supports secure transactions, but that it is secure in other ways as well. Nonsecure servers obviously don't have a way to protect information either coming from or going to an Internet user. This is why it now becomes an additional task to see that your server has the proper security levels to support safe customer transactions. Netscape servers are very popular with Internet businesses for this reason, as they come equipped with SSL. Future Netscape servers will soon support S-HTTP as well. Netscape servers come in a variety of configurations, offering various levels of security and ability to protect commercial transactions. More information on them can be found on the Web at *http://www.netscape.com*. There is also a company called OpenMarket with a Web site at *http://www.openmarket.com,* that offers servers supporting both SSL and S-HTTP protocols, as well as server software packages for Web merchants. These software packages include store-building tools and commerce tools such as real-time credit card payment and sales tax calculation capabilities.

Whether you choose to operate your own server, or pay someone to operate it for you, there are other security issues that must be dealt with. Protocols like SSL and S-HTTP only secure data during its transmission. They do not provide what is called end-to-end encryption. This means that when the credit card numbers are transmitted from your customer to your Web site or server, the data is already comprehensible. Clearly then, when this information is on your server, the server invites attack. If a hacker were to break into your server, he or she could steal huge sums of money via your unencrypted credit card information, much as Kevin Mitnick, the headline-making info-thief you'll read about in chapter 16 did. In light of this, credit card information, or any sensitive data for that matter, should not normally be stored on a computer connected to the Internet. If it is, it better be encrypted. You can also have what is called a "firewall," which is essentially a computer that stands in the way of your server. The firewall allows certain information to come in, but not to go out. This is another technical procedure you can either read about yourself or discuss with your ISP.

One problem that has arisen in affecting the progress of Internet security is that SSL and S-HTTP can't communicate with one another. If your server supports only SSL, then your customers must have SSL on their browsers. Consequently, if they have either Netscape Navigator or Internet Explorer as their Web browser, the two brands that together account for a huge percentage of those actually in use, there should be no problem, as both these browsers utilize SSL. At one time, there had also been a disparity in conformity between the two major credit card companies, Visa and MasterCard, a problem which now appears to be resolved. Originally, MasterCard and Visa had come up with separate security standards for their Internet transactions. MasterCard was working with IBM and Netscape to create one protocol, while Visa was working with Microsoft to create another. Having two different security standards would mean that merchants and banks would have to either choose one system or support both. With pressure from the banking and business sectors to create a unified standard rather than force the purchase of two different systems, MasterCard and Visa developed what is known as Secure Electronic Transactions (SET), which will soon become the new standard for Internet credit card transactions. The security protocol that the two companies will support is the S-HTTP. This future unified standard of Internet credit card commerce has brought together companies such as competitors Netscape and Microsoft, though it is still a likely bet that these companies will in some manner again enter into heavy contention to provide browser and server software for secure electronic transactions. As a result of SET, as well as its ability to support digital signatures, S-HTTP is expected to become the dominant security standard on the Web.

ELECTRONIC PAYMENT SYSTEMS

Electronic payment systems operate on a credit/debit system. A third party is necessary for the transactions. The two leading systems are

CyberCash, with a Web site at *http://www.Cybercash.com* and First Virtual with its Web site at *http://www.fv.com.*

CyberCash is one of the main electronic payment system companies. It was founded in August 1994, and it uses the public key cryptography system based on RSA technology to encrypt the consumer's credit card number. Electronic payment systems have some positive features that simple encrypted credit card systems do not. To accomplish security, an electronic payment system requires that a piece of specialized software be downloaded and installed into the customer's computer, and, as stated earlier, a third party. The specialized software makes the entire transaction a complete point-and-click affair, quick and easy. The software also offers end-to-end encryption. The third party can be thought of simply as a specialized banker who exists exclusively to process Internet sales, for with electronic payment systems, the entire payment transaction takes place 100 percent on-line.

CyberCash consists of three main parts: (1) the "wallet" for consumers; (2) the Secure Merchant Payment System (SMPS) for merchants; and (3) CyberCash's secure servers, which are now being operated by the CyberCash company itself on its site, but will eventually become available on a license basis to banks and processors. The CyberCash "wallet" is simply software that resides on a consumer's computer to enable secure transactions. This software can be downloaded free of charge at any time from the CyberCash Web site or through any participating merchant. Once the software is installed, CyberCash works with the customer's browser to connect to any participating merchant sites. The customer establishes a special wallet software, providing identification that binds the credit card to consumer identification for authentication purposes. The customer automatically opens his or her wallet by activating a point-and-click button displayed on the participating merchant's Web page.

The SMPS for merchants allows the merchant to conduct transactions with the customer. The software resides on the merchant's server and enables secure transactions. As a merchant, it doesn't really matter whether or not you have your Web site on an ISP or on your own server, the process is still the same. You simply download the SMPS onto your site and you are then able to conduct transactions through CyberCash's server. The software acts like an electronic cash register, from the time of authorizing the transactions, through providing receipts, to handling voids and returns.

CyberCash's server provides a link between merchants, customers on the Internet, and their banks. From a bank's point of view, arriving CyberCash transactions look exactly like traditional purchase transactions.

Cybercash's transactions are fully automated and take less than a minute to complete. The process starts with the customer visiting the merchant's site and selecting an item to buy. After the customer chooses, the merchant's Web page will display a payment icon. Then the customer clicks on the icon, which prompts the merchant's server to send the customer an electronic order form. The customer's browser software then automatically opens the wallet. The customer is given the option to select a mode of payment, either credit card or electronic checks. The customer sends the encrypted information to the merchant, and the merchant's computer sends both the customer's encrypted transaction information and the merchant's encrypted order form to the CyberCash server. The server proceeds to decrypt the message and authenticate the customer's wallet, as well as the merchant information, which is then sent to the off-the-Internet financial organization. The request is processed and sent back to CyberCash's server for forwarding to the merchant and on to the consumer. The merchant sends the customer a digital receipt. Transactions can be voided or returned. The customer's wallet is debited or credited accordingly and the merchant is likewise appropriately credited or debited.

The credit card information is passed on to the merchant and to CyberCash's server using the previously mentioned RSA public key technology. The customer's credit card number is normally invisible to the merchant but it can be supplied at the bank's option. Making the credit card number invisible to the merchant protects the consumer against "shell" storefronts that make an illegal practice of simply collecting credit card numbers and then disappearing. CyberCash charges a fixed fee of roughly thirty cents per transaction.

First Virtual (FV) became fully operational on October 15, 1994. FV is unique in that it does not use encryption for its electronic transactions, but uses a Personal Identification Number or PIN number in place of an encrypted credit card number to accomplish a secure transaction. Therefore, the customer's credit card number is never sent over the Internet or entered into his or her computer. FV does not need encryption since no sensitive information is transferred. If someone got hold of a PIN it would be worthless and meaningless. Instead, the data is stored off the Internet and assigned the PIN number associated with the customer's credit card, which is, in turn, used to make purchases. This requires a prearranged contract with First Virtual to acquire a special PIN number. All FV transactions are conducted and confirmed via e-mail.

To participate in the First Virtual Program the following items are required.

For buyers:

1. a private Internet e-mail account
2. a Visa or MasterCard
3. a completed FV registration form

For sellers:

1. a private Internet e-mail account
2. a bank account accepting direct deposits via the U.S. Automated Clearinghouse System—you don't need a credit card merchant account.
3. a completed FV registration form

The costs for the FV systems are as follows: For customers, there is a $2 annual fee to have a PIN number assigned. A fee is charged to the credit card when the customer registers as a buyer and annually thereafter. For sellers, there are payments of $10 per PIN, twenty-nine cents per sale, plus 2 percent of the selling price (the amount that Visa and MasterCard charge for using their credit card systems). There is also a $1 processing fee when sales proceeds are deposited in the bank account.

Additional storage and transaction fees are charged if a FV service known as InfoHaus is used. InfoHaus is a mall-like operation for products that are informational in nature. InfoHaus allows the buyer to review an information product before deciding whether to pay. Under these circumstances, it is obviously not possible for the seller to wait for the buyer to confirm a transaction before delivering the requested merchandise. Account activity of the consumer is reviewed on a continuous basis and abuse of this privilege will result in termination. Payment to the merchant is via direct deposit into the merchant's bank account.

A second way to take advantage of the First Virtual system is by having a Web site supported by the seller's own server. The merchant is then required to collect buyer's PINS and send them to FV by snail mail. More conveniently, the process can be automated with software provided by FV, or, alternatively, the merchant can write his or her own program. FV encourages the "try before you buy" policy when selling information products, but acknowledges that it is not appropriate for all products. A business that does not wish to be part of the InfoHaus Mall and also does not maintain its own server cannot participate in the First Virtual system.

DIGITAL CASH

The first two payment methods discussed here continue to include the use of credit cards to a greater or lesser degree. There are still many people who are hesitant about conducting transactions over the Internet by exchange of credit card information, no matter how it is masked or secured. Digital cash, also called electronic cash, might allay some of these fears by eliminating a portion of the buyers' and sellers' risk. In reality, electronic cash transactions are done daily by all the world's banks and are hardly a concept that is new, although at this time it should be noted that encrypted credit cards and electronic payment systems are much more prevalent on the Internet than are digital cash systems. Nevertheless, the technology is being made available to the general public.

David Chaum, cryptographer and recognized Internet guru, is one of the pioneers of electronic cash technology. Chaum compares digital cash to an ATM on the Internet; you can withdraw and deposit cash right on the Net. Electronic cash systems are based on exchanging real money for electronic money and allowing the consumer to make purchases over the Internet simply by an electronic cash transaction. These transactions are allegedly untraceable, just as if you were making a purchase using paper money. The anonymity that digital cash can provide has made the government, law-enforcement agencies, and many financial institutions wary of the technology. Law-enforcement experts believe that the speed with which an electronic cash transaction can be concluded, coupled with the anonymity, would provide the perfect environment for criminals to hide and launder illicit cash. Nevertheless, electronic cash is slowly making its way into progressively more commercial transactions on the Web. In fact, this technology fills a hallowed Internet goal: complete interactivity and autonomous use of the Web, free of support from other supplementary businesses or institutions. In addition, it could be beneficial to businesses on the Net. The leading company for electronic cash is DigiCash, found on the Web at *http://www.digicash.com.*

DigiCash is best known for its product, ecash, a form of digital money. Ecash is intended to secure payments from any personal computer through e-mail or sent over the Internet in any other manner. With the ecash client software, a customer withdraws ecash from a participating bank and stores it on his or her computer. Your hard drive literally becomes your wallet. A consumer can spend digital money at any shop accepting ecash, without the trouble of having to open an account there, or having to transmit credit card information first. Chaum's vision for ecash is that it become the actual currency of the Web, just like paper cash is in the physical world.

In October 1994, ecash started a trial phase called "Cyberbucks." Today, over thirty thousand people are using ecash worldwide, although, as was already mentioned, this is a significantly lower number than those using encrypted credit cards or electronic payment systems. The digital money used in the Cyberbucks trial cannot be exchanged for real money, but goods and services can be purchased in more than one hundred shops that have joined the experiment by agreeing to accept ecash. The Cyberbucks trial is now closed to further participants because the number of merchants allowed to be part of the test phase has been exceeded. Nevertheless, any business interested in accepting ecash can still do so by contacting DigiCash at the above Web address.

Real banks have also begun to use ecash. The Mark Twain Bank is the first U.S. bank to issue and accept ecash. To use Mark Twain, both consumer and merchant have to obtain and install the ecash software. A consumer can then move money to its own hard drive from the ecash mint. Once the money is on the customer's hard drive, it is held there until it reaches its expiration date or it is spent. Ecash can even be attached to e-mail for person-to-person transactions.

Ecash uses public key cryptography and digital signature technology for secure transactions. CyberCash gives full support to new shops setting up on-line. Both users and shops need no special hardware to operate. Anyone can start a business accepting ecash that takes real money through an ecash issuer like Mark Twain. Merchants get paid by redeeming ecash through participating banks, which transfers money into their accounts. Merchants pay a $5 to $25 monthly fee and a $150 to $500 start-up fee. There is also a 2 to 3 percent charge for exchanging ecash into real money.

MICROTRANSACTIONS

Currently, the practice of charging for transactions that cost ten cents or less, called more commonly microtransactions, has received a lot of attention because it is a great way to charge for the single use of a search engine or the reading of a magazine on a per-use or per-page basis. The same theory applies to any information or service commodity that can be issued in small increments. This is not presently feasible over the Web. With today's technology, if a business sold goods for ten cents or less, the cost of the transaction would exceed the profit. Methods are now being developed that would execute commercial transactions over the Internet down to a penny or even a thousandth of a penny. This would allow businesses to sell and consumers to buy in piecemeal increments instead of wholes.

Microtransactions could significantly alter the commercial environment of the Web and significantly diminish the multitude of free services presently available. Right now, many people consider the Web to be an ad-based medium, meaning most Web companies rely on advertising to make their profits. With microtransactions, this could all change. Imagine being charged for a look at one picture or reading a single page out of the *Wall Street Journal*. The Web would in essence become a transaction-based medium, with literally millions of these microtransactions taking place every day. Obviously, the objective of this technology is to make the thousandth of a cent purchase worthwhile, reducing the cost of transactions to many times lower than what they are today. Since, given the way the Internet is normally employed, the usage of this microservice is so frequent, it would still add up to a huge amount of money to be made.

Regardless of where the Web goes in terms of money transactions, it must be remembered that no matter how secure you think your Web site or server is, or how secure you feel about the electronic transaction you're conducting, there is no such thing as complete security. The only secure computer is one that is unplugged from the wall and locked in your closet. Even public key technology has its weaknesses. There will undoubtedly be people of great faith who choose to leave their private keys on their computers, unencrypted and unsecured. Hackers will take advantage of this. And, of course, the keys in the public key systems are simply codes. It is an Internet rule of thumb that where there is a code there is a code-breaker. The purpose of secure transaction systems, however, doesn't need to be that of complete imperviousness. They simply have to be economically unfeasible and not worthwhile for profit-motivated hackers to attempt code-breaking.

Commercial cryptography has doubtless come a long way. In fact, the government doesn't even allow the export of many of the cryptography systems used in the U.S. because they are too advanced. If companies like RSA want to export their products, they must downgrade the technology. Cryptographic products, you see, are illegal to export unless they meet certain criteria, meaning that they actually have to be made less effective. Cryptography is closely controlled by the International Traffic and Arms Regulations. It is actually treated as a weapon. Only registered international arms dealers can trade in this potentially dangerous commodity.

The government argues that the technological advances in civilian cryptography—those that used to be made only by government agencies—are threatening national security. They argue that criminals could use public key encryption systems to conspire and commit crimes in cyberspace undetected, that this technology in the wrong hands could be a lethal weapon. As a result, the government has responded with a highly controversial proposal called the Clipper Chip. Clipper is an encryption chip supported by the government and supposedly designed to balance the needs of law-enforcement agencies with those of security for private citizens and industry. To say that Internet advocates don't approve of the Clipper Chip would be a vast understatement. The Clipper Chip has brought out the virtual Internet soapboxes in force.

The Clipper Chip works under a theory called key escrow. An escrow is simply an account managed by a third party—in this case, the government. Key escrow would require that everyone place his or her *private* key in a government account. These keys would be made available only to the government or other authorized individuals when so directed by a court-issued warrant. The government's rationale is that they have a right to eavesdrop on someone if he or she is suspected of illicit activities, much like they could with a phone tap.

Hue and cry notwithstanding, the Clipper Chip has been accepted as a U.S. government standard. In fact, a number of vendors, including AT&T, have announced products based on the Clipper Chip. Besides the privacy rights issue, many people think that the Clipper Chip is too vulnerable to attack. The escrow agencies will be the first places hackers will attack. They also believe that the Clipper keys are not secure enough, and finally, that government control of the technology will lessen competition, ultimately resulting in the sale of slow and expensive chips. The general consensus on the Clipper program, however, seems to be that it will not be accepted by enough people to become a standard. This only serves to illustrate that the security vs. privacy issues will be with us both technologically and philosophically for some time.

13
Your PC—The Biggest Moneymaker You'll Ever Know
What Equipment Do You Need and How Do You Buy It?

THE COMPUTER REVOLUTION

Marching upon us with heavy footsteps are the forces of the computer revolution. Some may remember what it was like before fax machines and cellular phones were everywhere. A few may even recall life before photocopy machines. How did businesses manage? As much as other assorted developments in office machinery have brought about important changes in the ways we do business today, they pale by comparison with the effects of the computer. Nothing except the telephone has had a more profound impact. Companies once used computers only for accounting, storing records, and word processing. Virtual offices, where employees physically stay at home and telecommute to work via the computer, are becoming more and more commonplace. Companies are already using the computer to talk between themselves, communicate with their customers, and even read their daily newspapers. Within a few years, the computer is likely to supplant the telephone, fax, and regular mail as the primary means of communication. A number of newspapers and magazines, complete with advertisements, have already gone on-line. Soon, the computer may well be the principal medium for all advertising. As you already know, you can currently order a panoply of products and services through your home computer. The use of computers for marketing is about to explode.

As the computer revolution progresses, it is becoming more and more possible to transact business without actually speaking to anyone. Many people find a true feeling of security in being able to interact fully with the world while still managing never to leave the privacy of their homes. Internet junkies who just about live inside their computers are the extreme example of this syndrome. They don't understand or believe anything unless it appears in type on a computer monitor. Any other source is suspect. The reliability of whoever was ultimately responsible for placing the information in cyberspace is seemingly unimportant. Only the vehicle of communication matters. While people that far over the edge are still out of the mainstream, the increasing importance of computers in our lives is undeniable.

There is life outside of cyberspace and hopefully that will always be true. Nonetheless, those who try to stay away from computers will find the task difficult to impossible. The computer revolution has arrived. Viewed with an eye toward all that computers can and do help us achieve, try to rejoice over the part you will play in what is to be. Brace yourself. Here comes the worst of the technobabble, administered gently and with the promise to make it as easy and painless as possible.

What is a computer? We have considered at length how computers can help you make a fortune. Now it's time to take a look at the machines themselves. Computers are simply tools that organize, store, and transfer data. Although some computers have been given humanoid names, like "Hal," they are not living creatures. Computers aren't people. They have no feelings or emotions. Computers have no soul. Most important, they don't think for themselves. The seventeenth-century French philosopher Descartes, who made famous the quote "I think, therefore I am," would have been forced to conclude that computers don't exist. When it comes to computers, make no mistake, it is you who must do the thinking.

This brings us to a key question. Just how smart do you have to be to use a computer? So many of us seem intimidated by the mere thought. Can you read and write? Are you as intelligent as that airhead who mixed up your last plane reservation? Are you able to understand this book? If your answer to any of the above is yes, then you are more than smart enough to operate a computer expertly.

Probably the single biggest skill required to use a computer successfully is the ability to type. It's not a very glamorous thought, but true nonetheless. A computer keyboard, which looks much like a typewriter, is the vehicle used to tell your computer what it should do. Models of computers that listen to the spoken word are already on the market, but are still limited to very basic functions like word processing. As the technology improves, these voice-activated computers may become more commonplace. For now, however, typing is what it takes. By the way, if you don't already know how to type or need to brush up, there are computer programs available that will teach you, that is, if you don't mind learning something from a machine that can't think for itself.

MAC VERSUS IBM

Computers come in a number of different styles and they are evolving faster than the speed of light. About thirty years ago the first computers, with names like UNIVAC and RAYDAC, were as large as army tanks. They consisted of thousands of television-style vacuum tubes, took hours or even days to wade through difficult mathematical functions, and cost millions of dollars. Today, for less than a couple thousand dollars, you can buy a new computer that sits comfortably on your lap and calculates complex mathematical problems in a matter of seconds. Hardly a month goes by without the development of yet another new computer component that is faster, smarter, and ultimately cheaper than its predecessor. In choosing what type of computer to get, you might as well relax. No matter how much you spend today or how carefully you study up before making your purchase, the model you've selected will be obsolete in a matter of months. For that reason, when buying a new computer, simply make sure the one you pick can easily be upgraded as new technology comes out, and you won't have too much to worry about.

Here will be briefly discussed the most common types of computers to assist you in selecting your own. At the outset, however, it should be emphasized that just about any kind can be used successfully to make money on the Internet. The latest bells and whistles may expand your marketing options and add to your enjoyment, but they are rarely a business necessity. Computers come in different sizes, from mainframe computers that fill a room (which are becoming obsolete) to laptop portables that can fit inside a small briefcase. This discussion will limit itself to microcomputers, better known as personal computer systems, or "PCs."

These are the ones most individuals use and are what you will find being sold at your local store.

There are two basic types of PCs. One is the Apple system, known mostly as Macintosh, or Mac for short. The other is the IBM-based system, including IBM clones such as Compaq, Packard Bell, and Dell. When reference is made to IBM here, it indicates a general type of computer, not necessarily a product directly manufactured by the IBM company. Styles of IBM computers differ according to the kind of processor they contain. The processor is actually the brain of the computer, although physically it is about the size of a soda cracker. Interestingly, processors for most IBM machines are not even made by IBM but by another company known as Intel. The most common processing system is the Intel Pentium Model, with the newest being the Pentium Pro. The various IBM models differ in the speed and efficiency with which they handle data. Speed of data transmission is measured in megahertz. The speeds available for Pentium models range from 66 to 200 megahertz. The type of processor also affects the speed of the computer. A Pentium Pro runs at 200 megahertz but will be much faster than a regular Pentium processor operating at the same speed. The Pentium Pro chip simply processes data in a more efficient manner. Moreover, there are now future plans to have a Pentium Pro at 300 megahertz and above.

Both the Mac and IBM systems, in their most complex configurations, are extremely powerful and versatile. You can easily access the Internet or any other part of the I-way from either type of machine. If you already have one or the other, there is no reason to change. If you are buying a computer for the first time, you should consider that Macs are thought to be more user-friendly and handle computer graphics brilliantly, while the IBMs are considered better business computers, manipulating non-graphical data more efficiently than Macs. With new and improved graphical software programs, however, IBM is rapidly catching up to the Mac in graphics capability. At present, there is also more business software available for IBMs, but this may be changing.

Computer processors exist that will allow you to run either Mac or IBM programs from the same machines, although there are some definite drawbacks with this solution that you should take into consideration. These machines are not worth the cost for at least three reasons. First, the IBM side of this machine runs on a very slow Pentium 66 processor, which is already obsolete in the Pentium world. Second, they are weak on software. Third, and most importantly, if you have a problem with the machine, you won't know which part of the machine is malfunctioning, the Apple or the IBM side, until you get a computer geek to look at it. Most technicians are usually experts in either Apple or IBM, not both. In short, depending on your problem, you could end up paying more than one computer technician to fix things, making repairs quite costly. Mixing two technologies is a chancy way to go. Microsoft Windows, the best-known computer software package in existence, is used in IBM-type computers to assist you in moving easily between the various other programs you have purchased and installed on your PC. One thing that Windows can do is make an IBM look and act much like a Mac. The Mac purists, however, insist that their operating system is superior. In fact, the two systems look more and more alike all the time. It is pointless to enter here into the ongoing debate about which system is better. In reality, it is probably more a matter of personal preference than anything else.

MEMORY

When purchasing a new computer, one important question you will be asked is how much "memory" you will need. A computer has two kinds of memory. One is internal and deals with the capacity of the computer to process data. The other refers to the amount of data itself that the computer is able to store. The internal memory is also called Random Access Memory, or RAM for short. You will remember that each general function you want your computer to perform, word processing, for example, requires a different program. The more sophisticated the programs you use and the more programs you install on your computer, the more RAM you will need. Most modern PCs are equipped with a minimum of eight megabytes of RAM, but can be increased to many times that number simply by adding additional memory chips that plug into a special slot. RAM can be expensive, so when comparing prices of computers, make sure you are comparing systems with comparable configurations, including RAM. How much RAM you will require depends again on the type of software you will be using and whether or not your computer is part of a network. For most personal and simple business uses, eight megabytes will probably be adequate, but twelve or sixteen is better, allowing you room to upgrade software if necessary. Here again, though, there is not much to worry about if you make a mistake. Increasing a computer's RAM is one of the simplest types of upgrades. If your software seems to run very slowly, increasing the amount of RAM may cure the problem.

Another essential component of all computers is the operating system. An operating system is a special computer program that tells the machine how to handle basic functions. Software that you buy, such as word- or data-processing programs, must be purchased in versions compatible with the operating system you select. The most common operating systems are DOS, Windows NT, OS/2, Mac OS(Apple), and UNIX. Macs almost always run on their own proprietary system made by Apple Computer. IBMs usually run on an operating system called DOS (Disk Operating System). The overwhelming majority of DOS systems come from Microsoft. Indeed, this product started Microsoft owner Bill Gates on his way to becoming the richest man in America. Other operating systems can, however, be used with IBMs. IBM itself, in an effort to steal some of Microsoft's thunder, has now developed an operating system called OS/2, which requires a rather powerful computer to work properly. You can also put a UNIX operating system on an IBM-like computer or a Mac if you want to. If you use DOS, which is still the most common operating system, you should also use the Windows program mentioned earlier. Most of the large Internet computers that keep the Net going run on the UNIX operating system, although a version of Microsoft's Windows, Windows NT, a more user-friendly operating system than UNIX, is slowly gaining popularity on the Net. As yet, it still doesn't have the full-time operating stability, but it will soon. It is unlikely that when you get started you will use UNIX on your own computer.

Generally, if you are a beginner, the best idea is to select the most common operating system, Windows, because this is the one that has the most software available for it. Because it is used so predominantly, it is also easier to find people who can help you with it when you get stuck. Almost all the software being written for use on an IBM computer requires having Windows in place. As a practical matter, then, a DOS system by itself is inadequate to run most modern software. You will have to install Windows as well. As you get more experienced with a computer and have a better feel for your particular needs, you may decide that a different operating system will better serve your needs. For starters, DOS with Windows is the simplest way to go.

Only those who have advanced Internet business interests need to look at the UNIX operating system. You should consider a UNIX operating system if the type of Internet access you are planning is the very high-level leased line, which is discussed, along with other types of access, in the next chapter. As mentioned earlier, most of the Internet networks are based on UNIX. Most individual and small computer-users will have little or no familiarity with UNIX and could probably care less about that system because common software does not usually come in a UNIX version. Nonetheless, UNIX, having been developed in the sixties, is actually one of the oldest, not to mention the most powerful computer-operating system around. UNIX is considered superior to the other common operating systems for computer networking because UNIX was specifically designed to allow many computers to access the same programs and files at the same time.

Most UNIX systems usually operate on larger, more powerful, and therefore more expensive computers than Macs or IBM PCs. There are now, however, versions of UNIX that can even be installed on the less powerful PCs. Three of the most popular versions are Solaris, BSDI, and Linux. Linux is one of the more popular versions because it can be downloaded free off the Net. Installing UNIX is considerably more complicated than the other operating systems and is therefore best left to a hired computer geek.

Often, depending on the Internet service provider (ISP) you have selected, UNIX computers can be accessed and run by other computers not operating with UNIX. The easy-to-use Internet software, for use on Macs and IBM PCs, allows you to work on a UNIX network without knowing anything about UNIX. You simply execute DOS or Mac commands while the software then invisibly converts your commands to UNIX.

Even though you will probably not buy a UNIX-based computer as you begin your moneymaking activities on the Internet, you should at least know that they exist, since UNIX is still the predominant language of the Internet. There are other networking systems out there, including AppleShare for Mac, OS/2's Warp Server, Novell's NetWare, and Windows' NT. The latter two, as you may have guessed, run on DOS-based computers. Experts are now saying that Windows NT, because it is considered to possess greater user-friendliness than UNIX, will become a more popular networking system as more and more businesses move to the Web. This is because the average business doesn't want to deal with the complexities of UNIX. As previously mentioned, Microsoft's Windows NT, however, still lacks the full-time operating stability that

UNIX has. For now, if you ever do want a computer network and intend for it to be hooked into the Internet, UNIX is still the safest way to go.

If the Internet access you choose is a fairly low-level variety, then, for Net-marketing purposes, which operating system is on your own computer won't make any difference. That is because most people accessing the Internet will be doing so through the computer of an intermediary network or ISP. The commands you enter from your keyboard are actually manipulating programs that sit on the intermediary computer, which is almost always UNIX-based. Your operating system does not come into play. When you retrieve data from the Internet, it is sent to the provider's computer, although you may elect to copy it on to yours later. With this type of Internet access, it does not make a great deal of difference what sort of computer you are using, since all the real action takes place somewhere else.

DATA STORAGE CAPACITY AND DISK DRIVES

Some of the earlier personal computers stored data only on floppy disks. We have already discussed RAM memory. RAM is the memory used internally by the computer to process data. Floppies are a way of storing the actual information the computer processes. This includes your e-mail, customer information, inventory, accounting—any data you wish your computer to store. Floppy disks also are used, at least initially, to store the software you have chosen for various functions. Almost all software you purchase will come on floppy disks.

Floppy disks are small circles of magnetic tape, much like the tape used in a tape recorder. They are housed in plastic containers that are flexible, hence the name "floppy." These disks are inserted into a portion of the computer known as the disk drive. Although the floppy commonly used to come in two sizes, 5¼ inches and 3½ inches in diameter, almost all new computers no longer have a 5¼-inch disk-drive slot, as the 3½-inch floppy has now become the standard. The floppy disk's use as a repository for data is often convenient in many situations, because floppies are inexpensive and removable. All computers come with at least one floppy drive. Floppy disks, however, have relatively limited storage capabilities, and operate rather slowly on the computer when compared with the more advanced hard disk drives to be discussed in a minute. There are now floppy disks that hold twice as much data as the older ones did. The newest hold 2.88 MB but were never accepted as the standard, a position still maintained by the old 1.44 MB. They are still very slow, however, by comparison with hard disks.

All personal computers today have hard disk drives in addition to floppy drives. A hard disk drive looks somewhat like a miniature record player. A circular magnetic disk, housed in a metal cabinet, is accessed by a needle-like apparatus. Hard disks are usually installed inside the computer and are not meant to be removed (though there are now removable versions available). Hard disk drives operate very fast and can hold huge amounts of data. A typical hard disk drive containing 1 gigabyte of storage will hold as much data as roughly 710 of the 1.44 MB size floppies. Because of the large program size of most modern software, you'll need a hard drive to take advantage of it. The larger the storage space on the drive, the more it costs. Most of the new hard drives, however, holding at least 1 gigabyte, are more than sufficient to support a number of modern software programs on your machine at one time.

There is software out that compresses computer data, enabling a hard disk drive to store as much as double its normal capacity. If there is a system failure, compressed data is harder to retrieve, but such failures are rare. Not all data can be compressed. Certain types of computer files, particularly those containing nothing but text, such as e-mail or most word processing files, will safely compress into about half the space. Other types, including most program files, may not compress at all. It is quite likely that some disk space is taken up by noncompressible files.

Another relatively new data storage device is the compact disk, or CD, which has all but replaced phonograph records and cassette tapes for music lovers. These are round, plastic disks with digitized data permanently recorded on them. CD drives are, obviously, computer drives that can play back CDs. Unlike other types of data memory we've been discussing, the data on a CD is permanently encoded and cannot be erased, written over, or changed. All you can do is read the data on the disk. Hence the name ROM, meaning Read Only Memory.

As computer software programs become more sophisticated and complex, they are taking up more and more disk space. Some of the newest software programs fill up literally dozens of floppy disks. Besides just recorded music, CDs can be used to store any type of digitized data, including computer programs, and a single CD disk can hold as much data as two hundred of the newest floppy disks. Therefore, most software programs are now being made available on CDs, and, of course, that means you need a CD-ROM drive attached to your computer to use them. Almost every prepackaged computer comes with a CD-ROM player, usually located somewhere next to the disk drive slot. CDs are many times faster than the fastest hard disk drives. They are especially popular for multimedia functions, such as video, animation, and sound. If you want to take full advantage of the CD-ROM's multimedia capabilities, namely sound and graphics, you'll probably want to get quality sound and graphics cards, as well as some good speakers.

THE SOFTWARE FACTOR IN CHOOSING HARDWARE

The key to which computer you should buy lies, to a large extent, more in the software you want to use than anything else. You will remember that it is the software you select which will control what tasks your computer can perform. The operating system, the memory size, the speed and type of processor, all these features are there only to see that the programs run at peak performance. In the Cybersell® office we happen to use IBM-style Pentium computers made by Zeos, a mail-order manufacturer, because they are powerful and so handle UNIX, as well as many business and Internet programs, efficiently. If you know you will be using a particular type of software, a good idea would be to pick your computer system on the basis of which machine will run your favorite program best. If you haven't yet decided on your software, then, when shopping for your computer, the simplest strategy is just to look for the best bargain.

MONITORS

Now let us move away from the computer itself to the monitor. A monitor looks much like a television screen. Your computer would be virtually useless without one, since everything you send or receive on your computer will be in the form of an image and the monitor enables you to see that image. Monitors, like televisions, come in many sizes, in color or monochrome, which is a single color, usually green or orange. They are also identified by their degree of resolution, which, in English, means the sharpness or clarity of the image. Most of today's color monitors have a resolution much greater than that of your television set. Your new computer will probably come with a color monitor, called SVGA (Super Video Graphics Array). When it comes to Internet marketing, the monitor is another piece of equipment where what you select doesn't matter much, as the quality has no bearing on how other people will see your Web site. That all depends on and varies with the quality of monitor that each of your individual customers has.

KEYBOARDS, CURSORS, AND MICE

You will remember that typing is the most important skill needed to work with a computer. All computers are equipped with a keyboard, which looks like the main part of a typewriter. If you are buying one separately, you may test it by pressing the keys to see if one feels better than another. Beyond that, once again, it doesn't particularly matter which you select.

When you press a key on the keyboard, the letter or symbol on the key should show up on the monitor. The cursor, appearing as a blinking light, will also be flashing on the monitor screen to show you where you are. You can move the cursor around by pressing assorted keys on the keyboard, or you may acquire another piece of equipment for this purpose called a mouse. The "mouse," or pointer, first became popular when it began being used with the early Apple computers. A mouse is a plastic device with two or three buttons. Except for the absence of fur, this device really does look in size and shape like the rodent after which it is named. By sliding the mouse on a table or "mouse pad"—a protective foam rubber pad that sits on top of your table—you can move the cursor on the monitor screen. This makes it easy to jump around the screen without having to hit a lot of keys. The mouse is particularly useful with graphical programs, including all Mac and Windows applications.

MODEMS

The modem is perhaps the single most important piece of hardware you will need for your Internet venture. A modem is an electronic device that takes data from your computer, converts it into electronic impulses, and sends it through telephone lines to the Internet. At the end of the line, another modem receives the impulses you sent and converts them back into the same format the data was in when it left your computer. That is how computers communicate. Speed is the key element to consider when choosing a modem. You will be happiest with a high-speed modem of at least 28.8 "baud" or "bps" (bits per second). Baud and bps are a measure of speed, the computer version of miles per hour. The faster your modem, the easier it will be for you to communicate with the Internet. If your computer is not already equipped with a modem, you can buy a high-speed one at a discount store for around $150, with prices dropping all the time.

Over and above speed, there are two types of modems you can choose from: internal and external. You will probably not be surprised to learn that internal modems reside inside your computer while external ones sit outside. External modems have a series of colored lights that blink on and off as data is being transferred. The lights serve a variety of diagnostic functions. Most importantly, if the lights are blinking, you know you have a connection to another computer. With an internal modem, you can tell for sure whether you have made a connection only by an indication on the computer screen or listening for the telephone connections. An additional benefit to external modems is that they are easier to install. You only have to plug it into the back of the computer. Installing internal modems can sometimes be a hassle. On the other hand, internal modems usually cost a bit less. Most new computers come already equipped with high-speed internal modems. If you already have a computer, though, and are looking for a good modem, U.S. Robotics is the brand that is considered the industry standard. Most of the computer packages you buy today, in fact around 90 percent, come already equipped with a modem/fax and sometimes even voice capability. However, much of the built-in fax software doesn't really have multiple fax capability. If you wanted to use your fax software for business purposes, you might be better off buying additional software like WinFax, which allows you to send large volumes of faxes to a large number of people.

PRINTERS

A computer monitor lets you look at everything one screen at a time, but it does not let you carry the information away from the computer or give you a hard copy. For that you will need a printer. It should be mentioned here that computer printers are not absolutely necessary for doing business on the Internet, provided you will only be communicating with your customers electronically. If you want to take full advantage of your computer, however, for such tasks as word processing and record-keeping, a printer is required.

There are three basic types of computer printers. The first type is called a dot matrix, because it forms letters and other characters with little dots that strike a ribbon, much like a typewriter. Dot matrix printers are the least expensive, but they have many drawbacks. First, they are very noisy. If you use one, keep your telephone in a different room. You won't be able to hear a conversation while the printer is running. Second, the quality of print they produce is very poor. Actually, they make things look like they were printed on a computer. Lastly, they are slower than the other types of printers. Dot matrix printers are designated by how many ink pins they have. The more pins, the higher quality of print. Twenty-four-pin printers are the highest quality dot matrix and you shouldn't consider anything less.

The second and newest type of printer is called an ink-jet printer. Like a dot matrix, the ink-jet forms characters by using tiny dots of ink, but the way ink-jets transfer the ink to paper is very different. Instead of having a pin strike a ribbon, ink-jets have tiny nozzles and the ink is actually sprayed onto the paper. The result is an extremely sharp-looking image that produces a print quality close to that of the top choice, the laser printer, discussed below. Ink-jet printers can be purchased for about $250, and the most popular models are made by Hewlett Packard or Canon. They are much quieter than dot matrix printers, but are still a bit on the slow side, especially if you are printing out graphics. Ink-jets with full color capability are also available for less than $400. The quality of output is surprisingly high, although it takes two to three times longer to print out a full color page.

The third type of computer printer is called a laser printer. Laser printers offer the best of everything: high quality print, speed, and even color, although a color laser printer will cost you around $5,500. The popular HP has the Color Laser Jet 5 for around $5,800. The better laser printers can print out more than sixteen pages per minute, with a quality that, until a few years ago, could only be obtained with very expensive offset printers. Slower models can be purchased for under $500, with top-of-the-line machines, like the Hewlett Packard Laser Jet 4V, selling for about $2,000. If you can afford it, a laser printer is by far the best choice.

WHERE TO SHOP

Where should you go to buy your new moneymaker? Assuming you want the latest system and are not considering a used computer, there are three types of computer dealers from which to buy: discount department stores, mail-order houses, and specialty computer stores. If you know exactly the items you want to buy, then price is your only consideration. In such cases, you will probably choose to deal with a mail-order house. That is because you can easily shop by telephone until you find the best deal. You can locate the larger computer mail-order houses by looking for their advertisements in any computer magazine. There is absolutely no reason to fear dealing with a mail-order house. Their main drawback is that there will be no experienced salespeople to assist you. Returns can also sometimes be problematic with mail-order purchases, not because these companies are dishonest, but because of the time and hassle of repackaging the equipment, shipping it back, and then waiting to receive credit.

Discount department and electronics stores that have computer sections are another option. Examples of these are Sears and Best Buy. You will find that they usually offer a rather limited selection of brands and features, but generally have good prices on name products. In addition, the salespeople will probably be able to give you at least limited help. If there is a problem later on with the system you bought, you will have no trouble exchanging it or getting a refund. If you are only comfortable buying mainstream brands, don't need anything fancy, and want to see what you're getting before you lay down your money, the discount department store is your best bet.

Last, but certainly not least, are computer specialty stores. These include national chains, such as CompUSA and Computer City. There are also numerous locally owned and operated specialty computer dealers. These stores, like mail-order houses, usually have a wide array of products from which to choose, and in some cases may even be competitive price-wise. The larger chain dealers will offer name-brand products. Sometimes, however, a specialty dealer may be selling brands you haven't heard of. They may have been made by a larger company. On the other hand, they may also be locally assembled. It is not difficult to assemble computers from purchased components, and there are some computer "manufacturers" that are actually working out of basements, garages, or dorm rooms. This is not to say that the computers from such sources aren't any good. The problem is, you never know. The salespeople at specialty stores are likely to be more knowledgeable than at the other types of dealers. If you want an unusual configuration of computer components, such as an especially large disk drive to increase your computer's storage capacity, the larger computer specialty store should best be able to meet your needs.

Used computers are another option, attractive if you are on a budget. Many people buy computers and then never bother learning to use them. Tired of having them gather dust, they offer them for sale, sometimes at bargain prices. The main problem with used computers is that they are likely to be at least a few years old, and so not as powerful as those you can buy today. Also, because prices for new computers are steadily declining, even though the person selling a used computer may be discounting it considerably from what he or she originally paid, it may still turn out to be nearly as expensive as a brand-new, more powerful model. Finally, you won't have the comfort of a warranty that you get when you are a computer's first owner. Buying a used computer is a great option if your immediate financial resources are very limited. Besides, you can always move up to a newer one, once you've made your fortune on the Internet. Still, as with anything you may purchase from a private individual, let the buyer beware.

FORD OR CADILLAC

How much computer should you buy? As previously stated, virtually any computer can be used successfully for accessing the Internet and making money on the Information Superhighway. Nonetheless, buying the most powerful computer you can afford is always a good idea. Computer software is becoming increasingly complex and requires more and more sophisticated equipment to run it properly. Then, too, your expectations will probably change fast as you become more familiar with using a computer and more aware of how much it can do for you. Just because you don't need all that power today doesn't mean you won't want it in the near future. Although most computer systems can be upgraded, upgrading is always expensive when compared with buying the more powerful system in the beginning. Upgrading is an inexact science at best. Sometimes the upgrades just don't work because of a system incompatibility, and you end up buying a whole new computer anyway.

My first computer was an early version IBM PC with one floppy disk drive, 64K of memory, and an ugly monitor that produced a virulent shade of fluorescent green. It cost about $3,000 for that system. Today, the same amount of money will buy one of the highest-powered Pentium PCs available. Compared to those early IBMs, which cost a small fortune, the new and cheaper computers have over twenty-five times the memory capacity, hard disk drives that will store one hundred times as much data as the old IBM floppy drives, and incredibly high-resolution full-color monitors that will put your color television to shame. You can purchase new or used computers in virtually every price range, with the market prices for brand-new, respectable, Pentium-based systems readily available for around $1,500. Still, don't forget that with some minor upgrading, you could probably access the Internet with an older IBM. The total cost would be about $800. You wouldn't be able to have the array of software that you could have with the newer computers, and the computer might be a bit on the slow side, but it would still work. How much computer you need depends on the type of Internet access you want, the software you will run, the size of your pocketbook, and your personal pleasure.

You have now digested a sufficient amount of knowledge about computers to convince a computer store salesperson that you actually know what you're talking about. You've also learned all you need about equipment purchasing to make your way to riches on the Internet. The final word on all of this is to once again remind you to relax. No matter what you do, you're not going to make a fatal error. Any computer can get you on the I-way. A recent perusal of the Phoenix Sunday newspaper showed used computers being sold for less than $300, equipped with all the hardware and software you'll need. Of course, if you want to be at the forefront of the newest technology, feel free to indulge yourself. A computer system costing thousands of dollars will work well too.

1 4
How to Get Yourself on the Net

NOW YOU'RE READY FOR THAT BIG STEP. YOUR COMPUTER and modem are bought and in place. It's time to actually get on the Internet. But how? You begin by finding an Internet service provider (ISP).

The first things to consider as you look for Internet access are your particular needs. You will select an ISP on this basis. Your purpose is to market a product or service on the Internet. How many people do you think will be contacting you by computer? Hopefully, a lot. What type of marketing program do you have in mind? Will you need more than just e-mail and Usenet access or do you plan to use the Web? There are more than twenty thousand national newsgroups available on the Net, but some ISPs elect to carry only a fraction of them. This can greatly affect the buying audience you are able to reach. If your ISP decides to exclude groups that offer sales potential for your product, you are stuck. How about costs? What are you willing to spend? How sophisticated are you with computers and networks? What type of computer do you have? What services are available in your area? With these questions in mind, let's next consider the types of Internet access you may choose.

If you are affiliated with a university, you might begin looking for Internet access by going to the school's computer science center. There, you should ask if you are entitled to a free Internet account. Many universities provide them to all students and faculty members. Be aware, however, that there may be severe restrictions on what you are allowed to do with such accounts. Typically, universities will permit uses consistent only with academic purposes. Moneymaking is strictly taboo. There have been several documented cases on the Net where entrepreneurial students attempted to sell products or services over their university accounts, and quickly had those accounts pulled. Consider yourself warned.

A number of so-called freenets have been cropping up all over the United States. They are usually operated by city or state governments. Freenets, as the name implies, provide free Internet access to anyone with a computer and a modem who is a resident of the area served by the network. There is a freenet in almost every state, but it is not always easy to find them. The Cleveland freenet is the most famous. The state of Maryland recently announced formation of a freenet that will be available to any of its residents. Most freenets offer e-mail and bulletin board services and many give Usenet access as well. Call the office of your state or city commerce department to find out if now or in the not-too-distant future, free Internet access will be available to you. You might also want to check out *http://www.the list.com,* or have someone do it for you if you are not yet on the Net, for a fairly complete list of freenets and ISPs in your area. Also, the Budget Web Index (*http://budgetweb.com/budgetweb/index3.shtml*) lists over 100 of the most reasonably priced ISPs on the Web, along with a number of options included in their price. Another good site for finding ISPs with low-cost fees is The Budget Web Host List (*http://www.callihan.com/budget_abt.html*). Although this site is not as comprehensive as the Budget Web Index, it contains a useful little index of Web page publishing resources, along with hypertext links to each site.

It's hard to resist anything that is free. However, if you intend to log on to the Internet frequently or for long periods of time, as you will when you utilize the Internet for marketing purposes, freenets are not a good business solution. Freenets are not set up for volume use. They can handle only a limited number of users at a time. That is why you should not be surprised if you find yourself getting busy signals when you try to dial up. On a recent Sunday afternoon, it took nearly thirty minutes to get an available line to the Cleveland freenet. Once you do make a connection, many freenets limit the amount of time you can stay on-line. Again, looking at Cleveland as an example, you are permitted only one hour per day of on-line time, not nearly enough to do serious business. Freenets also offer only very limited space in which to store files and messages you receive. This is yet another serious drawback when you anticipate large numbers of responses from potential purchasers of the products or service you are selling.

Finally, as with college and university accounts, using freenets you will find yourself limited in the marketing that can be done, due to restrictions on types of usage. Freenets may be a good Internet learning tool, and a means of inexpensive recreation. Overall, it is not what you are likely to want for business purposes.

PAID ACCESS

Internet accounts can be opened from about $10 to $30 per month with unlimited use at no extra charge. Dial-up accounts, those that you can access with a modem over a standard phone line, typically cost $1 to $2 per hour for time you spend on-line. Some companies charge a flat fee of $20 to $30 per month including unlimited on-line access. However, make sure the company allows you to market for that amount. Many ISPs charge additional for commercial accounts, typically $40 to $60. Other more powerful types of access can run into thousands of dollars per month. How much you spend depends entirely on your needs and the size of your wallet.

There are five main types of Internet access accounts: SLIP, PPP, UUCP, Shell, and leased lines. In addition there are privately owned commercial on-line services that also offer Internet access. There are also Bulletin Board Services (BBSs), small private operations which do not give Internet access. With the exception of leased lines, all of them including BBSs utilize transmission through standard telephone lines and modems. The pros and cons of each one, including typical costs, will be explained here. In selecting your ISP, be aware that all types of services are not available from every provider. Another related consideration in choosing an ISP is the software you must use. Some Internet programs are easier to use than others, depending on the type of account.

Then, there is the matter of the telephone or long-distance charges you may have to pay. Using a modem carries with it the same charges as you would pay for any other telephone call. Some ISPs also levy a surcharge. A number of the larger ISPs offer local dial-up numbers in most major cities. Smaller outfits have dial-up service only for limited areas or the one place where they are physically located. If you choose a company without a local dial-up for your area you will be paying long-distance charges every time you log on. That in itself will cost much more than the fee you pay for Internet access itself. If you are on-line twenty-four hours a day, as many business people are, those long-distance charges can quickly become prohibitive. It is, therefore, essential to choose a company that offers a local dial-up for your area, if one is available.

COMMERCIAL ON-LINE SERVICES

The commercial on-line service is usually a large national provider such as AOL with its three million subscribers. The main positive feature of the commercial on-line services, in addition to the capability of their special forums and databases, is their proprietary software that is usually highly graphical and very simple to use.

The problems with on-lines are that often the speed of the connection given is very slow, as well as the fact that not all Internet standards are maintained. For example, TCP/IP, the name of the standard protocol used to communicate among the various heterogeneous computers of the Internet, does not apply to on-lines off the Internet. AOL uses its own net-working standards. This doesn't allow you to run any third party software packages you might be accustomed to using for e-mail such as the popular Eudora. Due to the pressures of the marketplace, most of the large commercial on-line services now offer full Internet access. These services, however, require modem access and their own proprietary software.

You'll notice that a lot of on-lines with Internet access don't carry all of the newsgroups, or may not tolerate advertising from their services. Be wary of this. While on-lines may often provide easy-to-use graphical interfaces to their services, they are not necessarily the best way to market on the Internet.

SLIP AND PPP

The great majority of ISPs offer SLIP or PPP accounts. SLIP stands for Serial Line Internet Protocol, and PPP stands for Point to Point

Protocol, and both are relatively inexpensive ways to become your own Internet host. Here we are talking about acquiring a direct link to the Net. SLIP and PPP accounts, therefore, allow you to market by putting up a World Wide Web site in addition to selling with e-mail and Usenet. As you will see, Shell and UUCP Internet access are more advanced accounts that require a knowledge of the Internet networking language, UNIX. When you use your ISP's computer as a host, as you do with a Shell, the host you are using can handle larger amounts of information more quickly. The speed and amount of information transferable on SLIPs and PPPs are its biggest limitations. Its strongest point is flexibility of use.

For your purposes, assume that SLIP and PPP are similar. PPP is a superior system and should work more efficiently than SLIP. If you have a choice, you should probably select PPP. It's almost always best to go with the latest technology in a field. PPP is now included with a lot of the operating systems on the market today. There is also an option known as CSLIP or compressed SLIP, which is an upgrade of a standard SLIP account. The availability of this type of account is somewhat of an equalizer with PPP, but PPPs still come out ahead with respect to speed and reliability of use.

SLIP and PPP are available through dial-up services. You may also choose dedicated access, a special phone line for use only with your computer. In either case, this time your ISP acts as no more than a connection point between you and the Internet. Your own computer connects out to the Internet by itself, again by use of special software. Once this is accomplished, your only limitations on what you can do on the Net comes from the software you select. For all types of Internet accounts, you will require a number of software packages. Each function—Internet, Usenet, and e-mail—has a separate one, as well as a modem communications package and a few others. Your ISP will most likely provide you with all the easy-to-install software you'll need, including browser, e-mail, and newsgroup software. If for some reason the ISP doesn't give you software, or you want something other than what they have offered, there are many places on the Web where you can download software for free.

The first thing you'll need is browser software, which, as you know, allows you to navigate the World Wide Web. The two leading browsers, Microsoft's Internet Explorer (*http://www.microsoft.com*) and Netscape's Navigator (*http://www.netscape.com*), can be downloaded free from each of their respective sites. You can also buy the commercial versions of these browsers. The advantage to this is that you get a few extra services, as well as technical support.

E-mail and newsgroup programs are also available off the Net. However, both Netscape and Internet Explorer now have their own e-mail and newsgroup software built into their browsers, so if you purchase Explorer or Navigator, all of your software problems are taken care of. The most popular stand-alone e-mail programs are Pegasus and Eudora. Both can be downloaded off the Web at *http://www.tucows.com*. Finally, if you want newsgroup access other than what your ISP provides, the most popular newsgroup software is Free Agent, and you can also get this at the "tucows" site.

Some good SLIP and PPP programs are available free on the Internet. Others can often be obtained at a nominal charge from your access provider. There are now a number of SLIP and PPP programs you can buy, which will run under both Windows and Mac. It is much easier to use software under these common operating systems than it is to function under the complex UNIX language. The basis for the Shell and UUCP types of accounts are discussed later. Commercial Internet access programs are sold at prices ranging from $100 to more than $400. The higher-priced programs usually allow you to operate your own network of computers, something you will want to consider only when your financial success on the Internet and technical capabilities grow.

SLIP and PPP accounts usually include a Shell account at no extra cost. The Shell account may be necessary in order to have a place to put your arriving e-mail when you are not on-line. Remember, with SLIP and PPP, you are now connected directly to the Internet. With Shell accounts discussed below, you have the advantage of an always-on-line host computer, where your mail can come in and wait for you. With SLIP or PPP, where you are your own host, the middle man is cut out and the mail has nowhere to go while you are off-line. The addition of a Shell to your SLIP and PPP solves this problem. It also simplifies some of the processes you would need to undertake for the sending and receiving of mail and Usenet data. When you are on the Net alone, without the aid of a Shell, you normally have to create your own news- and mail-sending and -receiving system, something well beyond the scope of a beginner. The addition of a Shell takes this big technical burden off your shoulders. Be sure to check whether the ISP you are considering offers this important added service.

If you expect to be on-line for more than a few hours per day, rather than relying on a dial-up account, it may be cheaper to get a dedicated telephone line for your SLIP or PPP access. The ISP can help arrange this at a flat fee per month. Costs for a dedicated line frequently involve initial setup fees of up to $1,000 and continuing charges of around $300 per month. You will then be on-line 100 percent of the time, and you will never have to dial into your provider to reach the Internet.

The main marketing advantage of a dedicated line is that you can allow potential customers to access your sales information through the World Wide Web twenty-four hours a day. It is certainly possible to set up a Web data site without a dedicated line, but doing so puts real limits on your customers' ability to reach your information. They will be able to get it only when you are on-line. Keeping normal business hours is not enough when you are dealing with varying time zones around the world and customers that often don't turn to computers for recreation and shopping until evening. Let's also not forget the large audience of obsessive Netters who stay on-line during all their waking hours and traditionally never sleep.

Other than full-time on-line marketing benefits, dedicated access has the same features, good and bad, of any dial-up SLIP and PPP account. The biggest limitations are the speeds of standard telephone lines and your modem. SLIP and PPP accounts probably can handle up to one thousand messages per day with respect to e-mail. In terms of Web access the SLIP or PPP can comfortably accommodate one or two people at a time. If you think of this as a two-line telephone, that should tell you if it will accommodate the business volume you have in mind, or if you need to move up one notch to a leased line.

Normally with dedicated SLIP or PPP access you will want to register your own domain name. Domains indicate the name of the Internet host computer. Since you have a direct line to the Internet, in this case the host computer is your own. There is, of course, a cost to register a domain name. (See chapter 7 for how to register a domain name.) Once you have your domain name, you must decide how to use it. You can have your ISP give you what is known as a static IP. This means your IP connection stays in one configuration, so that the path of access to you does not need to change each time, and you can therefore maintain a simple name. You can become, for example, *yourname.anynet.com*. Note that the name of the ISP is included here, so customers can still see that yours is not an independent operation. With the appropriate software, you could have a

Web page on your own computer instead of that of your ISP, and if you want a more professional look, most providers charge a little bit extra so that you can have something like *www.yourname.com* and there is no sign of the ISP's involvement at all. You can do just about anything with your service provider so long as you have appropriate funds. Having a business page on their servers can cost up to $200 if you want it to be *www.yourname.com* (or whatever your company name is). Most providers can, for instance, give you e-mail addresses with your company's name included and no sign of the name of the ISP. This makes your business appear a lot more professional. The set-up charge for a dedicated connection is usually around $200, with an additional $200 per month for usage. But this allows you to be on-line twenty-four hours a day without any extra hourly fees, or without the risk of having your account terminated for excessive use. The problem is that, since the highest connection possible is 33,600 bits per second, with 28,800 bits per second being the most common, your network connection will be very slow. This is where a leased line (discussed later) would be the only real alternative.

SLIP and PPP accounts are excellent ways to connect your computer directly to the Internet. They give you all Internet marketing options and work well when only a few people are accessing your computer or sending you data at one time. However, if you anticipate having a lot of customers contacting you and many employees, all of whom need to be on the Net at the same time, SLIP and PPP will not be adequate, even with a dedicated line and Integrated Services Digital Network (ISDN). If you generate thirty thousand e-mail responses in a few days, as the Green Card Lottery did, your messages are likely to become choked in the narrow bandwidth of your connection and you may lose much of your mail. For this reason, if you don't mind limiting your marketing feature to e-mail and the Usenet, you may be better off using a dial-up Shell account. It will handle masses of e-mail better than PPP or SLIP.

SHELL ACCOUNTS

With Shell accounts you can use the marketing techniques supported by e-mail and the Usenet. You cannot create World Wide Web sites with a Shell account, although you can access and look at the sites of others. All other Internet features, including Talk and Chat are available. Shell accounts are also among the more difficult to use. With a Shell account, you are connecting to an Internet host computer rather than being one yourself as you are with PPP or SLIP. Since the host is used for heavy commercial purposes, it is very powerful. With a Shell account, you just dial into your ISP and log in with the user name and password that the ISP provides or you choose upon registering for an account. From then on you make use of the ISP's server as a bridge between you and the rest of the Internet.

When accessing the Internet with a Shell account, your own computer is, in effect, a dummy terminal. By using just your PC and a modem over a standard telephone line, you can connect with the host computer and utilize space on it, making that power your own and thereby getting access to most Internet features. With a PPP account, the data you transfer, such as large e-mail messages, all your Usenet posting, etc., will use your telephone line to transfer the information. Therefore, you are limited to the speed of your 28.8k bps modem (which is 28,800 bits per second without compression). While more difficult to use, a UNIX Shell account lets you transfer data once from your computer at 28,800 bits per second, and the ISP handles the majority of the data transfer from that point on at a much higher speed.

For example, suppose you were to send out a thousand e-mail messages over your PPP account. It would take a long time since they would all be transferred at 28.8K. If you transferred it once to your UNIX Shell account, though, you could use it to send the thousand e-mail messages at more than a million bits per second. This is something that needs to be looked at if you are transferring large amounts of data.

While using a Shell account is a lot faster, the work that you do over it is more noticeable to those in your ISP's company. If you send out thousands of e-mail messages using your Shell account, the system administrators might not appreciate you using their server as a bouncing point and might suspend your account for using up too much traffic. This is something you should consider when choosing between Shell and PPP accounts.

To tie into the host computer, which is the one you will in reality be using with a Shell account, you will need a standard communications program, also called a terminal program. Qmodem and Telix used to be the programs most used. Now, not surprisingly, Windows has provided the standard for this function. Windows 3.1 comes with a program called "Terminal" and Windows 95 comes with "Hyper-Term." There are also commercial products available at almost any store that sells software. All are fairly easy to use. When you operate a Terminal program, the only thing you control is whether your own computer sends or receives data. Other than that, your keyboard acts as if it were connected directly to the computer of your ISP. Your provider has actually set up a directory for you there. In fact, when you decide to store a file, you are storing it not on your own computer but on that of your provider.

If you want to send e-mail, you must first place the message on the computer of the ISP, and then send it to the destination. You cannot send anything to the Internet directly. Don't forget that the term "access," as it is used here, means you can look at anything on the Net. You still cannot develop your own data site with a Shell account.

Shell accounts may not really give you a direct connection to the Internet. You will remember it was stated earlier that with a Shell, your own computer is, in effect, a dummy terminal. However, a Shell account is a giant step closer to the Internet than UUCP discussed below. The difference is easy to understand. With UUCP, data is simply being transferred back and forth between you and the Internet, with the ISP's computer acting as a stop along the way. With a Shell account, you actually obtain space on your access provider's computer for the time you are online and you can, therefore, do almost anything from your computer that your ISP, with its heavy-duty equipment, can do. Shells, utilizing this powerful computer as a host, can be quite fast and versatile. E-mail sent from a Shell goes directly to the Internet via your ISP's computer in a matter of seconds. E-mail on a UUCP account sits on the provider's computer until someone or something decides to send it out, maybe once or twice a day. Shell accounts, besides affording you easy access to viewing virtually all Internet goodies, are usually very inexpensive.

The word "Shell" is a UNIX term for a special kind of program. If you ever see strange names such as Bourne and Korn pop up on your screen, they simply refer to two of the more popular types of UNIX Shells. The software you use to access features of the Internet is the software on your ISP's computer. Forget about Mac or Windows. Forget the programs you've installed for yourself. You are now using UNIX. The UNIX language, if you were to see it written out, would look to you like a series of weird codes and general gibberish. A UNIX Shell allows you to tell the computer what to do, using plain English. As stated earlier, UNIX is a powerful computer language but it is also quite advanced. Even though through the Shell you can execute UNIX commands in words that will be recognizable to you, you still must learn those commands. Most of us are too busy struggling with DOS and Windows to digest UNIX in any depth. However, if you are among the more ambitious computer-users, you can master enough UNIX commands to meet your Cyberselling needs without too much trouble. Alternatively, you can always fall back on the option of hiring someone to help you out until you learn what you need to know.

One of the most useful features of the Shell account is the ability to use UNIX scripts. Scripts are extremely simple automated programs meant to carry out special functions. It was a script that enabled the Green Card Lottery message to be posted in six thousand newsgroups automatically by typing only one word, "masspost." The script then took over and sent the message to each group, one at a time, in a matter of about ninety minutes. Were you to do this over a PPP account, it could take you hours of on-line time. To do it manually would have taken days. Script programs are written in English, not computer language. If you want to use scripts to mass post to Usenet, mass post e-mail, or any other purpose, but don't have programming ability yourself, once again, think geek or order one of the programs now being sold for these purposes.

As time goes on, more and more ways are being offered to free you from the need to learn even a few commands in the relatively complex UNIX language. Many ISPs are now offering their own graphical software that will allow you to use commands from Microsoft Windows, translating such commands automatically into the UNIX language. All these programs feature easy point-and-click graphics. Windows now has its own Internet access program. When you choose one of these options, you do not need to know any UNIX yourself. You don't even have to know that UNIX exists.

In many respects graphical software programs are a joy to use, especially for the person who is not technically oriented, but this ease of usage comes at a very significant price. As explained in chapter 7 on the World Wide Web, graphics require the computer to operate huge files of electronic instructions. This really slows operations down. Without fast modems or ISDN, these software interfaces cause your computer to work so slowly that handling volumes of mail or other data becomes virtually impossible. In addition, remember that with a Shell account, you are going through a host computer. This puts one more computer between you and the Internet, one more machine that could break down or garble the huge file of data graphical interfaces require.

In addition to the limitations of graphical software, there are other possible problems with Shell accounts. Your ISP may limit the storage space you can use on his computer. A five or ten megabyte maximum is typical. If you exceed that amount, you may incur additional charges. The main Green Card Lottery posting resulted in more than one gigabyte of mail in the first few days. This is equal to a thousand megabytes. Many ISPs charge a storage fee of a dollar per megabyte. Keep this in mind when comparing prices.

Graphical Shell accounts are great for personal use, to play with the Net, and learn how it works. You may want to consider one for your first steps into cyberspace. You can certainly do Usenet or e-mail postings from them. Windows even has a special feature called Recorder that allows you to write a script without knowing how to program that will work on a Shell account. It works by entering into memory a series of the keystrokes you first performed manually to achieve a certain function, and then playing them back over and over. In the long run, though, as you become more comfortable with the Internet, you will probably not be satisfied with a Shell. You will then probably want to lose the pretty software in exchange for more power and flexibility.

UUCP

UUCP stands for UNIX-to-UNIX copy. UNIX, you will remember, is the computer operating system or language that ties together most computer networks. UUCP accounts lack speed, flexibility, and availability of the more sophisticated Internet features such as the Web. UUCP accounts also frequently charge on a per-message basis, which can make them very expensive if you are doing extensive business on the Net.

UUCP is what is known as a file transfer system. Technically, it does not give you true Internet access. Instead, you dial into a remote computer, in this case the one owned by your ISP. This remote computer transfers the data from newsgroups, as well as e-mail, and sends it back and forth from the Internet at regular intervals. When you log on, the data from your provider's computer is copied to your own, where you can then read it. If you want to send data out, the procedure is simply reversed. UUCP, then, really only gives you e-mail functions to the Internet. Even your newsgroups come in the form of e-mail.

Direct access to the most popular functions like the World Wide Web are not available with UUCP systems. Neither will it allow you to engage in Talk or Chat. Most such accounts do have a method that allows you to research Internet databases by retrieving files on other systems. Once again, this is accomplished by sending an e-mail request to your UUCP ISP's computer. This computer then forwards the message to a second computer that does have a direct Net connection. It is the computer second down the line that actually carries out the search or retrieval you requested. Then the result comes back via e-mail to your provider's computer. There it will sit until you log on and retrieve it to your own computer. If the thought of all this makes you dizzy, it won't surprise you to learn that the process can take a number of hours or sometimes even days. When you have a more direct access to the Net, you can do the search yourself, perhaps in a matter of minutes.

The most important thing you need to be concerned with here is that the circuitous procedures of the UUCP system limit the type of marketing you can do. You cannot develop Web sites for your customers to reach. Everything on a UUCP account must go through sporadic e-mail transmissions which get sent out to the Net itself only as often as your ISP chooses. In many cases, that is only once a day. One thing computer customers don't like to do is wait, but they will have to wait with UUCP. Finally, let's not forget those charges. If you are retrieving a lot of data, perhaps as many as thousands of e-mail messages from your customers each day, the per-message or per-minute charges of UUCP accounts can run up a significant bill, often higher than the standard PPP or Shell account.

Why, then, would anyone ever want a UUCP account? There are two possible reasons. First, these accounts are very simple to operate. The easy-to-use graphical software discussed earlier that runs under the standard Windows or Mac operating systems is usually available free from UUCP providers. If you are an extremely inexperienced computer-user, or are interested only in e-mail and very limited employment of the Usenet, these accounts may make sense. The other reason to choose a UUCP account is that it may be the only one available with a local access number. Remember, the business of providing Internet access is a new industry. The day when all types of services are available to everyone, everywhere, is still not complete. Under most circumstances, the few advantages of a UUCP account rarely outweigh the many limitations. Since most providers allow Shell or PPP accounts, it is not recommended that you utilize UUCP for your marketing needs unless you have no other choice available.

ISDN

The reason why SLIP and PPP deliver data transmission that is relatively slow is that standard telephone lines weren't really invented for this purpose. Telephone lines usually handle what is called analog data, which works well for voice transmission. Computer data is digitized to occupy a much smaller space than analog data. Therefore, a lot more of it can go over a line at one time. The only problem is that a special line, able to carry digital rather than analog data, is required. The digital ISDN phone lines discussed earlier are now available in most major cities around the country, but certainly not everywhere. The availability of these transmission lines is giving a high-speed twist to SLIP and PPP. ISDN telephone lines carry data at a speed of between 64 or 128 kilobits per second. Compare this with the 28.8 kilobits per second speed or even the 36.6k, the highest-speed modem currently available. An ISDN link to the Internet will operate 2.25 to 4.5 times faster than a traditional modem over regular phone lines.

ISDN is available with either dial-up or dedicated lines. Many other ISPs offer this service, and it would be a good idea to see if your local access provider is one. It does cost a bit more than dedicated SLIP and PPP access, but should be well worth the difference if you anticipate significant volumes of traffic from your Cyberselling efforts. An ISDN account should be able to handle a number of different users at the same time with no sacrifice in speed.

Under any circumstances, your account remains subject to any restrictions placed on it by the ISP, and your allocated storage space may be limited. If you are handling a large volume of messages, you probably won't want to trust another company's computer anyway. You'll much prefer to control everything yourself. For that you need a leased line.

LEASED LINES

When a 28.8k, 33.6k, or even an ISDN connection to the Internet just doesn't seem fast enough, the next step up is a leased line. Leased-line connections require special modems and hardware, as well as special telephone lines, to communicate with the Internet at high speed. A leased telephone line is the ultimate solution to marketing freedom on the Internet. It is a permanent connection between your computer and your Internet access point, usually an ISP. A leased line keeps your Net connection up around the clock just as a dedicated line does, but with a leased line, your power, control, flexibility, and volume capability is the greatest you can get short of becoming an ISP yourself. In fact, depending on what kind of leased line you get, you may be able to do just that. The size and power of your own computer is the only limitation on what you can do. Since you are on-line all the time and control your available storage by the capacity of your own computer disks, you may have hundreds of customers contact your computer directly to retrieve information through FTP or World Wide Web servers. All Internet features are available. With respect to speed, a leased line provides a full range of options. Speed of data transmissions is measured in units known as bits. You may select the speed or size of your leased line, ranging from 56,000 bits per second, known as a 56k line, at a cost of about $1,500 per month, to 1,540,000 bits per second or even faster.

A reasonably speedy option is known as a T1 connection. The faster the line, the higher the cost, but the greater the volume of traffic it can manage. A T1 connection will probably cost you under $3,000 in start-up expenses, excluding needed equipment, which will cost from $1,500 to $7,000. Another $1,500 to $3,000 per month will be spent in operating costs. However, you will be able to put hundreds of people on the Net at the same time. A T3 connection is the fastest option and can run at a level some twenty-six times faster than the T1. If you choose to go the leased-line route, be wary of who you get your connections from. There are various small ISPs that only have a T1 connection to the Internet for themselves, yet they sell off twenty or thirty T1 connections to clients. This means that your T1 connection from them is shared with thirty other people. Make sure your provider has enough resources to give you the service that you require. Ask for a point-to-point T1 connection. This enables you to have 1,540,000 bits per second flowing through your own computer at all times without having to share it with anybody else. The alternative to point-to-point is known as a frame connection and means you are sharing the same T1 with others. This difference between frame connections and point-to-point is the answer to the question of why some T1 connections cost more than others. A point-to-point leased-line connection can sometimes be twice as expensive as a standard leased-line connection, but it's very well worth it.

In deciding whether to proceed with a leased line, you should keep in mind that, in addition to the higher cost, leased access also requires the greatest level of technical expertise to operate. Leased lines are for those on the Internet fast track. It is unlikely that you will be able to set up your own system without a lot of help. In this case a few hours of geek time aren't going to do the job either. Using leased lines almost always requires you to work with networked computers, called Local Area Networks or LANs. LANs are used to string together relatively small networks such as all the computers within a single company, for example. These function best under the UNIX operating system. Although it is technically possible to do it with DOS, Windows NT, or Mac computers as well, the result will be disappointing. It is also more difficult to find leased-line Internet access than it is simpler types of accounts. If you are interested, it is suggested that you contact one of the following national Internet providers for assistance:

Network MCI: 800–955–6505
Performance System International: 703–620–6651
SprintLink: 703–904–2156
UUNET: 703–204–8000

All are reliable and provide extremely high network speeds.

COLOCATION

A new trend among many providers is called colocation. That is, physically bringing your computer down to the offices of your ISP and getting "hooked up" to their Internet network. Colocation is often a good idea because, if your provider has a T3, your site gets to share the T3 with them. Make sure that your ISP has enough bandwidth to go around though. You wouldn't want to colocate with a company that can barely support itself at a reasonable speed. Some companies that provide colocation actually limit the amount of usage your computer can have. This rarely happens, but be aware that sometimes it does.

Colocation can cost anywhere from $300 per month to $3,000 per month, depending on what type of contract you have with the company. While having a T1 leased line to your office may cost you upwards of $1,500 for installation, $1,500 per month, and a $2,000 one-time charge for the equipment, colocation charges are often less than $500 and offer use of high-powered equipment as well as a staff already in place.

Make sure that the service contract with the company you choose is favorable in other ways as well. For example, there is no worse feeling than having your computer crash on a Saturday and not being able to have anyone reboot it until the following Monday. Most ISPs offering this service have separate offices or rooms just for colocated companies, and provide them with twenty-four-hour access to their equipment as long as someone from the ISP company is present. Because this is a relatively new trend, there are no set ways on how people handle colocation.

Why, in addition to price, would someone want to colocate when they can have a leased line all to themselves? Colocation is often a lot less expensive. You don't have to pay for the installation, the hardware required to run the leased line, nor do you have to deal with maintenance on the leased line itself. Your provider deals with all that.

Choosing the right type of access and the right access provider is a difficult decision. With all these options, what would the best method for mass marketing on the Internet be? Costs may narrow your choices significantly. If you are new to the Net, you will probably want to dip your toes into the water first before jumping in all the way. A PPP account with graphical software would be a good choice. After you have been on the Net for a while and can see what direction your business is taking, you can better decide if a stronger and more expensive Internet connection is warranted. In reality, the best choice is an ISP that offers a Shell and a PPP in one package. Almost 80 to 90 percent of ISPs now have this available, although the number is decreasing because it is so much hassle for the ISP.

If money is a concern, but your heart and business plan are set on a leased line, the best recommendation is probably getting a domain name and having your provider handle your Web pages and e-mail for you. Ask about "Virtual Web Hosting" and "Virtual Mail Hosting." This means that you bring all your equipment to the site of your ISP, but the ISP runs the operation. This makes it look to the outside world like you have your own servers running your company, when in reality, everything of yours sits on your provider's servers but is aliased to look like it belongs to you alone. This can cost as little as $100 per month and provide sufficient speed. A word of caution in evaluating costs: per-hour fees on any type of account can mount up faster than you think. Long-distance charges, however, will probably add up even faster than the charges from your access provider. A number of access providers offer toll-free 800 dial-ups, but be careful. They always charge a per-minute fee for the 800 service. This can sometimes be even higher than the actual long-distance charges. In considering the comparative costs, take a good look at your long-distance carrier's discount plans. Sprint, for example, offers a very large discount to the number you call most. Such discounts might bring long-distance charges down sufficiently to make an ISP, with many good features to offer but no local dial-up, competitively priced with a local company.

MONEYMAKING PROSPECTS FROM THE COMMERCIAL ON-LINE SERVICES

It has already been mentioned several times that the commercial on-line services are separate networks from the Internet. Due to the pressures of the marketplace, the vast majority of these on-line services are now offering varying degrees of Internet access. CompuServe and AOL, for example, provide very close to full Internet access.

Although they may not be well connected to the Internet, the commercial networks are still part of the I-way and do offer additional moneymaking opportunities. CompuServe alone has over two million subscribers. The primary problem with promoting products or services on the private networks is the fact that their main reason for being is to make money for their owners. To accomplish this, they must charge you a lot! If you already have an account with one of these companies and are not quite ready to get on the Internet itself, a good use of your commercial access might be a test-run of your sales messages. All of these commercial networks have bulletin boards or forums, which work much like the Usenet. On certain boards, it is permissible to post commercial messages. Try it on those where such postings are allowed and see what happens. The numbers you will be reaching will be considerably less than with the Usenet itself. However, it is likely that you will have enough success to make you eager at the prospect of jumping in headfirst on the Internet. For those of you who have yet to make your first connection with a network of any kind, you should look at the commercial services as moneymaking outlets only after you have established your main Internet storefront. Once you are firmly entrenched in the larger part of the market, you may then want to consider reeling in the important but much smaller group of potential customers that can be found on the commercial services.

1 5
Do It Yourself or Find a Geek

MAYBE YOU'RE REALLY TURNED ON BY THE LIMITED technical material that was unavoidably presented in the writings of this book. If, instead, the technical aspects of Cyberselling serve only to bring on a violent headache, there is a solution—the geek. Geeks don't mind the use of the term. To them, it is not an insult but a badge of honor. Computer geeks aren't like you and me. Cyberspace may be a fictional place, but the true geek is trying to move there nonetheless. This probably accounts for the otherworldly aura that surrounds them and explains why they have difficulty communicating through speech. You probably knew a geek in high school or college. You remember, the one with the thick glasses and silly laugh. He who laughs last, laughs best. Now, thanks to the computer revolution, many geeks make ten times as much money as you do, and if you've read the chapter on investing in computer companies, you'll understand why. Were you nice to the geek when you both showed up at your last class reunion? If not, you'd better change your attitude fast. At some point, unless you're already an Internet computer expert, you may well need him.

How much technical expertise is required to make your fortune on the

Internet? It really depends on where you are starting from and the degree of your dedication to knowing the technical end of the business yourself. If you've never even used a computer before, there is certainly quite a bit of learning required. On the other hand, if you can already turn on your computer, operate Microsoft Windows or the Macintosh desktop, and memorize a few short commands, you can easily start a profitable marketing campaign with Usenet and e-mail right now. Even building your own Web site is becoming easier with the development of new software for that purpose. The Internet, however, is a vast resource and some of its features require more expertise than others. If you wish to venture out into sophisticated areas, or even if you don't have the personal time to master Internet basics, you may need some professional help.

Finding that help is not one of the easiest tasks you will ever face in cyberspace. Perhaps it is because the medium and technology are so new. Perhaps it's because geeks love to keep nongeeks confused. You can't beat the independent feeling that comes from being able to do everything for yourself, but if you are eager to get started and don't want to take the time required to scale the learning curve, finding some technical support may be the answer.

My personal first landing on the Internet was done the hard way. It soon became apparent that using CompuServe for a number of years was no preparation for the Internet, which was unexplored territory. No one took the trouble to explain how it worked. There was no obvious source where you could get an understanding from a technical standpoint of what Internet Service Providers (ISPs) did. You certainly weren't in a position to choose between types of accounts when you knew nothing about any of them. More to the point, when you had found the name of only one company to call, who else could you call? Nonetheless, this first arrival on the Internet was, for better or worse, eventually managed, and it was easy enough to figure out how to send individual e-mail as well as post to Usenet groups. Soon, however, a situation arose that no one in our office could readily handle. The earlier Green Card Lottery postings had resulted in nearly a thousand responses and there was no obvious solution as to how to deal with answering that kind of volume efficiently. What needed to be done was obvious; even a vague idea how to do it was not. Shortly after the first Usenet postings, an e-mail message came back saying "just what we needed, geeky lawyers on the Internet." Unfortunately, we weren't sufficiently geeky to solve technical problems.

A technical expert was needed to help automate both the posting and mail-answering tasks.

The search for an expert began with studying the yellow pages. There was no shortage of listings under the heading Computer Consultant. This was going to be easy, we concluded smugly. It seemed of no concern that none of the ads in the phone book mentioned the Internet. A computer's a computer, after all. That seemed logical enough! The calling around process began. About half the consultants didn't know what the Internet was. Most of the rest recognized the term but had never actually accessed the Internet themselves. The remaining few claimed to know all about the Internet and to have had extensive experience. The interviewing commenced. Nine different allegedly experienced individuals came to the office. Seven could not identify the Usenet.

THE PSEUDO GEEKS

Numbers eight and nine, however, managed to sound sufficiently Internet savvy that we decided to give them a try. Growing desperation didn't hurt their chances much either. Although for the most part, they were really very different from each other, they were also quite similar in some important ways. Each of them exuded confidence over his knowledge of the Internet. Each had enough grasp of Internet jargon to convince us to hire him, not a difficult task to accomplish, given our own limited knowledge at the time. Unfortunately, in spite of the fancy talk, each turned out to be shockingly ignorant of the subject in which he purported to have expertise and each cost us a lot of money before we eventually had to fire him for being totally incapable of getting the job done.

THE GENUINE ARTICLE

A third attempt finally turned up the real thing. He was only twenty years old. He had started college but dropped out temporarily for financial reasons. Besides, all the hours he spent accessing the Internet left little time for school. Mr. Genuine Article had been cohabiting with a computer since he was nine years old. He absolutely loved computers, loved the Internet, loved UNIX, and thought the $12-an-hour salary we offered him was indeed a fortune. Mr. G. designed all the programs we needed in a few days. He was having so much fun, it didn't really matter much to him whether he was paid or not.

Mr. G. was not, however, problem-free. As with most geeks, his ability to communicate on a real-life human level was limited. He evidenced no appreciation of business concerns. He was operating on a different level. As long as our needs and his happened to coincide, all was well. If he had something better to do, we had to wait. You've been told the stories about the Net fanatics who were up in arms about Usenet advertising. Strangely enough, Mr. G. was one of them. In addition to getting the programs written, he undertook to indoctrinate us with the gospel of the Net. "We must respect the Internet," he would preach. We didn't much care for being lectured to by our twenty-year-old employee, especially when he was telling us it was morally wrong to mass post to the Net, even as he was having the time of his life creating the program that would help do it. The program worked, as you already know, but when the media took hold of the story, the Genuine Article began to fear that his friends on the Net would find out the role he had played and ostracize him. No other form of banishment could be worse. Mr. G. flew back out into cyberspace where he came from. He requested anonymity and we were happy to oblige.

HARD LESSONS

Even though it took a while, we did finally manage to find effective help. It may have been no picnic, but the results were worth the effort. If you don't want to learn about computers and the Internet yourself, there are geeks out there you can hire to do the work for you. At this time the Internet is no longer the mystery it was when we were first looking for assistance. There are now many more people with strong computer backgrounds who have taken the time to learn about the Internet. However, the fact is that many of the so-called experts out there still don't know a great deal and levels of knowledge vary greatly from one individual to another. Accordingly, you should still be able to benefit from the experiences related here when trying to choose a useful geek to help you with your Internet project. We found out a lot that should assist you in avoiding mistakes. First of all, don't forget that anyone can call himself a computer consultant. We discovered that many of them who do know little more than how to use a few mainstream computer programs, like the ones with which you probably are already familiar. In the case of some, even that is asking too much.

Be aware that you are looking for help in an area of computerdom still new enough that there are relatively few people who truly know their way around it. Don't make the mistake of believing that someone with extensive general computer experience is necessarily all that familiar with the Internet. The Internet, its programs and functions, are highly specialized. You yourself now know a little about the Usenet, the World Wide Web, and other assorted special Internet features. If you run into a computer consultant who is unable to talk knowledgeably about these subjects, don't assume that because of experience in other areas, he will be able to figure out the Internet any better than you can. We learned the hard way that that just isn't so. When you interview a prospective geek for hire, ask direct questions about the Internet specifics described to you here. If you see no sign of recognition in your prospective consultant's eyes, go on to the next candidate.

Any real Internet expert knows UNIX even though it is no longer necessary information for an average user, due to the proliferation of simplified Internet software. There is a special problem in finding the right kind of help in this area because UNIX comes in so many different versions, some operating only on larger computers that you can't buy at the local computer store. Although all UNIX versions are similar, there are sufficient differences that someone with experience in one cannot be presumed to know how to work with another.

There are all kinds of people out there billing themselves as computer consultants, and the prices they charge careen wildly over a huge spectrum. If someone asks you for a fee of $100 per hour and tries to tell you that is the going rate, don't listen. From everything we have observed, there is no going rate. More important, a high price tag on a consultant's time is no assurance that you are getting what you pay for. Just because someone has a lot of degrees or years of computer experience doesn't mean he or she should automatically be paid a high salary. The ability to produce results in a specific area, the Internet, is what counts. Fancy credentials are in themselves meaningless. In negotiating with computer consultants, arrange for payment based on results, not time. Anyone who is a true expert will have confidence in his or her ability to get the job done and will not mind being paid on this basis. Those who object to being paid only for results are telling you they aren't sure they can deliver. The technical knowledge you will need for executing the marketing techniques described in this book is not extensive. The most unusual thing required was the writing of the simple script that did the mass posting. Today, building uncomplicated Web sites has become greatly simplified. Unless you are trying to achieve something truly exotic, and even if you are, a real Internet geek should be able to help you reach your goals quickly and easily. Anything else is an unnecessary waste of your money.

Overall, your best bet in locating an effective computer geek is to contact a college or university. Try the student employment office or go directly to the computer department. Remember, almost every institution of higher learning provides Internet accounts to its students free of charge. While knowledge of the Internet has yet to become truly widespread among the public in general, it is common to college students. When there is a computer department at a university, there is usually a veritable hotbed of geekdom. You are much more likely to find people who know the territory here than anywhere else, and the prices they charge, pizzas included, are usually quite reasonable. Another source of geek help not available at the time of the Green Card Incident is your ISP.

Stereotype humor aside, many computer wizards have unusual personalities. If you want to hire someone who is really good with computers and the Internet, you may find the individual possessing such skills difficult to deal with. A cousin who is head geek for a large New York financial firm says all of them suffer from attention deficit disorder. Real computer buffs tend to care only about the fascination they find in exploring areas of the computer field they deem interesting. Your deadlines and business requirements mean little to them. Often, even money doesn't provide a truly effective incentive for giving you what you want and respect for an employer is not a concept they have easily accepted. If you find a truly talented person, it is worth it to show some tolerance for the quirky geek personality. At the same time, you must be firm or you will find yourself covered with geek footprints. It often takes a strong and forthright approach to get through to someone living in cyberspace. When your geek flies too far into orbit, say what you must to bring him back down to Earth.

Your own skills, time availability, and personal preferences will dictate how much you rely on the technical skills of others. There is help out there if you want it. You just have to look until you locate the right person. Perhaps you will decide to delegate all the computer chores to someone else and concentrate only on marketing and other aspects of your business. It is possible to do this and make a fortune on the Internet without ever knowing how to operate a computer. Indeed, with respect to the World Wide Web, a new job title has been created, that of Webmaster, for people who do nothing but supervise, update, and keep operational a company Web site.

Maybe, though, you will become fascinated with computers and want to master it all yourself. Books, computer tutorials, classes, and your ISP can all assist you in learning what is essential. To engage in Cyberselling you don't need to be a computer engineer. In addition to helping you get started, one thing a geek can do is teach you what he knows, so that eventually, you won't need him anymore. The day you say good-bye to a geek will probably bring you warm memories for the rest of your life.

16
Crimes in Cyberspace

YOU'VE NOW LEARNED WHAT YOU NEED TO KNOW ABOUT how to make a fortune on the Internet. You understand why it works so well and how to execute the marketing techniques available. You have a fine, salable product or service ready to go. You are aware of what you can expect in the way of both risks and rewards and you've made the decision to go forward. All of the information you've received here so far is related to solid, practical considerations that can lead to a satisfying financial result. Now here is a word of caution. Unfortunately for Cybersellers and everyone else, some of the biggest stories about the growth of the Internet focus on a new brand of high-tech crime. It's not pleasant, but it is reality.

Cyberspace has given rise to some completely new breeds of criminals in an equally new techno-environment. The courts are in turmoil, as they attempt to impose order on a wide array of troubling and unprecedented circumstances. Here is what you need to know.

THE COMMUNITY THAT ISN'T

It is important for you to understand well that what is often referred to as the cyberspace or Internet community is not a community at all. It is

simply a huge and ever-expanding heterogeneous group of people accessing the Internet for an endless variety of reasons. A lot of folks watch television for entertainment. That doesn't make them a community. A lot of
people go to the library for either entertainment or educational purposes.
That doesn't mean all library patrons form a community just by checking
out a book. Almost everyone uses a telephone. Picking up a receiver does
not equate with the instant purchase of a residence in Phonesville. The
Internet is no more than a library, entertainment center, and telephone all
wrapped up into one. You don't join a community by using it.

The idea that there is a separate Internet community with special laws
and standards of behavior differing from those that you will find in actual
society is a notion harking back to a set of circumstances that no longer
exists. In the days when the Internet was only a way for Defense Department employees to communicate among themselves, there was arguably a
small and like-minded enough group to which the term community could
be applied. Even when usership expanded to include academic and industrial researchers, there were still severe limits to the vocations and group
affiliations of people who could access the Internet. It was understandable, then, that certain conventions arose that were well suited to the interests and temperament of most Internet-users at that time. The National
Science Foundation's no-advertising policy existed primarily because the
U.S. Government cannot, by law, finance private commercial ventures.
Still, the computer geeks loved the idea that they had something of value
that the slick, commercial outside world couldn't touch. As for other matters such as pornography, privacy, or defamation on-line, that are now
headline-making issues, in the old days, before most people even knew
what the Internet was, these matters didn't come up.

Nonetheless, there is in certain quarters a held-over belief that when
an individual operates on the Internet, he or she should receive special
treatment under the law, and indeed the courts have sometimes recognized a particular imperative in the Internet as a unique communications
vehicle, the one that most allows the general public to have a voice. As a
result, many issues of well-settled law are being reexamined in the light
of Internet technology, and numerous legal protections, such as those for
copyrights and trademarks, are being put at risk.

ABOVE THE LAW

The death threats and mailbombs elicited by the Green Card Incident
are a sampling of what is still happening on the Internet. Forged mes-

sages were and are a common Usenet practice. In my own case, people electronically signed my name to messages that I had never sent. One of those messages advocated the assassination of President Clinton. Indeed, by this time, President Clinton himself, as well as Newt Gingrich, have joined the ranks of those who have been both mailbombed and the objects of forged messages. These practices have served to make cyberspace a world filled with doubt, where the origin of any message received is constantly questioned. It would appear that such acts should be prohibited by already existing laws. Most of them, however, and other activities similar to them, have yet to be specifically tested by the courts or addressed by statute. Legal authorities currently believe that the laws forbidding questionable practices in other venues cover the same activities on the Net. This will be confirmed when the court tests inevitably come.

The Joy of Anonymity

In the past, those who didn't want to be bothered with the creativity that forgery demanded simply sent messages through the Anonymous Server located in Finland. This Scandinavian-based computer, previously mentioned in chapter 10, was often used as a vehicle by which pornography was distributed without fear of police intervention. Another of its uses was for the purpose of defamation. The Anonymous Server could "launder" messages in the same spirit that money is laundered through small Caribbean island nations.

Finland's server was really pseudoanonymous because the operator and other administrators of the system did know the sender's e-mail address. The Finland server simply "stripped away" the sender's true name and address from the header, replaced it with a dummy address, and forwarded it to the correct destination. The system was only as secure as the integrity of the operator and administrators. Finland's server, run by Johan Helsingius, was the most popular and most trusted Anonymous Server. Nevertheless, the security of the server was compromised when someone used it to post materials concerning the Church of Scientology (CoS). The CoS retaliated by requesting that the Finnish police look into the matter. Even Interpol became involved. The Finnish police subsequently obtained a search warrant to investigate Helsingius, who was then taken to court and compelled to reveal the name of one of the CoS posters. Because his service was no longer able to offer anonymity, and because of the many accounts of pornography allegedly found to be funneled through the service, Helsingius decided to shut down the server. He is presently appealing the court decision.

Now, however, there are scores of other anonymous servers, popularly called "remailers," that are available on the Net, and remain a boon to the pornography industry. There are also a number of software programs known as "remailer" programs for sale, which will enable you to send anonymous e-mail messages without help from anyone. The latest and ostensibly greatest class of these remailer programs is called Mixmaster, which allows you the highest level of anonymity, making e-mail sent through it extremely difficult to track. In fact, the security of the Finnish server pales in comparison to the security of remailers like Mixmaster.

Obviously these remailers have given rise to a number of legal and ethical questions. Nevertheless, a Philadelphia federal court opinion on the constitutionality of the Communications Decency Act, discussed at length in chapter 10, addressed this issue by noting that anonymity is important to Internet-users who seek to access sensitive information, such as users of AIDS data, and those seeking support material for gays, rape victims, etc. Other arguments for the retention of remailers include anonymity for victims of oppressive regimes, whistle-blowers, and people posting to newsgroups dealing with subjects such as drug addiction, alcoholism, and gambling.

I Thought of It First

The theft of intellectual property is another crucial cyberspace crime currently being litigated. There are two major issues in the intellectual property conflict. One is standard copyright or trademark infringement, and the other is the efficacy of domain names as protected trademarks. These issues are creating complex matters for the courts. The laws of copyright and trademark essentially do apply to use of material on the Internet, so if you use works created by others, be sure you are complying with these laws as they presently stand.

There is an overwhelming number of copyright violations on the Net and the nonchalance of the users in violating these laws is part psychological and part technological. In simple terms, copying and disseminating the work of another that is displayed on the Net is just too easy. The expense and effort required to print and distribute material to millions of people, that once acted as a deterrent to the breaching of this particular law, has been reduced to no more than a few point-and-click procedures. Psychologically, the intangibility of the written word as it appears on the Net has the effect of making it seem less like the theft it actually is.

In Chapter 7, you were introduced to the problems caused by the pirating of domain names, a practice commonly called "domain name grabbing." A more in-depth inspection of this practice reveals a minefield of disputes waiting to explode. The first-come-first-served method of registering domain names, irrespective of prior trademark registration, creates open season on even the most established of company names. McDonald's was involved in a domain name dispute when a reporter, writing an article for *Wired* magazine, beat McDonald's to the punch and registered the domain name *ronald@mcdonalds.com*. This left McDonald's with three options: buy the name back, file suit, or do nothing. They chose the first option, and the reporter, in a burst of altruism, requested McDonald's to contribute $3,500 to a public school in Brooklyn, earmarked for setting up a high-speed Internet connection.

A conflict where the holder of the registered trademark decided to sue did not have a similar storybook ending. In February 1996, federal district court judge William Dwyer rendered what may be the first court ruling on domain names. Hasbro, Inc., the famous toymaker, had, to its understandable dismay, the name of one of its children's games, Candyland, expropriated by an adult entertainment site on the Net. The *candyland.com* site, owned by Internet Entertainment Group, Ltd. (IEG) was sued by Hasbro and the court ordered IEG to remove all contents from the site.

The differences between trademark and domain registration rules are in many cases problematic. Trademark laws allow identical registration of names, provided the products or services of the companies using the name are different. In domain registration, a name can be used only once, by the one who is first to register. Trademark registration does not allow registration of generic terms such as oranges, oatmeal, or soda. Domain registration does. How, with these differences, can a fair, uniform, and comprehensible system of name protection be devised for businesses? It remains to be seen.

As for InterNIC, the registering body of domain names, they have left the various issues entirely to the courts, and will not remove a domain name unless presented with a court order to do so.

Hacking for Fun and Profit

Among the most flagrant criminals in cyberspace are the hackers. The hacker stereotype is well known. Like most stereotypes, the perception of the hacker as a human cartoon isn't altogether accurate. Still, one thing does seem to be typical of many hackers, they don't believe that their actions on the Internet are criminal when in fact they may be. A famous early example of Internet activity that led to criminal charges is the David La Macchia case. La Macchia, an MIT student, ran an electronic bulletin board out of an MIT workstation. At one point, he allegedly invited his subscribers to post to the bulletin board software manufactured and sold by private companies so that anyone wanting it could simply take it free of charge. The companies who produced the software viewed this as piracy and La Macchia was criminally indicted. Eventually the charges were dropped on the basis that the criminal statutes required the perpetrator to have profited from the piracy, and La Macchia had not. Still, piracy remains an important issue and leaves the civil intellectual property rights involved an open question.

Like most early groundbreakers, those who came after La Macchia reached heights of media infamy La Macchia never dreamed of. There could be no better example of this than the notorious Kevin Mitnick. Mitnick made a career of breaking into university, corporate, and personal computers on the Internet. He was a well-known hacker, who was convicted for stealing $1 million worth of software from a Silicon Valley company known as Digital Equipment Corporation. He served a year in prison and eluded authorities for two years after violating probation. All this, it turned out, was simply prologue.

Mitnick achieved major criminal notoriety early on by discovering how to steal credit card information through a security weakness in the Internet. To do this, he utilized an intricate methodology called IP (Internet Protocol) spoofing that allowed him to pilfer millions of dollars of software along with 20,000 credit card account numbers. He was eventually caught by a computer security expert, Tsutomu Shimomura, who chronicled the entire hi-tech chase in a popular book called *Takedown*.

In his book *Cyberia*, which chronicles the behavior of the cyberspace culture, author Douglas Rushkoff paints a chilling picture of the computer devotees who deem themselves part of the entrenched hacker community. In describing the crimes of the hackers, Rushkoff quotes former

Arizona assistant attorney general Gail Thackery. "I see a ruthless streak in some kids. Unlike a street robbery, if you do a computer theft, your victim is unseen. It's a fiction. It's an easy transition from Atari role-modeling games to computer games to going out on the network and doing it in real life." Maybe the hackers can't tell the difference. The rest of us, including law enforcement authorities, obviously can.

Industrial-strength Hacking

Some hackers, like Mitnick, operate for the glory and the challenge. Others have a much more business-oriented agenda. Companies that are Internet-based or, for that matter, any business relying on computer technology for conducting daily operations, which in reality covers just about all of them, now have a new enemy lurking in the digital shadows of cyberspace—hackers from other companies. It seems that real-world corporate one-upmanship has migrated to the Net, creating one of the most active areas of Internet crime. This trend is expected to grow with the increasing commercialization of the Internet. Electronic security breaches are already up ninetyfold from a few years back.

Inside jobs seem to be a common problem. One very well-known case involves an Intel employee, William Gaede, who decided that he wanted to steal the blueprints of the Pentium computer chip. Because Intel had put in special security measures that prevented the downloading of sensitive materials from off-company sites, Gaede was not able simply to download the blueprints into his home computer files. Instead, Gaede set up a video camera in front of the computer monitor and recorded the blueprints on videotape, circumventing Intel's security measures. Once in possession of the tape, Gaede fled the country, but was subsequently arrested for transportation of stolen property and mail fraud. He eventually pleaded guilty to both.

In spite of such incidents, outside attacks are what the companies guard against most, taking aggressive and costly security measures to make their systems hacker-proof. With the vast array of electronic weaponry available, and the generally crafty nature of many hackers, these companies have their hands full.

When companies are successfully attacked, they are understandably reticent to let word of the problem get out to customers. Here is one particularly scary story that saw daylight in a big way. It was recently reported in *The Times* of London that City of London financial institutions have been paying vast sums of money to gangs of "cyberterrorists" that threaten to destroy computer systems. *The Times* reports that up to approximately $600 million has been paid in secret ransoms to international terrorists worldwide by banks, brokerage firms, and investment houses in the U.S. to avoid a complete computer system infiltration. News investigative teams discovered that British and American agencies were looking into over forty attacks on financial institutions in New York, London, and other European banking centers since 1993 on the basis that blackmailing hackers, who have shown companies just how they intend to stop trading with information warfare techniques, have been paid up to $20 million at a time to refrain from making good on these threats. Some have reportedly sent encrypted messages at top security levels that read: "Now do you believe we can destroy your computers?" The majority of the attacks are thought to originate in the U.S. The National Security Agency (NSA) estimates there are four main cybergangs, one of which is based in Russia. Victims, including a brokerage house, a bank, and a defense firm reportedly gave in to the blackmailer's demands within hours, transferring the ransom money to offshore bank accounts. Both European and American authorities have established special units to deal with the cybergangs, and a group of information warfare experts met in Brussels in 1996 to discuss ways to combat the newest threat.

SEX, DRUGS, ROCK 'N' ROLL

Probably the most publicly condemned behavior practiced on the Internet has to do with sex. The vast array of pornography readily available on the Internet that has parents up in arms and police in hot pursuit has already been described, as well as the Robert and Carleen Thomas case where a California couple were convicted of sending pictures showing acts of bestiality and sexual fetishes over a computer bulletin board run out of their home. Because their conviction came from a court in Tennessee, not California, the difference in community standards in varying locales was pinpointed as a problem in applying law to the Net. Certain factions believed that any activity of this kind deserved the most liberal handling, so that one group's standards would not be imposed on another. It would appear, however, that the majority of both the public and the courts is not buying into this theory, because an appeal of the Thomases' conviction was denied.

Another aspect of this issue as it applies to pornography was highlighted when CompuServe elected to ban more than two hundred pornographic newsgroups as a result of federal prosecutors in Germany claiming that the content of these groups violated German law. Most of these groups carried pornographic pictures in binary form and irrespective of the hotly debated issue over differences in various community standards as spelled out in the laws of differing locations, one cannot help but again be struck with the large amount of sexual material broadcast on the Internet.

California, the home of the quasifamous Thomases, also leads the way in another favorite pastime of the Net community: drugs. In spite of the "Just Say No" initiative of the eighties, the as yet unfinished war against drugs still rages on, with so-called designer drugs coveted as boutique items and psychedelics enjoying a major comeback. While groups of Net denizens are hardly the only ones engaged in heavy drug use, they are in the forefront of the movement. Based primarily in San Francisco, maintaining close proximity to Silicon Valley, the true believers engage simultaneously in computer development and substance abuse. Indeed, they see a relationship between the two. Just as LSD is purported to expand the mind with new perceptions of the world around you, connectivity to the vast reaches of the Internet supposedly does the same thing. Just as you may shape your computer environment through virtual reality, so too can your real surroundings be altered to suit by taking the correct combination of drugs. It is not for nothing that drug-takers of today call the acquisition of new insights they receive by distorting their minds with chemicals "downloading."

The Power Seekers

Another philosophical theory left over from the early research-only days of the Internet is that no one controls the Internet. Because it began as a voluntary cooperative of networks at the beginning of its move into national prominence, a picture was drawn by the press of a utopian village where the residents functioned peacefully together without the restraints of formal control. By this time it should be obvious that in practice, especially taking into account the drastic difference in demographics of today's Internet from its earlier incarnation, human nature, as well as law and commerce, inevitably took over, and there are now many groups determined to run the on-line show at all costs. One of these was the original Net research faction, and it is not difficult to understand why this is so. Every person on the Internet then came from a strongly academic background. Free accounts at universities promoted heavy usership among students as well as faculty. Even when industry got involved, it was only the research and development people who were permitted by law to be Internet participants.

Enter Vice President Gore and suddenly a favorable and extremely bright spotlight was turned on the Internet under the sobriquet Information Superhighway. And who were the experts in this new medium that was fast becoming an obsession with the international press? The nerds! Suddenly, they were yanked from their normally obscure life into prominence. There was every indication they liked it that way. The newspapers sought their quotes. Publishers sought their manuscripts. People wanted to know what hackers thought. The real-life revenge of the nerds was well under way.

These people all knew each other and were close-knit. Their bid for control was based on a platform of anticommercialism, freedom of speech, even as it applied to already outlawed forms of pornography, and the Internet viewed as a community separate from the rest of the world. Their game plan for gaining influence was mainly through use of media influence. Howard Rheingold, a San Francisco-based journalist who was one of advertising's fiercest critics, wrote about members of a Bay Area network called the WELL (Whole Earth 'Lectronic Link) of which he is part and parcel. The WELL, located near to Silicon Valley, appears to be still one more throwback to the sixties—a commune with a computer spin. Rheingold, Rushkoff, and all the other Internet genre writers related the adventures of the Netters, new objects of curiosity who gave themselves nicknames like Acid Phreak, Phiber Optik, and Poptart. (Nicknaming is a standard Net practice, a custom similar to the one observed by CB radio operators.) The Electronic Frontier Foundation (EFF) is an organization publicly presenting itself as a proponent of free speech issues in the same mold as the ACLU. EFF Founders Mitch Kapor of Lotus development fame and John Perry Barlow, a rancher best known as a songwriter for The Grateful Dead, are active participants in the WELL electronic commune, where Internet writer Howard Rheingold is a leader. Ex-WELL director Cliff Figallo became the first director of EFF when it opened its Washington office. Since then, it has relocated to California, closer to its friends and philosophical roots. The Internet Society is the original Internet organization to which all of these individuals belong. EFF attorney Mike Godwin writes columns for the Internet Society News. He is also a regular columnist for Internet World, a commercial magazine, published by the highly promotion-minded Meckler corporation that for an entire year had an article in every one of its issues criticizing Usenet advertising, Cybersell®, and its owners personally. The Internet Society, among other things, makes sure that ISPs, all of whom are Society members, uphold the party-line philosophy, even as the Internet becomes ever more commercially important. Well-known and much quoted Net guru, Nicholas Negroponte, head of the MIT Media Lab, whose acolytes were the fiercest mailbombers of "spammers," wrote articles for one of the Net's most commercially successful publication, *Wired* magazine, that began its days in a staunchly anticommercial mode. One of the first books about how to do business on the Internet was written by a librarian at Boston College. This university professor, who had been in an academic environment for the past twenty years, was often quoted by the press as an authority on her subject, even though she'd worked in business hardly a day in her life.

Finally, and ironically, this group's efforts to control the Net as an organized force lost steam because more and more original Net founders took highly paid positions in the private, profit-oriented sector. Eventually, *Wired* magazine, the publication that had once refused an advertisement for the first edition of this book, printed a highly even-handed article on an individual who billed himself as the Spam King. Nicholas Negroponte was named as a major stockholder when the ostensibly iconoclastic *Wired* magazine became the highly profitable subject of yet another IPO. Rheingold, the proponent of the virtual commune and opponent of advertising, found himself as a paid spokesman for a computer equipment company in a national TV commercial. The college professor is still writing books about the Internet. Vinton Cerf, president of the Internet Society, often called "the father of the Internet," took a lucrative position as vice president with MCI for the purpose of expanding their Internet market share, and like the other members of the original power-seeking group, found happiness, money and, yes, power, from a different source.

As much as the original Net faction gave tacit approval to control of the Net via vigilantism, interestingly, there is now competition from newbies for vigilante control of the Net that had once been the exclusive province of the early Net community. It seems that, of all people, Curtis Sliwa, cofounder and commandant of the famous Guardian Angels, has decided to extend his "jurisdiction" to cyberspace. Sliwa now oversees the CyberAngels, who are actually run by fellow Angel, Colin Hatcher, using a single PowerBook 150. There are currently over a thousand CyberAngels. Sliwa got the idea to start up the CyberAngels when he began receiving e-mail from concerned citizens complaining of being harassed on-line, from pornographic sites to lurking pedophiles. Sliwa's requirements for becoming a CyberAngel are fairly loose: there is no age requirement and one does not have to be at all familiar with the Internet. There will no doubt be other newbie factions who try for power on the Net, recent Net arrivals being no less human than those who preceded them.

The courts and official lawmaking bodies cannot help but be one of the contenders for control of the Net. It is their job. When the public cries foul about something like pornography, obscenity, or theft via hacker tactics, government agencies must do what they are paid to do as well as what is politically expedient. In addition, to the extent that the Internet spells big money, politicians want to see that the interests they support are advanced. You have already learned about a number of areas ripe for legal regulation and the litigation already completed or under-way, and there is no need to repeat them.

The final contenders and undoubtedly most likely winners of the Internet power struggle are the huge corporations trying to gain com-plete control of the World Wide Web. Here the two major contenders are Jim Barksdale, CEO of Netscape, developers of the vastly popular Web browser Netscape Navigator, and the world-famous Bill Gates, head of Microsoft and developer of the Web browser Internet Explorer. Since it is widely accepted that the Web is by far the most important part of the Internet, the theory that he who controls the Web controls it all is a strongly held belief.

Defamation Versus Free Speech

Let us leave the moneymakers now and examine another legal prob-lem that has caused much controversy on the Net: defamation. As pointed out earlier, nobody, from lawyers to judges to legal scholars, has figured out whether or not the laws of the real world should be imported as is to the virtual world, and this is no less true of defamation. Like the raft of pending legislation and litigation actions in many areas of Internet law, experts are taking the cautious approach. Generally, if it's illegal in the real world, then it is likely to be illegal in the virtual world as well. So far this is the theory that applies for issues of libel. In fact, you would be smart to be even more careful on-line than off, because you have the ability to reach more people in a shorter amount of time over the Internet, and the results that affect damage awards can be easily multiplied. In addition, on-line messages don't go away until somebody erases them, an event which potentially may never happen.

When defamation does occur, a major issue is whether the ISP who transmitted it can be held liable. An example of the courts' position on defamation can be seen in the *Cubby v. CompuServe Inc.* case discussed in chapter 10. This suit failed because the court decided that CompuServe, as an ISP, could not be held responsible for remarks made by its users over which CompuServe had no knowledge or control. However, had Cubby sued the person actually making the libelous remarks on-line, an action on this basis would probably have been successful.

ISPs as Regulators of Speech

Unfortunately for both the public and themselves, the ISPs are in the front lines of the various legal battles about what goes over the Net. Now there are thousands of ISPs, where once there were hundreds, and ISPs are, in large part, responsible for and profiting handsomely from the influx of newbies. The fact is, however, at the inception of the Internet's commercialization, ISPs have been put in the unenviable position of having a foot in two opposing camps.

The role of the ISP is especially uncomfortable when some of the more conservative Net factions ask them to assume the task of controlling newcomers who do not agree with old-line practices. On the other hand, several prominent legal cases that have already been reviewed in chapter 10 in connection with the Communications Decency Act are instances where ISPs have strongly asserted that they should not be held responsible for what their customers put on the Net. When you consider that the Internet is a free resource, it hardly seems appropriate that private companies who have no proprietary connection with the Internet should decide what those who access it may and may not say. Nonetheless, while they rightly attempt to deny responsibility for controlling content in the courts, in conducting business, they do try to exercise control where it suits their purposes. Thanks to the Green Card Incident, many ISPs now make their users sign contracts promising to limit advertising activities.

Again, this is done in spite of most ISPs' court positions denying responsibility for client behavior and seeking common carrier status.

The refusal of ISPs to truly limit their role on the Internet to that of a common carrier which, like the telephone company, does nothing more than convey communication without censoring content, is a truly terrifying aspect of how the Internet is now operating. Moreover the most recent court action in this area supports the right of the ISP to exercise control, a sad development, especially for Internet marketers. The AOL and CNC cases, limiting the ability to use mass e-mail as a selling technique, has already been discussed in chapter 5. The reasoning in these cases both rest on the specific acts of one mass e-mail company and do not outlaw mass e-mailing per se, but the direction these cases are taking is certainly not promising for the future of mass e-mailing as a marketing technique. Hopefully, those who have an interest in seeing this marketing method preserved will heed the warning before it is too late.

Netiquette

The repetition of Netiquette in the early days of the Net's popularity is another element that has lost a considerable amount of steam since the time it was first repeated continuously in the press. Nevertheless, here, for your reference, is the standard dogma:

1. Spend several weeks reading the newsgroups in which you are interested before contributing any of your own messages. That way you will have an idea of what is going on and will, therefore, be better able to make yourself fit in.
2. Don't ask stupid questions. "Stupid" refers to those questions that have been asked before. Each group maintains a FAQ file (frequently asked questions). Netiquette advocates recommended that you read these before saying anything that your newfound Net friends might deem offensive.
3. When replying to a newsgroup article, summarize the article to which you are replying so others will be able to follow the conversation.
4. Don't put a word in all capital letters. It's considered shouting.
5. Don't break the law by posting copyrighted works.
6. Keep your messages short.
7. Don't post off-topic of the group.

8. Don't clutter up newsgroups with empty statement such as "me too" or "I agree."
9. Don't use poor grammar and spelling.
10. Don't flame someone who uses poor grammar and spelling.
11. Don't post private messages meant for one person to a newsgroup.
12. Keep your signature short.
13. Don't be rude and abusive to others. Be polite and show some consideration.
14. Keep in mind that what you are saying is public and will be read all over the world.

Whew! If you had to worry about that much every time you opened your mouth in the real world, you would probably never say anything at all. It is equally true that if everyone to whom you spoke criticized your behavior for failing to follow all these rules, there would be more fist fights than conversations. It's not hard to understand why no one is paying much attention to this stuff anymore.

If you tune into a Usenet group, recalling the elements of Netiquette just listed here, you will see that asking you to abide by them is a question of "do as I say, not as I do." Among the most widely used phrases you will find as you peruse Usenet groups is, "I know I shouldn't be saying this, but . . ." Just for fun, let's take a look at what a person shouldn't be saying, but does anyway. Here is a conversation between two Netters whom we'll call Mr. X and Mr. Y. Mr. Y has his Internet account with AOL. Apparently, Mr. Y had criticized AOL's posting system. Mr. X thought Mr. Y's comment stupid. He, therefore, concluded that Mr. Y must be a newbie and sent him an unsolicited beginners' guide on how to act on the Internet. Here, Mr. Y lets Mr. X know he was not happy to receive the guide and Mr. X demonstrates his disdain for Netiquette as well as for Mr. Y.

Mr. Y: Obviously, I'm not the first person you've sent this [new users' guide] to, and it seems I'm not the first person who has been offended by your accusation of ignorance.

Mr. X: It wasn't an accusation of ignorance until you began your whiney little tirade. It isn't even an accusation of ignorance now. It's a simple fact, one that you have proved beyond the shadow of a doubt: AOL users in general, and YOU, in particular, are worthless, whiney, clueless fuckstains who should be driven off of a tall bridge on the "information superhighway" and left to crash to the jagged rocks below.

Mr. Y: Maybe you should take the angry responses to your mailing as a clue.

Mr. X: I have. I now am clued to the fact that you're the stupidest whiner I've ever corresponded with.

Mr. Y: If you want to be helpful, perhaps you should ask first if the person would like your assistance.

Mr. X: Sure thing. I'll send mail to guy who probably doesn't know which button to push if he wants to answer it. Brilliant fucking idea, son.

Mr. Y: Certainly better than randomly sending off mail that says, "First of all, welcome. [. . . H]ere's a little introduction I wrote a while back for new users," to someone who has a definite history with the Internet and is by no means a new user.

Mr. X: Ohhhh, would YOU QUIT FUCKING WHINING ABOUT HOW GODDAMN EXPERIENCED YOU ARE?
If you were not a novice, you'd know better than to get this hissy-pissy attitude with someone who, I remind you AGAIN, was trying to help you.

Mr. Y: I skimmed through your little guide and found the tone to be overwhelmingly condescending and the advice to be barely useful to someone who had been on-line more than a week.

Mr. X: Yes, fuckstain, it might appear so. But if today was your first time on-line and you don't know what the fuck you are doing, it won't help you very much if email you [sic] source code for a newsreader and tell you to compile it. It WILL help if you know how things work, where to go for help, etc.

Mr. Y: Nobody wants that kind of help. . .

Mr. X: Do me a favor. Since you represent only 1/5,500,000,000th of the population of the earth, don't tell me what "nobody" wants.
Here is your final clue, pal.

Mr. Y: I'm not your "pal."

The above exchange hardly requires further comment. It speaks eloquently for itself. It also bears out the truth of the criticism that language and attitude on the Net may be a problem in its future development.

The argument has been made that all newsgroup messages, because they are mainly text, require Netiquette-like conventions, so that nuances of the speaker's meaning can be transmitted without the listener having the benefit of hearing voice intonation or observing body language. There are also symbols meant to serve this purpose. For example, if you type a colon followed by a dash followed by a closing parenthesis, you get :-), which is called a "smiley." Turn the top of this page ninety degrees to your right and you will see why. A smiley at the end of a sentence indicates that you were only kidding about what you just said. If you replace the parenthesis with a capital *D* and you get :-D, a smiley that is laughing. Replace the colon with a semi-colon and you get ;-), a smiley that is winking. Had enough? Who can blame you.

Don't misunderstand. In this discussion of Netiquette, no one is arguing in favor of rudeness and against good manners. Consideration for others is always a valuable objective and there is far too little civility exhibited on the Internet or anywhere else, for that matter. The point here is not to get rid of politeness but that no special convention devised and dictated by any group, especially one with no recognizable expertise or authority, is required for successful transmission of ideas on the computer. After all, expressing thoughts through writing is nothing new. If, for example, something you read is meant in a joking manner, can you tell that from context, or do you require the use of a smiley face lying on its side to make you understand? This writer has great faith in your ability to perceive the meaning of written words without extra help from the folks who bring you Netiquette. Likewise, do you really need a special code telling you to mind your manners when you turn on your computer? If you resent the condescending attitude inherent in Netiquette, you are not alone. The end result is that this code, in its heyday, probably caused as much contention as it dispelled.

FLYING LIKE SUPERMAN

Hopefully you've found your dark-side tour of the Net informative. It is always valuable to see all aspects of the environment in which you are dealing. This was not intended, however, to scare you. There is no reason the crimes in cyberspace should intimidate you, even though that's what they were meant to do. The criminal element is in the overwhelming minority. Of the tens of millions of Internet participants, probably less than a few thousand exhibit the antisocial behavior described here. Only a very small group are prepared to trade their homes and families on Earth for a room with a view of the I-way. It would certainly be better for all concerned if the strident, criminal factions in cyberspace were gone. Like any other part of our real-world society, there are some elements we could well do without. Still, the number of those who commit crimes in cyberspace is small. They are just very noticeable because, in addition to being the most undesirable, they are also the loudest.

As an example of this, I'll use the event to which I was personally closest and one that should be of interest to Internet marketers. Watching the newsgroups where discussions of the Green Card Incident were going on, it was noticeable that the same names appeared over and over again. In all but about five of the approximately ten thousand then-existing groups, talk stopped a few days after the posting. Looking at the final numbers, our firm received somewhere over twenty thousand polite e-mail requests for information and an equal number of flames. Of the flames, often several hundred or even several thousand would come from a single person. Strictly counting heads, the vote came out in Cybersell's® favor. What, then, can we assume about the 9,600,000 who didn't bother to weigh in on one side or the other? We can assume they went out and mowed the lawn, caught a movie, or read a book. Then they got into bed and went to sleep, totally unaware that some unhappy souls on the Internet believed they were facing Armageddon in the form of a 171-word Usenet posting.

Not long ago Penn Jillette, one half of Penn and Teller, the popular magician duo who often appear on television, wrote a column about the evolution of the Internet. Jillette, a nine-year Internet veteran, gave two examples of the influx of undesirable new elements onto the Net. The lawyers who spammed the Net was one of them. The other was Teri Hatcher, the stunning actress who plays Lois Lane in the television series *Lois and Clark: The New Adventures of Superman,* and has since become one of the Internet's most popular female personalities. Jillette, it seems, did a guest shot on an episode of *Lois and Clark* and during the course of the taping, Miss Hatcher, learning of Jillette's Internet expertise, invited him to her apartment so she could learn more about it. Was Jillette happy to help out? Was he gracious? No way. He was suspicious of Hatcher's motives. He waxed sarcastic, observing that Hatcher could certainly, to use his words, "do better than a big ugly son of a bitch with a square head" like him. He complained that she wanted him only for his Net access. Then, he exultantly addressed his Internet compatriots about how great all of this was for them. "She invited me because I know people like you! Get it? It's more proof that we have won. The beautiful people want to be us. Even our Deadhead vice president is talking about how hip it is to be on the Internet." Jillette worked Teri Hatcher over verbally for a few more paragraphs before moving on to me. When he was finished, he concluded that once the advertising lawyers and the Teri Hatchers of the world wanted onto the Net, the party was over.

Well, there it is in a nutshell. The "nerds" want the "beautiful people" to want to be like them. When the smoke clears, it's an old story. Everybody wants control. But Mr. Jillette is wrong. It's people like you and me and almost everyone else who now represent the Internet. Bless the nerds, but they are no longer the only ones. The fact is you don't need to be a geek to profit from the Internet, unless, of course you would care to emulate the likes of the incredibly rich ones who made huge fortunes by, among other things, commercializing the Internet. Personally, if I had to pick a role model I'd be more partial to Superman. Besides being strong and able to fly, he's also a law-abiding citizen and a really nice guy. Sadly, that is more than you can say for the Net's criminal element. Anyway, Superman was created by the late Jerry Siegel, who must certainly be a long lost relative somewhere down the line. Whoever it is you may admire, whatever your personal code of belief, you don't need to transform yourself in order to prosper on the Internet. As you seek your fortune on the Internet, if anyone tells you otherwise, let them know it's a bad idea to tug on Superman's cape—or the hem of Lois Lane's skirt.

17
What It Means to Be a Pioneer

WHEN YOU BECOME A CYBERSELLER, YOU'RE JUMPING headfirst into largely uncharted territory. The Internet and other parts of the I-way are a new frontier, and it has been said that those of us who are among the first to undertake its exploration are pioneers. If the word "pioneer" conjures up romantic images of the Wild West, wagon trains forming circles to protect the settlers from attack, singing around a campfire, and looking up at the stars while feasting on the day's kill, well, that's not at all what cyberspace is like. This is about as far from a natural setting as you can get. The only similarities to the Old West you'll find here are a small degree of lawlessness, and the desire of most Internet travelers to see a better tomorrow for themselves and their families. In that, the goals of Cybersellers and others on the computer frontier are one.

The computer revolution, especially the spread of networking, is impacting society like no other recent event in history has. As a businessperson, your future success will depend on how well you understand what is happening and learn to fit in. The description of this plan for making a fortune on the Internet is going to end with a tour, not of the future, but of the present. During this description of the computer-driven changing scene, think of what opportunities you might find for yourself there.

You can begin by realizing what many of the original developers of the Internet can't grasp: The basis for pioneering is usually economic. This is as true for the frontier of cyberspace as any other. Even in its relative infancy, the computer revolution is affecting the worldwide monetary picture. Countries fail or flourish based on the extent of their ability to develop and apply computer technology. The stark contrast between rich and poor, both individuals and nations, is reflected precisely in the differences found between the technological haves and have-nots. Even in the United States, we have seen our economic fortunes rise, fall, and then rise again with new achievements in the computer field. Alan Greenspan, chairman of the Federal Reserve, has pointed out that our nation's salable output is consisting more and more of information products like computer software, instead of durable goods like automobiles. The world's best and most advanced computer components and software are now invented and manufactured in the United States. America is also far ahead of its industrial peers in overall computerization and networking. As a result, this country, after several decades of falling behind less developed nations in manufacturing jobs, has again taken a leadership role based on its supremacy in computers.

The computer revolution is not only good for our country as a whole, but for you as an individual as well. Computers have put us back on top, and as a result, you, the marketer, now have many healthy areas of the economy in which to operate. Moreover, if you are a businessperson just starting out, you won't need huge amounts of money to stand a chance of success. The emphasis on information means your ideas will be valued as much as your ability to raise venture capital. The many businesses that have grown in a year or two from the confines of garages to the grandeur of multimillion-dollar public offerings prove this. The Internet, where you have ample opportunity to market any product or service you can think of without a huge cash outlay, is the perfect example of this principle in action.

YOUR WORK LIFE

To plan how you can take your place as a successful pioneer on the computer frontier, you must look hard at the impact computers are already having on daily life. Most of us sense what is happening, but never really give much thought to its dynamics. Let's step back for a moment and observe the events taking place in our world that, among other things, probably led to your reading this book. Computers are taking over, much as science fiction accounts of them that proliferated in the fifties predicted they would. In the workplace, the resulting decrease in the need for human labor has completely and permanently altered the job market. Alan Greenspan observes that the need today for the physical labor of the unskilled worker has all but disappeared. Everything is done by machine and even the machines are operated, not by people, but by computers. The well-paid assembly-line worker is becoming a thing of the past. And why not, when the jobs of one hundred semiskilled workers can be replaced by a handful of highly trained technicians and a computer or two? Even a simple job like that of cashier in a fast-food restaurant requires some computer ability. More and more, finding work is tied to computer skills. Prospects for the computer illiterate are becoming increasingly bleak. It is equally true that the future is bright for any who will take the trouble to absorb the necessary knowledge.

Nowhere is the influence of the computer more apparent than in the office. Word processors have cut the need for secretarial help easily in half. Automatic banking machines, not live tellers, now hand us our money and receive our deposits. Telephone voice-mail systems have replaced switchboard operators. So pervasive have these systems become that many of us face on a daily basis the frustration of never dealing with a live person. Everyone has experienced telephone gridlock, where answering machines leave messages for other answering machines and two people who need to have a discussion can never reach each other. However exasperating we may find this, it is clear that anything that can be mechanized will be mechanized.

Even white-collar workers are not immune to the effects of computerization. Accounting software has greatly reduced the need for bookkeepers and accountants. A business that fifteen years ago required a full-time bookkeeper can now manage with one person entering data into a computer for an hour a day. Desktop publishing programs and high-quality laser printers are significantly cutting into the sales of the printing industry. With graphics software, an artist can put together a complex design for a magazine or book cover in a few minutes without ever picking up a pencil or paintbrush. No matter, it still takes the artist to develop the concept. The articles for the magazine cannot write themselves. As we stated in the very beginning of this book, computers can't think. Intellectual ability and human creativity are not devalued but heightened by what the machine can achieve.

Computers are not only eliminating certain types of office workers, they are eliminating the offices themselves. Virtual offices, where workers spend most of their day at home or in their cars, telecommuting with portable PCs, cellular phones, pagers, and fax machines, are becoming commonplace. Such virtual offices depend on networking capabilities just like the ones supporting the structure of the Internet. A corporate buzz-word of the nineties is "downsizing," the term given to cost-reduction strategies. Virtual offices accomplish this goal. Not only has computerization enabled many companies to lower their workforces without decreasing work production, but, with virtual offices, physical plants can be made smaller, saving on rent and other office overhead. As more employees work away from the physical office, the location of that office becomes less important, and companies may save even more money by putting plants in lower-rent districts. Meanwhile, you get to stay at home and avoid rush-hour traffic.

Everyone today is dealing with the realization that to keep up and stay competitive, computers absolutely must be integrated into his or her daily existence. If you are contorting your face into a grimace at this prospect, stop. It is not a difficult or unpleasant adjustment to make. Remember the vast difference between inventing a computer and learning to use one. The learning process can be interesting and exciting. The evidence of this is how readily people are making computers a part of their home life. Surprisingly, the fastest growing segment of the personal computer market is not for business, but home use. Instead of buying a set of encyclopedias for the children, parents now purchase a personal computer, and, by the way, an entire set of encyclopedias can be had on a CD-ROM disc for less than $50. IBM recently made the startling announcement that selling to the home market will now become its top priority. Most schools have already accepted the reality that learning how to use a computer is as much a necessity as knowing how to read and write. Instruction in computer operation has evolved from an educational innovation into a basic, and the kids love it.

As you contemplate these changes, do not imagine finding your economic place has become more difficult. To the contrary, if you will think about the scene we've just described, you won't covet the jobs computers do. Most of them are tedious. That's why computers were invented, so that you could escape boring tasks and perform work taking full advantage of your talent and intelligence. In addition, the more situations change, the more chances for those who make the most of the changes to prosper. While computers eliminate many jobs, they also create others. Whole new industries are springing up. Someone, after all, must make the computers, program them, service them, and, of course, operate them. Someone must train the operators. Someone must even take on peripherally created jobs such as office relocation for downsized companies. The increasing reliance on computer networks gives rise to the need for new businesses that adapt services traditionally obtained elsewhere to the recently developed networking facilities. The computer marketing plan we've described for you here is only one way of profitably fitting into the technological evolution taking place.

YOUR PERSONAL LIFE

In personal terms, a common condition of cyberspace frontier existence is a marked reduction in face-to-face human contact on every level. The advent of the virtual office means the absence of water-cooler camaraderie. The growth of the virtual mall means a decline in the social sport of mall-crawling. Video conferencing, still in its infancy, will all but eliminate the need for most business travel. Time with the family may increase, but interaction with everyone else will become more and more dependent on the computer itself. Computers as communication devices, when depended upon too much, seem to detach us from our fellow man, creating a feeling of emptiness and a craving for interpersonal connectivity. This has been observed in some of the larger corporations, such as IBM and Arthur Anderson, during their efforts to convert many of their employees to telecommuters. Suddenly, the executive who finally gets the corner office after years of climbing the corporate ladder finds it taken away. Instead, as a reward, he or she is sent home with a PC and a modem. The satisfaction of walking through oak-paneled hallways with the admiring eye of those with lesser positions turned in his or her direction is taken away. Ultimately, if users are eased into this new situation carefully, they usually grow to prefer the freedom offered by the virtual office. Still, there is a wrenching change in the adult system of relationships and rewards to which we are accustomed. It may be that in the near future, one way of making a fortune on the Information Superhighway will be to offer new face-to-face gathering places to those who have been on-line one day too many.

For those to whom computers are becoming a drug, they can never get enough. Cyberfanatics living in their virtual communities on-line, breaking away from their computer screens only long enough to sleep, are the new addicts and there are plenty of fortune-seekers who unwittingly act as their suppliers. That computers enable a person to interact with others but not to really see or talk to them is a mixed blessing. The painfully shy or those suffering various physical and psychological disorders may thrive in a computer environment, where they can maintain a high degree of privacy. They also may lose incentive to deal with problems in a direct manner. The practice of flaming is thought by many psychologists to be a manifestation of the particular type of personality that built the Internet and now uses it as a shield from the real society where they feel unwelcome. For those who really want to envelop themselves in their computer terminals, several companies are now contriving so-called virtual-reality helmets. This headgear puts a small screen directly before your eyes, providing a 3D view of cyberspace, while blocking out the physical world completely. For those who have seen the futuristic murder mystery *Wild Palms,* you may have seen such a device demonstrated. Like much high-tech fiction, it is all closer to reality than you might believe.

The fact that computers can isolate people from face-to-face encounters is widely recognized as one of the main reasons cyberspace crime is so rampant. Those who are comfortable using computers draw a sense of power or control from the experience. Some handle the power correctly, deriving from it a useful, confidence-building experience. To others, like the cyberspace criminals we've described, power is a feeling with which they are unaccustomed and they misuse it. This is a dangerous situation that must be controlled. By bringing real-world law to the computer frontier, there are attorneys whose fortunes are starting to be made addressing these serious problems. Those who mourn the passing of the early days in cyberspace, nostalgically thinking of it as a golden era, will be relatively few. The anarchy that is the old buzzword for freedom on the Internet is giving way to an order and values that are comfortable for its new, wider audience. Though the process may be long and painful, as the transition progresses, everyone will have increasingly better opportunities to make a fortune on the Internet.

BEATING COMPUTER PHOBIA

Perhaps the biggest challenge of the computer frontier is to eliminate computer phobia. Don't imagine this is just a casual or humorous term. It is a real problem and there is now a whole raft of psychologists studying it. People seem to be either enamored of or completely repelled by computers. Many enjoy using them because they provide direct and immediate feedback. If you make a mistake carrying out a computer function, you'll find out about it right away. Likewise, if you do something correctly, you'll get the instant reward of seeing it work. Those who don't enjoy feedback find computers their natural enemy. If they make a mistake, they'd rather not know. Computers don't allow for that kind of escape unless you turn them off.

Everyone who may be computer phobic can take heart in the fact that a good deal of the fear originally came about from a difficult situation that no longer exists. Computers are not inherently user-friendly. It takes a lot of specialized know-how to make them that way. In past years, as computer processes became more complex, the knowledge required to operate them increased as well. Original programs like those that run the Internet were written by computer technicians for their own use. They didn't care if others could understand how to use them. In fact, they may even have preferred to keep it all a convoluted mystery in order to ensure their own technological supremacy. Those not falling into the geek category, then, were somewhat at the mercy of programmers, who might or might not choose to undertake simplifying the incomprehensible.

In today's computer world, populated not only by the technological elite, but by just about everyone else, a goal of programming is user-friendliness. Since most civilians are now insisting on access to all the advantages computers and computer networks offer, there is plenty of motivation for the technology crew to pursue this objective. The greatest fortunes in the computer business have been made by those who have devised effective solutions to the user-friendliness problem. Thanks to this profit-driven initiative, extensive technical skill is not even close to being necessary in order for you to find your place in computerdom. The complexities of UNIX we have so feverishly tried to shield you from in this book were faced by all computer-users until the advent of point-and-click graphics. Even typing, which had been so essential to efficient computer use, is now less important with the coming of Mac and Windows. As a result, children who can barely read or write, let alone type, can now be taught to use computers. Learning about computers at such an early age ensures that it becomes second nature. The generation growing up now and those that will follow won't ever have to deal with computer phobia.

As the excitement over computers and computer networks grows, what everyone with a pioneer outlook is going to see is not a lessening of job possibilities but a broadening of opportunity for wealth. Prospects for those tuned into the computer revolution, even in a largely nontechnical way, will skyrocket. The gap will continue to widen between the technology haves and have-nots, but that is no different from what happens in any age to those who choose to let new developments pass them by. Today's technology "haves" are well educated, with promising futures ahead of them. As a consumer group, they are among the most desirable for marketers to reach. Soon, it is inevitable that Cyberselling will be the main way marketing is done. A report from Forrester Research Inc. of Cambridge, Massachusetts, predicted that on-line shopping would grow more than twentyfold between 1994 and 1998. What other words of encouragement need be said to you, the computer marketing pioneer, than that?

The early pioneers faced a dangerous existence. They didn't experience the romanticized frontier we all enjoy watching in movie westerns. Instead, they underwent tremendous hardship for one main reason: the federal government literally gave away land by the acre, to anyone willing to stake a claim and work the property. Homesteading typically resulted in ownership of forty acres or more. That land was about as raw as it gets. No electricity. No roads. No well-mapped-out plan for the future. The earliest settlers formed the foundation of great wealth for their descendants, but struggled mightily in their own lifetimes. In cyberspace, the homesteading race is on. Hoards of anxious trailblazers are prospecting for the best locations in cyberspace. At the moment, everything seems up for grabs. We've staked our own claim. We've explained to you how to do the same. While you may need some of the pioneer spirit to get involved in Cyberselling, the good news is that you won't have to live in a tent and brave the elements to make your fortune. The worst you will have to deal with is some misguided electronic vandals and the foolishness of a few flames. You won't be laying your life down for the enjoyment of your grandchildren. You'll see results quickly. That's one thing about the I-way, it's built to make things move fast.

Anything can be sold on the Internet. As for how to go about it, you are limited only by your own imagination, and, in this early stage, where the newness of the medium makes even the most standard marketing practices controversial, acceptance of your role as a pioneer. You are advised, however, to act fast. There is still plenty of room, but the ground-floor opportunities won't last much longer. Fortunes are in the making right now. The largest retailers are starting to move in. A new position being established in the upper management levels of the retailing giants is that of Director of Interactive Technology. It takes no contemplation at all to understand what that means. As for the position of Webmaster, that, too, is self-explanatory.

Right now, all companies, even the big ones, are starting out on the Information Superhighway from largely the same place. In a sense, all fledgling business ventures involve pioneering. Every new product or service is initially an experiment. The smartest business gurus cannot flawlessly predict the future. Companies spend millions test-marketing products before offering them to the public. In spite of those efforts, many new products fail. The largest companies can ride out the failures, but most of us can't. This is the single biggest reason start-up businesses falter. It's not because some big company necessarily knows something they don't. Rather, the cost of trial and error eats up resources faster than revenues come in. One of the most attractive features about I-way marketing is that it is so inexpensive, you can afford to make mistakes. A small business might drown in the cost of a few big-city newspaper advertisements. On the Internet, the expense of experimentation, test-marketing, and general advertising becomes negligible. The single greatest resources required are no longer money, but creativity and the willingness to try something novel. You can give your pioneering instincts full range of expression without risking the family farm in the process.

As for personal experience, it was just a matter of taking a familiar product and bringing it to an audience that would logically want it, and it turned out to be a correct assumption. If it had been a mistake, no one's survival was on the line. There were no worries about spending a year's worth of house payments on advertisements. Not only did the voyage on the Internet cost very little, but it turned up to be what many people were looking for. Cyberselling works! A fortune was made and there was an amazing bonus, too, the discovery of a completely new and largely uncharted world where you can sell virtually anything at minimal cost. The so-called Green Card Incident defined the future of Internet commercialism for nearly everyone, friend or foe.

Those who invented the Internet technology were understandably reluctant to see their creation pass into the hands of others. Sadly, they wouldn't take the wide public use of their invention for the compliment that it is. They couldn't at the time understand that unless their creation was utilized to change lives for the better, it would never be more than a technological curiosity. Those who utilize the Internet for all sorts of purposes, including marketing, will complete the job the computer technologists began. Cyberselling is the future of marketing. This book has attempted to share what has been learned with you so you can be among the first to try it out. You are encouraged to stake your claim to your piece of cyberspace. Cyberselling is new. It is unknown. Think back to those early homesteaders and the vast family fortunes that were created. Some people say there are no more good opportunities left in the world, but how can you know about the Internet and still believe that is so? Sit down at your computer and begin the journey to a dazzling future for yourself and your family. Not only will you make a fortune, but you'll have a good time on the trip.

INDEX

Filo, David, 171
Financial institutions, and "cyberterrorists," 246–47
First Virtual, 191, 192–94
Flames, 4, 53–54, 264
Floppy disks, 206
Flowers, 144
Food, 145–46
Foreign Affair, A, 160
Fortuna Alliance, 181
Fraud, on-line investment, 180–82
Free access, to Internet, 216–17
Free Agent, 220
Freenets, 216–17
Freeware, 10
FTP, 104–5
Fundlink Web site, 170
Funeral homes, 146

Gaede, William, 246
Gardner, David and Tom, 175
Gates, Bill, 165, 204, 251
Geeks, hiring, 233–39
General Motors, 140
Genie, 8
Genius T-shirts, 145
Gibbens, Karlyn Wolf, 95–96
Gibson, William (*Neuromancer*), 8
GIF, 120
Godwin, Mike, 249–50
Go on line, 4
Gopher sites, 104–5
Gore, Albert, 5, 249
Graphical web browser, 102, 219–20
Graphical software programs, 225
Graphic Interchange Format (GIF), 120
Graphics, formatting, 120
Graphic User Interface (GUI), 90
Great Business Hot Links, 148
Green Card Lottery, 20–28, 56, 58–62, 64–65
Greenspan, Alan, 260, 261

Hackers/hacking, 245–47
    corporate-level, 246–47
Hahn, Harley, 53
Hardware, 9–11
    data storage capacity and disk drives, 206–8
    IBM vs. MAC, 201–3
    keyboard, cursor, and mouse, 209
    memory, 203
    modems, 209–10
    monitors, 208–9

operating systems, 204–6
printers, 210–11
processors, 202
software factor in choosing, 208
Harris, C. Dodd IV, 136–37
Harvard Graphics, 132
Hasbrok, Inc., 244
Hatcher, Colin, 250–51
Hatcher, Teri, 257–58
Hellman, Martin, 185
Helsingius, Johan, 158–59, 242–43
Hewlett Packard printer, 211
Hierarchy
    of e-mail address, 77
    of newsgroup names, 49–50
Hobbies, 145
Home pages, 98
    see also Web site; World Wide Web
HTML, 120, 131–32, 189
http, 104
Hypertext links, 102–3, 133
    attracting people to your site with, 111, 114–15
Hypertext Markup Language (HTML), 120, 131–32, 189

IBM-based system, 202–3, 204
    running Macintosh programs on, 202
IBM vs. MAC, 201–3
IBM-based system, 202
Icons, 102
Indirect advertising. *See* Web site, World Wide Web
Individual Investor's Guide to Computerized Investing, 180
InfiNet's Cool Site of the Day, 111
InfoHaus, 193
Information, to sell, 141
"Information Superhighway" concept, 1–2
    term, and alternates, 5
Infoseek, 103
Initial Public Offerings (IPOs), 170–74, 178
    Netscape, 164
Ink-jet printer, 211
Inktomi, 103
Integrated Services Digital Network (ISDN) lines, 37, 106
Intel, 202, 246
Intellectual property, theft of, 243–44
Intelligent Interactions, 100–101
Intel Pentium Model, 202
Interactive television, 106
InterNIC, 244
Internal memory (RAM), 203